Hard sell

Manchester University Press

STUDIES IN POPULAR CULTURE

General editor: Professor Jeffrey Richards

Also published in this series

Christmas in nineteenth-century England   Neil Armstrong

Healthy living in the Alps: the origins of winter tourism in Switzerland, 1860–1914   Susan Barton

Working-class organisations and popular tourism, 1840–1970   Susan Barton

Leisure, citizenship and working-class men in Britain, 1850–1945   Brad Beaven

Leisure and cultural conflict in twentieth-century Britain   Brett Brebber (ed.)

The British Consumer Co-operative Movement and film, 1890s–1960s   Alan George Burton

British railway enthusiasm   Ian Carter

Railways and culture in Britain   Ian Carter

Darts in England, 1900–39: a social history   Patrick Chaplin

Holiday camps in twentieth-century Britain: packaging pleasure   Sandra Trudgen Dawson

History on British television: constructing nation, nationality and collective memory   Robert Dillon

The food companions: cinema and consumption in wartime Britain, 1939–45   Richard Farmer

Songs of protest, songs of love: popular ballads in eighteenth-century Britain   Robin Ganev

The BBC and national identity in Britain, 1922–53   Thomas Hajkowski

From silent screen to multi-screen: a history of cinema exhibition in Britain since 1896   Stuart Hanson

Smoking in British popular culture, 1800–2000   Matthew Hilton

Juke box Britain: Americanisation and youth culture, 1945–60   Adrian Horn

Horseracing and the British, 1919–39   Mike Huggins

Popular culture and working-class taste in Britain, 1930–39: a round of cheap diversions?   Robert James

Amateur film: meaning and practice, 1927–77   Heather Norris Nicholson

Films and British national identity: from Dickens to *Dad's Army*   Jeffrey Richards

Cinema and radio in Britain and America, 1920–1960   Jeffrey Richards

Looking North: Northern England and the national imagination   Dave Russell

The British seaside holiday: holidays and resorts in the twentieth century   John K. Walton

Hard sell
Advertising, affluence and transatlantic relations, c. 1951–69

SEAN NIXON

Manchester University Press

Copyright © Sean Nixon 2013

The right of Sean Nixon to be identified as the author of this work has been asserted by him in accordance with the Copyright, Designs and Patents Act 1988.

Published by Manchester University Press
Altrincham Street, Manchester M1 7JA, UK
www.manchesteruniversitypress.co.uk

British Library Cataloguing-in-Publication Data is available

Library of Congress Cataloging-in-Publication Data is available

ISBN 978 1 7849 9105 0   paperback

First published by Manchester University Press in hardback 2013

This edition first published 2016

The publisher has no responsibility for the persistence or accuracy of URLs for any external or third-party internet websites referred to in this book, and does not guarantee that any content on such websites is, or will remain, accurate or appropriate.

Printed by Lightning Source

STUDIES IN POPULAR CULTURE

There has in recent years been an explosion of interest in culture and cultural studies. The impetus has come from two directions and out of two different traditions. On the one hand, cultural history has grown out of social history to become a distinct and identifiable school of historical investigation. On the other hand, cultural studies has grown out of English literature and has concerned itself to a large extent with contemporary issues. Nevertheless, there is a shared project, its aim, to elucidate the meanings and values implicit and explicit in the art, literature, learning, institutions and everyday behaviour within a given society. Both the cultural historian and the cultural studies scholar seek to explore the ways in which a culture is imagined, represented and received; how it interacts with social processes; how it contributes to individual and collective identities and world views, to stability and change, to social, political and economic activities and programmes. This series aims to provide an arena for the cross-fertilisation of the discipline, so that the work of the cultural historian can take advantage of the most useful and illuminating of the theoretical developments and the cultural studies scholars can extend the purely historical underpinnings of their investigations. The ultimate objective of the series is to provide a range of books which will explain in a readable and accessible way where we are now socially and culturally and how we got to where we are. This should enable people to be better informed, promote an interdisciplinary approach to cultural issues and encourage deeper thought about the issues, attitudes and institutions of popular culture.

Jeffrey Richards

Contents

	List of illustrations	*page* ix
	Foreword	xi
	Acknowledgements	xiii
	Abbreviations	xv
	Introduction	1
1	The advertising industry in the age of affluence	16
2	Apostle of Americanization? J. Walter Thompson, advertising and Anglo-American relations	36
3	Understanding ordinary women: consumer research and the mass-market housewife	66
4	'A challenge both alarming and alluring': the birth of television advertising	95
5	'All mod cons': television advertising, the housewife and domestic life	119
6	Welcome intrusion? Television advertising and the viewing public	141
7	'Trading on human weakness': advertising, morality and consumer desire	164
	Conclusion	187
	Bibliography	197
	Index	207

List of illustrations

1 Total advertising expenditure as a percentage of GNP, 1952–69   20
2 Advertising expenditure and product groups, 1967   21
3 Advertising expenditure by media (as percentage of total spend), 1960–70   21
4 Parker Pens, JWT Chicago, 1951 (courtesy of John W. Hartman Center, Duke University/J. Walter Thompson)   53
5 Parker Pens, JWT London, 1954 (courtesy of John W. Hartman Center, Duke University/J. Walter Thompson)   54
6 Parker Pens, JWT London, 1966 (courtesy of John W. Hartman Center, Duke University/J. Walter Thompson)   56
7 Richard Shops, JWT London, 1966 (courtesy of Arcadia Group)   57
8 Richard Shops, JWT London, 1966 (courtesy of Arcadia Group)   58
9 'A remarkably accurate marketing tool', JWT, 1959 (courtesy of John W. Hartman Center, Duke University/J. Walter Thompson)   67
10 'Pin-Up', JWT London, 1950 (Pin-Up Perms Ltd)   75
11 'Oxo', JWT London (courtesy of Premier Foods)   82
12 Duncan Ross, Dorland advert, 1954 (Admark Publishing Company Ltd)   102
13 JWT television workshop, 1956 (courtesy of John W. Hartman Center, Duke University/J. Walter Thompson)   105
14 Modern Kitchen, *Design*, 1955, issue 75 (Design Council / University of Brighton Design Archives, www.brighton.ac.uk/archives)   124

Foreword

The Americanization of Britain has been the subject of many books arguing that the United Kingdom has been conquered and colonized by American culture and ideas, particularly in the twentieth century. But another subtler and more nuanced view has emerged recently suggesting that the process was not as simple and one-sided as has been claimed. Instead it is suggested that a process of hybridization between the two cultures, British and American, often went on. Adrian Horn advanced this idea in his book on British youth culture between 1945 and 1960, *Juke box Britain*, published in this series in 2009. Now Sean Nixon examines the history of advertising in Britain in the 1950s and 1960s from a similar perspective. Although by the 1960s, six of the top ten advertising agencies in Britain were US-owned, Nixon rejects the idea of the emergence of a common Anglo-American advertising culture and argues that American techniques and practices were adapted, hybridized and indigenized when introduced into a British context. This process required American advertising agencies to modify their approaches to take account of cultural differences between the two countries. So far from subordinating the British advertising industry, Nixon argues that American commercial and cultural influences should be seen as a valuable resource and stimulus to British advertisers.

The 1950s and 1960s saw the rise of consumer society in Britain and the dawn of the age of affluence to replace the austerity of the war and the immediate post-war years. The situation was memorably summed up by Prime Minister Harold Macmillan when he said in 1957: 'Most of our people have never had it so good.' Advertising was integral to this new world and the 1950s saw television join the traditional methods of product promotion – newspapers, magazines and posters. Since women were the key purchasers of consumer goods, much of the advertising was aimed at them. Nixon therefore examines the development of market research, the grammar of television advertising, the construction of the ideal housewife and the ideal home and the reaction of consumers to the new television advertising. He concludes by discussing how the advertisers responded to the growing chorus of criticism from socialists, moralists, clerics, academics and traditionalists accusing them of promoting Americanization, materialism and cultural banality. Thoroughly researched, engagingly written and wholly persuasive, Sean Nixon's book provides a valuable revisionist interpretation of a formative period in British cultural life.

Jeffrey Richards
November 2011

Acknowledgements

This book closes the circle on a body of research on advertising, commercial culture and social change which I have undertaken over the last twenty-five years. It follows two other books, *Hard Looks* (UCL Press, 1996) and *Advertising Cultures* (Sage, 2003), which explored developments in the 1980s and 1990s. *Hard Sell* moves the analysis not forwards but backwards in time and focuses on the 1950s and 1960s. Given the historical focus, archives and libraries have figured centrally in the research for this book. I am especially grateful to the staff at the History of Advertising Trust for their help and support in exploring the written archives of British advertising which they hold. Margaret Rose has always made my visits to HAT enjoyable and Chloe Veale, Edward Vanderpump and David Thomas were immensely generous with their knowledge, time and patience in the face of my many requests. Eve Read and Maggie Cammiss kindly helped with the tracking down of copyright for the images used in the book. The late Michael Cudlipp and Barry Cox were both genial and supportive chief executives of HAT during my numerous visits. Governors of HAT were also supportive of my research and many gave their time for the 'Advertising Lives' oral history project which I undertook in 2008. In particular I am grateful to Archie Pitcher CBE, David Bernstein, Graham Hinton, Sir John Hegarty and Winston Fletcher. Jeremy Bullmore, John Salmon, Peter Mead and David Puttnam also generously agreed to be interviewed for the project.

Librarians at the John W. Hartman Center for Sales, Advertising and Marketing History were extremely helpful during my visit there in the summer of 2004, as were staff at the National Archives, Kew; the British Library; Unilever Archives, Port Sunlight; Mass Observation Archives, University of Sussex; the National Galleries of Scotland, Edinburgh; and the University of Essex, especially Nigel Cochrane. The research would not have been possible without the support of the study leave arrangements at the University of Essex and its research promotion fund. I also benefited from a British Academy small research grant. This funded research by two research assistants, Rachel Duffet and Lorena Rivero de Beer. My thanks to them and to the British Academy. Travel to Duke University in 2004 was supported by a travel grant from the Hartman Center.

The ideas developed in this book have benefited from being aired at various seminars and conferences and I am particularly grateful to audiences at the Hagley Museum and German Historical Institute, Delaware; Centre for British Studies, Humboldt-Universitat, Berlin; Dublin Institute of Technology; Institute of Historical Research, University of London; Department of Sociology and Social Policy, University of Southampton; Department of Media and Communications, University of Leicester; Centre for Research in Economic Sociology and Innovation, Department of Sociology, University of Essex; and to all participants at the 'Rethinking Affluence, Socio-cultural Change in Britain c. 1950–2000' event hosted by CRESC, University of Manchester.

Many colleagues and friends have shaped my thinking and offered good advice over the years. A special thank you to Michael Bailey, Ted Benton, Robin Blackburn, Kerstin Brückweh, Suzanne Burke, David Clampin, Paul du Gay, Peter Gurney, Stuart Hall, Mark Harvey, Clark Eric Hultquist, Angela McRobbie, Mike Savage and Stefan Schwarzkopf. Frank Mort was an important sounding board in the early stages of the project and provided helpful comments towards the end. Bill Schwarz has been an important source of support and encouragement and has read and commented upon a number of the chapters. Mike Roper read a complete first draft of the book and commented on later versions. His perceptive comments and support (at times beyond the call of duty) have added much to my final arguments. Claire Nixon has lived with this book and offered thoughtful comments at various points. Her humour, love and wisdom have made its completion possible. The book is dedicated to her, with love.

Abbreviations

AA	Advertising Association
IPA	Institute of Practitioners in Advertising
JWT/Duke	J. Walter Thompson Company Archives, John W. Hartman Center for Sales, Advertising and Marketing History, Duke University
JWT/HAT	J. Walter Thompson Company Archives, History of Advertising Trust
PRO	The National Archives, Public Records Office

Introduction

When Edward G. Wilson, the head of the International Department of the US-owned advertising agency J. Walter Thompson (JWT), arrived in London in the evening of 10 February 1954 on the final stage of what he called 'My Trip to Europe', he had been away from his New York office for a week and had another week's work to undertake in London before he could return to the United States and to his family.[1] The trip had been tiring and had stretched his capacities as he got to grips with the local trading conditions of the company's offices in Antwerp, Frankfurt, London and Paris. Freed from the linguistic difficulties posed by his limited French and German and knowing that London was one of most profitable and largest of JWT's subsidiary companies, Edward Wilson began to relax.[2] He talked with London colleagues about routine client matters, as well as about the imminent arrival of commercial television in Britain, a matter which was exercising them.

Wilson's account of his travels, written for the benefit of his relatives and friends and as a way of 'getting the trip out of my system', was shot through with perceptions of the differences between Europe and his homeland. Stimulated by new sights and experiences, he detailed the variations in clothing, furniture and home interiors. In relation to Paris, for example, he mentioned not only the kinds of furniture in the office that he visited and people's clothes, but also made a point of describing the kitchen of one of his French colleagues, concluding that it was 'good for Paris, but the stove and refrigerator are tiny'.[3] In his comments on London, the contrasts were more subtle. Having lunch in the offices of JWT's lawyers he revealed how 'the windows in the dining room were open half way. In deference to me, these were closed until it became too stuffy for the Englishmen.' If being accustomed to less comfortably heated rooms set the British apart from their American visitor, then Edward Wilson was additionally struck by the fact that British staff did not use the old-fashioned lift but preferred to walk up the stairs. This prompted him to suggest that the 'English are hearty'. Wilson also described his shopping expedition in London. Like American tourists before and since, he was especially taken with Harrods, suggesting 'It is a tremendous department store without seeming to be.'[4]

Edward Wilson's interest in drawing a set of contrasts between the consumption norms of Europe and America was shared by other post-war American visitors to Europe, including Britain. For these tourists and business travellers, the lack of modern lifts in hotels, poor heating and the generally lower levels of material comfort prompted a sharp sense of cultural difference. As Richard Pells observes, these visitors tended to judge Europe not so much by its art and culture as by the shocking standards of its kitchens and bathrooms.[5] Peter Mandler makes a similar point when he notes how American tourists to Britain went looking for one old country – the old country of cathedrals and Shakespeare and Walter Scott – and found another – a new old country of inadequate plumbing and heating, tiny packets of food, shabby clothing and 'quaintness'.[6] American tourists were not alone in drawing these consumerist comparisons between the New World and the Old. Such contrasts preoccupied commentators on both sides of the Atlantic. Among them were American business people and policy makers who, in the late 1940s and 1950s, recurrently saw the products of US industry and its mass consumer society as visible proof of America's triumph over not only Soviet-style communism, but also over the older cultures of Western Europe.[7] The status of Americans as 'people of plenty', in David Potter's memorable phrase, contributed much to Americans' self-confidence abroad. America became the norm against which many Europeans came to judge their own way of life as they encountered the products of US commerce and culture on European soil, or else experienced them on visits to the USA. As the young would-be writer Malcolm Bradbury noted on a trip to the United States in 1955,

> I left behind an England … that was in the process of losing an empire and had not yet found a washing machine … America was where all that was freest and most novel came from: the best movies, the best clothes, the best ice-cream, the best gum, the best cars, the best comics, the best jazz, even the best books.[8]

It was not surprising that an advertising person like Edward Wilson should be attuned to the differences in the material comforts of life between America and Western Europe, since it was the role of advertising to sell dreams of abundance and a consumerist vision of the good life. Confident in the capacity of rising material affluence to deliver social progress, these commercial persuaders were advocates of a vision of social change carried by an expanding world of goods.⁹ Moreover, advertising agencies were important conduits through which the norms of American consumption experienced by Wilson at home – and the source of his contrasts with Europe – travelled eastwards across the Atlantic. This movement of the ideals, if not the actuality, of American standards of living went hand in hand with the transfer of US techniques of advertising and promotion. JWT was deeply implicated in this process as a pioneer of US advertising on European soil and the office which Wilson headed, the International Office, grew out of the agency's expansion into Europe in the inter-war years. It aimed to help JWT's subsidiary offices reproduce the advertising techniques and styles of the parent company and in so doing assist them in delivering American standards of advertising and service for their clients, both American and local.

This book explores the Anglo-American dimensions of the trans-Atlantic advertising relations in which Edward Wilson, and advertising people like him, participated during the 1950s and 1960s. These relations matter because they shaped the way that advertising agencies in Britain both understood and sought to give direction to an expanded consumer culture. The consolidation of this culture was a central part of the remaking of post-war Britain and advertising's contribution to it was shaped by the way that American advertising ideas and practices crossed the Atlantic, particularly through the good offices of US-owned advertising agencies in Britain. In my exploration of this transfer of knowledge and practices, Wilson's agency, J. Walter Thompson, figures prominently. JWT was a leading player not just in the US advertising industry, but also within the international advertising business and was one of the biggest agencies in Britain in the 1950s and 1960s. Reading post-war developments in advertising in Britain through the lens of JWT allows me to explore in some detail the way American advertising techniques, practices and forms of expertise came to Britain and developed in distinctive directions. In doing so, I argue that US advertising methods and approaches were, in many instances, adapted, hybridized and indigenized in their transporting to the British context.[10] These were processes of reworking and translation that were not only shaped by the cultural sensibilities of practitioners working in this country, but were also driven by the recognition from agencies of the cultural differences between British and American consumers. As Ken Shaw, a senior figure at JWT New York, conceded when reviewing the London office's television commercials in the late 1950s, 'Hard sell, as we know it in the US, is lacking, but bearing in mind the differences in the respective audiences, this makes sense.'[11] The brute reality of cultural difference forced US-owned advertising agencies like JWT to modify and rework their established ways of working. In the process, they could, as we will see, shed or soften their American-ness and go native.

To insist on this process of hybridization and indigenization is not to claim that a common trans-Atlantic advertising culture developed in this period. Nor it is to suggest that British and American advertising people were engaged in a set of reciprocal relations in which their practices converged.[12] The two industries remained distinct and different from each other even as they were joined together by commercial traffic across the Atlantic. Moreover, the power relations shaping Anglo-American advertising relations worked to position the British industry in a subordinate position, militating against reciprocity. The dominant direction of influence was definitely eastwards, with US advertising agencies, fuelled by the power-house of the US economy, exerting their influence upon the British. This was dramatically evidenced by new arrivals that joined established US agencies like JWT in Britain between 1957 and 1967 as American advertising went on an acquisition spree in London. By the end of the 1960s, six of the top ten advertising agencies in Britain were American-owned.[13]

In recognizing this dominance of US advertising over the British industry and the wider authority of US models of advertising and consumption, it will also be clear, however, that I part company with those accounts which have tended to emphasize the wholesale transfer of American advertising techniques and forms of expertise to Britain. Historians of this period, like contemporary commentators before them, have sometimes understood this as a process of 'Americanization' and privileged the influence of what Victoria de Grazia has termed America's 'market empire' in their exploration of trans-Atlantic relations.[14] This attention to US commercial hegemony has rightly emphasized the dominance of US advertising and commerce over countries like Britain in the post-war period. However, to acknowledge this is not to accept that British advertising and styles of consumption were transformed from top to bottom, or even all transformed in the same way, by the power of US advertising on British soil. Against the assertion of the 'irresistible' force of the US 'market empire' when applied to the subaltern British advertising industry, my book explores the way US commercial and cultural influences constituted a resource and stimulus to British advertising practitioners, but one which was reworked and combined with more local cultural resources. This worked to produce distinctive British styles and techniques of advertising and approaches to the mass market. This was the case, I suggest, even within a US-owned multinational advertising agency like JWT in terms of how its London office went about its business.

The book explores these trans-Atlantic influences upon advertising in Britain during a distinctive period of social and cultural change. I move across two decades in the course of the pages that follow, covering a period which begins in the last days of post-war austerity in the late 1940s and finishes amid the first signs of a slowdown in economic growth in the late 1960s. The book, however, does not follow a chronological progression, but rather moves across this time frame in each of the chapters. The years between 1955 and 1969, the central period that the book focuses on, were a time of ongoing social change. For sociologists and social critics the expansion of private-sector consumption was one of the defining features of the period. While the precise social effects of this were much debated, especially in relation to established working-class culture and identities, there was a broad consensus among contemporary sociological commentators that growing material affluence in the immediate post-war decades marked a watershed moment.[15] In fact, for both sociologists and later historians of post-war Britain, growing popular consumption was enshrined as one of the building blocks of the distinctive kind of society that emerged after 1945, alongside the creation of the Welfare State, policies to sustain full employment and political consensus.[16] Moreover, 'affluence', the term used to capture the rise in standards of living for the mass of the population, continues to be a key term through which economic and cultural historians have sought to understand the changed character of British society in the 1950s and 1960s.[17]

Underpinning the new patterns of consumption noted by sociologists and historians was not only the ending of the final austerity controls on private-sector consumption in 1954, but also the increase in average earnings, which nearly doubled between 1950 and 1959. The purchasing power of average households was also increased by cuts in the standard rate of income tax and by a buoyant labour market in which the supply of jobs in many sectors outstripped demand.[18] The existence of near full employment and rising wages were further bolstered by changes in hire-purchase which made credit easier to secure and helped household income to stretch further.[19] A reduction in the price of domestic electricity increased discretionary income for many households and made the purchase and running of electrically powered domestic technologies more economically possible. Electrical consumer durables like televisions, refrigerators and washing machines, all of which had been part of middle-class consumption in the inter-war years, were among the goods whose sales rose rapidly as consumer spending steeply increased from 1956 onwards.[20] Average consumption per head rose 20% between 1950 and 1959, and spending on household commodities rocketed by 115% during the 1960s.[21] The boom in consumer spending was linked with developments in the supply side of the consumer economy. Processed and convenience foods, first developed in the inter-war years, took a larger share of consumer expenditure, with sales of frozen food booming between 1953 and 1960.[22] The way consumers bought food and household goods was reshaped by the rise of self-service retailing and by the associated arrival of the supermarket. High-street shopping was transformed by Marks & Spencer's post-war growth as a major supplier of mass-market clothing.[23]

Advertising was an integral part of these developments in the consumer economy. The industry expanded on the back of growing demand for its services and by the late 1960s total billings for advertising agencies in Britain stood at a post-war high of approximately £590 million, following sustained year-on-year growth since the mid-1950s.[24] Much of the demand for advertising came from the big consumer goods manufacturers and it was the commodities produced by these companies which dominated advertising expenditure in the late 1950s and 1960s. In 1960, for example, the top twenty advertisers were made up of the manufacturers of detergents, washing powders, toiletries and confectionery, with cigarette manufacturers and oil and petrol companies also represented.[25]

The goods produced by many of these big-spending advertisers were not only important to the billings of advertising agencies. They had a deeper social significance in that they were central to the transformations in post-war life, bringing new kinds of comfort, convenience and cleanliness to the domestic lives of British households, especially those among the working and lower middle classes. Women were the key purchasers of many of these goods, accounting for 90% of all expenditure on food and household commodities and they were the key consumers at the heart of the social transformations in the domestic lives of subaltern groups.[26] So while advertising agencies worked across a whole range of commodity markets – from de luxe goods, motor cars, travel and tourism – and targeted consumers ranging from elite social groups and the new urban middle class to young people and children, it was products aimed at women, especially married women, which dominated advertising, particularly on the new medium of television.

This book focuses on how advertising connected with and helped to shape the transformations in post-war domesticity in its targeting of these consumers. At the heart of this was the way that advertising contributed to the elaboration of the post-war ideal of the 'modern housewife' at the heart of domestic, home-centred consumption. Advertising helped to generalize this ideal from its more middle-class roots in the inter-war years into the lives of working-class and lower middle-class consumers. Such an endeavour threw up competing images of the housewife. Showing how these advertising representations shifted and the way they articulated competing public fantasies of 'ordinary femininity' is a key purpose of the book. The assembling of the housewife, however, did not stand alone. Bound up with her representation was the promotion of an ideal of the post-war home over which she presided. The book focuses in particular on the way that television advertising represented one important aspect of post-war domesticity. This was the 'modern kitchen' equipped with labour-saving devices, fitted cupboards, vinyl flooring and a picture window. At a time when many consumers lived in pre-war housing that had been subject to limited interior modernization or else lived in poorly designed post-war homes, advertising was important in establishing the normative status of the 'modern servantless home' and the newly important room of the kitchen.

Images of the post-war home and the housewife within advertising were also intimately connected to the ways in which American models of consumption took distinctive directions in Britain in the 1950s and 1960s. The post-war home and the housewife not only had their roots in inter-war consumerism, but also in the model of mass consumption and domestic life developed in America. Advertising was important in disseminating this model of the 'new household'.[27] But at the same time, advertising worked to shed any American associations of this form of domesticity. Through the details of home interiors shown in the commercials and in the casting of the housewives in adverts like those featuring the Persil 'Mum' and Oxo's Katie, TV advertising rendered the housewife and her home as distinctively British entities. If the roots of the ordinary housewife, then, were at least partly in US commercial culture, she emerged within British TV advertising as a recognizably English-British social type overseeing a recognizably British home.

While television had a major influence upon the way that advertising agencies shaped the new cultures of home-centred consumption and the role of the housewife-consumer, its arrival also changed the advertising industry. In this regard the arrival of television advertising in 1955 is a seminal event in the story of post-war advertising that this book tells. Historians of television have recently begun to produce fuller accounts of the early post-war years of the medium and to describe how it established itself as a national habit in Britain in the late 1950s and 1960s, transforming cultural life in the process.[28] They have shown how a distinctive television culture was formed and how broadcasters assembled the styles and modes of address of popular TV. Television advertising was a central part of these developments and yet the place of television commercials in this expanded culture of TV has barely been addressed by historians of the medium.[29] My account seeks to explore how TV advertising developed in Britain and to reflect upon the challenges that it posed not so much for television as for the advertising industry. Television's rapid rise as an advertising medium, eclipsing the press and outdoor advertising by the early 1960s, helped to transform advertising agencies, including their relationship to consumers. It gave advertising practitioners access to a vivid and immediate form of communication that had many advantages over the established, dominant media of press and posters in its ability to demonstrate products in use and to offer viewers comic and entertaining forms of persuasion. Agencies responded to the opportunities which television offered by developing and deploying a distinctive range of advertising techniques. These included jingles, product demonstrations, comic turns and emotional 'slice of life' dramas that elaborated a world of everyday consumption. Yet the coming of television also posed challenges to an industry rooted in the idioms and technologies of print culture and, over time, contributed to the reshaping of advertising as a commercial practice. Grasping this contradictory aspect of TV for advertising agencies – the challenges as much as the opportunities – is central to my argument. One might even suggest, following Michel Callon, that television, along with other innovations in the 'technologies of persuasion', encouraged the reconstitution of advertising as a 'market device', changing in fundamental ways how it represented goods and their relationship to consumers.[30]

If television changed advertising, then it also changed how others saw advertising. Exploring the reception of television advertising forms a further key dimension of the arguments developed in the book. I focus on two aspects of this reception. The first concerns how consumers, the viewers of commercials, responded to the new medium. Drawing on a range of evidence, including letters written by viewers to advertisers about their commercials, the book seeks to capture a distinctive post-war moment in the history of advertising and how the new sense of immediacy and directness which came through the technology of television could stir viewers into direct engagement with it. Television adverts were part of the novelty and immediacy of TV and prompted an imaginative investment by viewers in them. Viewers were often drawn to the emotional domestic dramas of commercials or their humour. As *The Times* noted in 1967, 'as entertainment advertising clearly has a special place in modern life. Cartoons, animals, children, pretty girls, a luxury setting, travel themes and a good story are liked by most people.'[31] But the immediacy of TV advertising could also cut in a different direction, provoking an antagonistic response. For viewers, commercials interrupted their favourite programmes, they were repetitive and intrusive. Sometimes they were even seen as loud and vulgar, a far from welcome intrusion. Viewers' reactions to TV advertising were also subtly mediated by the popular press. While television's arrival represented a profound challenge to the commercial fortunes of newspapers, the daily press remained influential in the 1950s and 1960s and responded in part to the competition that it faced from TV by treating the new rival, including its commercials, as newsworthy. In doing so, they helped to weave the new intrusive form of advertising in the home into the fabric of national life through the way they discussed it on their pages.

Though the popular press saw TV advertising as a legitimate part of ITV's service, a paper like the *Daily Express*, the second most popular newspaper of the period (just behind the *Daily Mirror*), could also be highly critical of advertising. This negative reaction to TV commercials was also evident in the response from educated opinion and the political classes. In fact, the arrival of ITV and with it TV advertising served to rekindle long-standing antipathy from these sections of British society to advertising's social role. Key sections of the main political parties were joined by social and cultural commentators, churchmen, consumer activists and even by the BBC in their opposition to the advertising industry. Across this swathe of opinion an almost obsessive fascination with and scrutiny of advertising flourished. For these critics advertising was seen as a celebration of acquisitiveness, snobbery and crass materialism and a harbinger of American 'hard sell' techniques of salesmanship within British business. Part of the emotional dislike of advertising undoubtedly came from not only its perceived American influences, but also its close relationship with apparently banal and trivial products. Certainly advertising's involvement with washing powders and cleaning products associated with dirt and disorder, as well as medical and personal products linked to hygiene, the body and its materiality, could stir aesthetic as well as moral prejudices among advertising's critics. While some advertising people may have shared these impulses, leading figures in the industry responded to these attacks by engaging in an ideological battle over the meaning and significance of popular prosperity and their role in these changes.[32]

Exploring this debate about advertising and 'affluence' is central to understanding advertising's broader engagement with social change. It means not just entering the corridors of advertising agencies but also the committee rooms of the inquiries and commissions in which advertising people came face to face with their critics and those policy makers concerned with the broader governance of commercial life and consumption. In responding to their various interlocutors, advertising people developed an optimistic defence of advertising's economic and social function. This saw the industry helping business and trade to flow both at home and abroad and so contributing to rising standards of living. Advertising people also advanced an expanded defence of the pleasures of mass consumption. This proposed a more self-expressive model of consumer subjectivity that challenged the puritan ideal of self-control and self-restraint promoted by the critics of advertising and affluence.

However, advertising practitioners were also prompted by the critique of their industry to be on their best behaviour. This reinforced the trend, already well established within parts of the industry, to emphasize the intelligent content and aesthetic standards of British advertising. Against the charge that advertising was crass and banal, industry leaders and its 'respectable reformers', including senior figures at an urbane agency like JWT, sought to emphasize its cleverness, intelligence and entertaining appeal to consumers. These responses, however, revealed the way that cultural reservations about advertising, especially from within educated and elite circles, worked to contain and contour the practices of commercial persuasion. This had notable effects upon US-owned agencies like JWT's London office, further encouraging them to soften what were typically seen as more brazenly commercial American techniques and approaches to the mass market and, in the case of JWT London, to reinforce its identity as a very British agency. In this sense, the critical reception of advertising played its part in shaping the distinctive directions that US advertising influences took in Britain.

Chapter one begins by setting the scene for the post-war developments in advertising. I explore the institutional developments in British advertising and the wider shape of the market for advertising services in the 1950s and 1960s. The industry experienced strong growth from the mid-1950s as advertising expenditure recovered from its contraction between 1938 and 1955. Advertising in the food and groceries markets led the way in the boom in advertising expenditure, especially in the form of television advertising. The chapter explores the relationship between each of the main advertising media and the factors which contributed to the distinctive range of products, such as soap powders, cleaners and confectionery, which dominated the new medium of TV. At the same time, I detail the growing internationalism of the advertising industry in Britain, including the increased presence of US-owned agencies in London.

Chapter two explores how the concern with the apparent 'Americanization' of British commerce advanced by a range of commentators both inside and outside advertising and driven by the so-called 'American invasion' of British advertising played out within the industry. I focus in particular on the consequences of this debate for an American-owned agency like JWT. Considering its relationship with its parent company, the chapter explores the dynamics of Anglo-American advertising relations within the company. It argues that ideas derived from the parent company in the US took distinctive directions in Britain. Rather than being an assertive advocate of the American vision of its head office, JWT London sought to soften its American-ness and go native. It did this by adapting, revising and rejecting elements of its parent company's approach and ethos. The chapter explores these processes through an attention to the organizational culture of the London office of JWT and its press advertising.

Chapter three explores the uses and development of market research within JWT London and allied companies. While it had been used by advertising agencies in Britain in the inter-war years, market research expanded rapidly in the 1950s and 1960s. It was transformed by the impact of a range of new techniques and ways of understanding consumer behaviour and consumer motivations. These included the influence of psychological models of human behaviour, together with sociological analyses of social change. Crucially some of these ideas travelled eastwards across the Atlantic to help inform market research practices in Britain. The effect of these diverse approaches to understanding markets was to enlarge the 'cartography of consumption' that advertising agencies and market research companies were engaged in and to generate inventive new ways of understanding the linkages between particular goods and the routines and rituals of 'ordinary consumers'. The chapter explores how these techniques were used to generate ways of understanding the 'mass housewife'. In doing so, it challenges claims made about market research's growing sophistication in the 1950s and 1960s under the influence of the psychological sciences. I also seek to bring a more expanded conception of consumer subjectivity into accounts of market research and to challenge the technical and limited view of consumer subjectivity proposed by sociological approaches to commercial devices like market research.

Chapter four explores how advertising agencies in Britain learnt to piece together the grammar of TV advertising, sometimes against their own reservations about its usefulness as an advertising medium. Detailing how many agencies walked backwards into the new world of TV, the chapter argues that agencies often looked towards the more 'advanced' world of US advertising, film and TV in order to help smooth the transition to television. These US influences, however, were combined with more local cultural resources and personnel. These included not only staff from the BBC, but also – more crucially – film makers from the field of sponsored documentary film. These latter practitioners worked not for the advertising agencies but for the production companies which agencies hired to produce the commercials. It was the legacy of British documentary film making which helped to give a distinctive British character and feel to many of the early TV commercials produced in the 1950s and 1960s.

One of the key genres in which US-derived ideas were combined with the traditions of British documentary film making was the 'slice of life' drama. This was a genre much favoured in advertising aimed at the housewife. In chapter five, I explore how commercials addressed and represented the housewife. Drawing on developments in the inter-war years, advertising people, like policy makers and others within commercial culture, saw the role of the 'modern housewife' as socially progressive in character since it allowed women to escape, they argued, from the domestic drudgery of old. This ideal of the modern housewife, however, did not stand alone. It was intimately connected to the creation of the idea of a 'new household'. The chapter explores how television advertising played an important role in the dissemination of both the ideal of the housewife and that of the new household. In doing so, I focus not only on the representation of 'Mum' within commercials, but also on the way a central aspect of the new home was depicted – the kitchen. Among advocates of the new household, the kitchen occupied a privileged position and it was seen as central to healthier, more hygienic and less labour-intensive forms of living. The chapter explores the ways in which TV advertising represented this key aspect of modern domesticity by focusing on commercials which promoted washing powders, washing machines and convenience foods. If, as cultural historians have contended, the example of the new household and the image of the modern housewife were first and foremost American models, then the commercials that I discuss show how US ideals were tailored to the British market.

Chapters six and seven address the reception of these commercials. In chapter six, I explore viewers' reactions to commercials, drawing on evidence from research conducted by the advertising industry and also from letters that viewers wrote to the advertisers about their commercials. I also discuss how the popular press responded to the arrival of commercial television and TV advertising. The way papers like the *Daily Express* and *Daily Mirror* reported upon commercials helped to colour how the new form of advertising was viewed by the public and fed into their own reception of the adverts. In chapter seven, I consider the reception of advertising by cultural critics and by those concerned with the broader governance of commercial life and consumption. If the arrival of TV advertising stirred critics to challenge both the cultural values promoted by TV adverts and the wider social role of advertising, then advertising people locked horns with their critics in a defence of their practices and of the wider social benefits of rising material affluence. In doing so they offered a positive and spirited defence of the role they performed and the pleasures of mass consumption in the age of affluence.

Notes

1. 'My Trip to Europe', February 1954, Edward G. Wilson, J. Walter Thompson Company Archives, Edward G. Wilson Papers, JWT/Duke, Box 19. See also, 'Diary, Trip to Europe, May 19–June 4, 1962'; 'Notes on My Trip to Europe', Jan 31–Feb 10, 1962, Edward G. Wilson, JWT/Duke, Box 19.
2. India was the next biggest with 544 staff, though the majority of its 25 international offices had fewer than 100 staff. International Offices, January 1962, JWT/Duke, Box 8.
3. Wilson, 'My Trip to Europe', JWT/Duke, Box 19, p. 6.
4. Wilson, 'My Trip to Europe', JWT/Duke, Box 19, pp. 11–12.
5. R. Pells, *Not Like Us: How Europeans Have Loved, Hated and Transformed American Culture since World War Two*, New York: Basic Books, 1997, p. 137.
6. P. Mandler, 'How modern is it?', *Journal of British Studies*, 42(2), 2003, pp. 271–5.
7. V. de Grazia, *Irresistible Empire: America's Advance Through Twentieth Century Europe*, Cambridge, MA, and London: The Belknap Press of Harvard University Press, 2005. Such thinking was articulated, among others, by the Marshall Plan. The plan was funded by the US Treasury and ran from 1948–51. Paul Hoffman, who led the Marshall Plan administration, counterposed the values of the 'American assembly line' to the 'Communist Party Line' (cited in M.-L. Djelic, *Exporting the American Model: The Post-war Transformation of European Business*, New York: Oxford University Press, 1998, p. 78).
8. M. Bradbury, *Dangerous Pilgrimages: Trans-Atlantic Mythologies and the Novel*, London: Secker & Warburg, 1995, p. 164.
9. As Stanley Resor, Edward Wilson's boss and chairman of JWT, put it in a in-house publication in the late 1950s, 'Never have the people of the world faced greater opportunities to increase their standard of living … never have we as a company had … a happier prospect of making outstanding contributions to this advance';

S. Resor in *Advertising as a Career for Women*, JWT, 1958, JWT/Duke, p. 1.

10 This understanding draws on J. Zeitlin and G. Herrigel (eds), *Americanization and its Limits: Reworking US Technology and Management in Post-war Europe and Japan*, Oxford: Oxford University Press, 2000; P. Gilroy, *Ain't No Black in the Union Jack: The Cultural Politics of Race and Nation*, London: Routledge, 1987, and *The Black Atlantic: Modernity and Double Consciousness*, London: Verso, 1993, chapter 1. The idea of cultural syncretism developed by Gilroy draws on the work of Roger Bastide. See M. Despland, *Bastide on Religion, the Invention of Candomble*, London: Equinox Publishing, 2008.

11 'Impressions of JWT London television department and British television generally', memo from Ken Shaw to Howard Kohl, 18 August 1959, Edward G. Wilson Papers, JWT/Duke, Box 10.

12 S. Schwarzkopf, 'Transatlantic invasions or common culture? Modes of cultural and economic exchange between the British and American advertising industries 1945-2000', in J.H. Wiener and M. Hampton (eds), *Anglo-American Media Interactions, 1850–2000*, Basingstoke: Palgrave Macmillan, 2007, pp. 254–74.

13 A. Sampson, *Anatomy of Britain Today*, London: Hodder & Stoughton, 1962, pp. 627–8; J. Pearson and G. Turner, *The Persuasion Industry*, London: Eyre & Spottiswoode, 1965, pp. 182–3; S. Fox, *The Mirror Makers: A History of American Advertising and its Creators*, New York: Morrow, 1984, p. 173.

14 De Grazia, *Irresistible Empire*; Djelic, *Exporting the American Model*; Zeitlin and Herrigel (eds), *Americanization and its Limits*; J. Killick, *The United States and European Reconstruction 1945–60*, Edinburgh: Keele University Press, 1997; F. Williams, *The American Invasion*, London: Anthony Blond, 1962; N. Tiratsoo and J. Tomlinson, 'Exporting the "Gospel of Productivity": United States technical assistance and British industry 1945–60', *Business History Review*, 71, spring 1997, pp. 41–81.

15 D. Lockwood, 'The new working class', *European Journal of Sociology*, 1, 1960, pp. 248–59; J. Goldthorpe and D. Lockwood, 'Affluence and the British class structure', *Sociological Review*, 11(2), 1963, pp. 133–63; J. Goldthorpe, D. Lockwood, F. Bechoffer and J. Platt, *The Affluent Worker in the Class Structure*, Cambridge: Cambridge University Press, 1969; M. Abrams, 'The home-centred society', *The Listener*, 26 November 1959, pp. 914–15; M. Abrams, 'New roots of working class Conservatism', *Encounter*, May 1960, pp. 57–8; M. Abrams and R. Rose, *Must Labour Lose?*, Harmondsworth: Penguin Books, 1960; S. Hall, 'A sense of classlessness', *New Left Review*, 1958, 5, pp. 26–32; S. Hall, 'The big swipe', *New Left Review*, 1959, 7, pp. 50–3; R. Hoggart, *The Uses of Literacy*, Harmondsworth: Penguin Books, 1957; R. Samuel, 'Dr Abrams and the end of politics', *New Left Review*, 1960, 9, pp. 2–9; R. Samuel, 'Class and classlessness', *New Left Review*, 1959, 6, pp. 44–50; E.P. Thompson, 'Commitment in politics', *New Left Review*, 1959, 6, pp. 50–5. Other recent commentators on the period from within political history have focused on the way the main political parties responded to an enlarged consumer society. See L. Black, *Redefining British Politics: Culture, Consumerism and Participation, 1954–70*, Basingstoke: Palgrave Macmillan, 2010; L. Black, *The Political Culture of the Left in Affluent Britain, 1951–64*, Basingstoke: Palgrave

Macmillan, 2003; M. Jarvis, *Conservative Governments, Morality and Social Change in Affluent Britain, 1957–64*, Manchester: Manchester University Press, 2005.
16   B. Conekin, F. Mort and C. Waters, 'Introduction', in *Moments of Modernity: Reconstructing Britain 1945–64*, London: Rivers Oram, 1999, pp. 1–21.
17   A. Offer, *The Challenge of Affluence, Self-Control and Well-being in the United States and Britain since 1950*, Oxford: Oxford University Press, 2006.
18   D. Sandbrook, *Never Had It So Good: A History of Britain from Suez to the Beatles*, London: Little, Brown, 2005, pp. 107–10; G.D.N. Worsnick and P.H. Ady (eds), *The British Economy in the 1950s*, Oxford: Oxford University Press, 1962; J. Tomlinson, 'Inventing decline: the falling behind of the British economy in the post-war years', *Economic History Review*, 49, 1996, pp. 731–57; G. Hughes, A. Lipeitz and A. Sigh, 'The rise and fall of the Golden Age', in S.A. Marglan and J.B. Schor (eds), *The Golden Age of Capitalism: Reinterpreting the Post-war Experience*, Oxford: Clarendon Press, 1990, pp. 39–125.
19   Sandbrook, *Never Had It So Good*, p. 112.
20   I. Zweiniger Bargielowska, *Austerity in Britain: Rationing Controls and Consumption, 1939–1955*, Oxford: Oxford University Press, 2000.
21   Sandbrook, *Never Had It So Good*, p. 112.
22   Ibid., p. 120.
23   R. Hoggart, 'Changes in working class life', in *Speaking to Ourselves: Essays on Society*, Harmondsworth: Penguin Books, 1971, pp. 45–61; P. Hennessy, *Having It So Good: Britain in the Fifties*, Harmondsworth: Penguin Books, 2007, p. 19.
24   P. Doyle, 'Advertising expenditure and consumer demand', *Oxford Economic Papers*, 20(3), 1968, pp. 394–416.
25   *The Times*, 18 August 1961, p. 13
26   'The housewife – a sitting target', *The Times*, 18 October 1962, p. vii.
27   De Grazia, *Irresistible Empire*, p. 428.
28   J. Corner (ed.), *Popular Television in Britain*, London: British Film Institute, 1991; J. Thumin, *Inventing Television Culture*, Oxford: Oxford University Press, 2004; R. Turnock, *Television and Consumer Culture*, London: IB Tauris, 2007; C. Johnson and R. Turnock (eds), *ITV Cultures: Independent Television over Fifty Years*, Maidenhead: Open University Press, 2005.
29   Though for notable exceptions see Turnock, *Television and Consumer Culture*, and Thumin, *Inventing Television Culture*.
30   M. Callon, C. Meadal and V. Rabeharisoa, 'The economy of qualities', *Economy & Society*, 13(2), May 2002, pp. 194–217; M. Callon, Y. Milo and F. Muniesa (eds), *Market Devices*, Oxford: Blackwell, 2007; M. Callon and F. Muniesa, 'Peripheral vision: economic markets as calculative collective devices', *Organization Studies*, 26(8), 2005, pp. 1229–50.
31   *The Times*, 13 June 1967, p. 67.
32   For a self-critical account of advertising see 'Writing the ads', *New Left Review*, 1966, March/April, pp. 15–20. Although published anonymously, the piece was written by JWT copywriter, Jill Neville. Sister of Richard Neville, the editor of *Oz*, Jill Neville eventually left advertising behind and established herself as a published author.

The advertising industry in the age of affluence

When *London Life*, the fashionable magazine edited by Mark Boxer, the founding editor of the *Sunday Times* colour section, threw a party to mark the opening of the GPO tower in central London in May 1966, it invited a number of advertising people among a guest list that included the fashion photographer Terence Donovan, the designer Ossie Clarke, the pop artists Peter Blake and David Hockney, the model/actress Una Stubbs and the musician Georgie Fame.[1] The inclusion of advertising people in this gathering of the great and the good of fashionable London was not unique. Advertising men and women regularly figured in *London Life*'s pages, including its feature 'What People Are Wearing', where they were shown as contemporary leaders in fashion and style alongside pop singers, actors, designers and boutique owners.[2] Elsewhere in the magazine advertising people surfaced in coverage of London's club scene, in a feature on the new breed of young Cambridge undergraduates who were being drawn to the worlds of publishing and advertising and in occasional commentary upon advertising campaigns.[3] In depicting advertising practitioners as part of what journalist Christopher Booker called 'the glamorous world of communication' in his study of the making of 1960s London, *London Life* echoed a broader fascination with and desire to mythologize London's new cultural and commercial elites, including advertising people. This was the same pantheon of creative talent captured in one of the most celebrated depictions of the new breed of celebrity associated with 'Swinging London': *David Bailey's Box of Pin-Ups*. Designed by Mark Boxer and with a text by *Queen* and *Sunday Times*' journalist Francis Wyndham, the book showcased the work of David Bailey, the most famous of the group of 'new wave' fashion photographers. Described by Booker as 'virtually a Debretts guide to the New Aristocracy', *David Bailey's Box of Pin-Ups* included two actors, eight pop singers, one interior decorator, four photographers, two managers of pop groups, one film producer, three models, one dress designer, one milliner, one discotheque manager, two East End criminals and one creative advertising man.[4]

While this depiction of advertising people registered their increasing cultural and commercial salience in sixties London, it was not entirely new. *Evening Standard* journalist Douglas Sutherland suggested that the 'ad executive' had been the most emblematic figure of the changes that saw London emerging from the gloom of the immediate post-war years. In 'a dark grey suit armed with his lavish expenses account … [he] commanded the best tables in the most expensive and exclusive restaurants'. For Sutherland these advertising practitioners were the 'most symbolic figures' of the 'new air of buoyancy' in London's expanding consumer economy of the mid-1950s.[5] At around the same time, in mid-1950s Chelsea, Mary Quant, the fashion designer and key shaper of the 'fashion revolution' at the heart of what became 'Swinging London' in the mid-1960s, identified advertising men as among the 'go-ahead' types who shaped the social milieu in which her first boutique, Bazaar, flourished. For Quant, her 'co-revolutionaries' and future clientele in the Kings Road were 'painters, photographers, architects, writers, socialites, actors, con-men and superior tarts. There were racing drivers, gamblers, TV producers and advertising men.'[6]

The placing of advertising practitioners at the heart of the commercial and cultural renaissance of the capital city during this period by magazines like *London Life* and commentators like Sutherland and Quant registered important changes in London's post-war economy. Employment in manufacturing and the docks fell sharply between 1961 and 1973. At the same time employment in sectors like fashion, design, magazine publishing and advertising brought nearly a quarter of a million jobs to London in the 1960s. These employment trends consolidated the already dominant position of service work in London. In 1951, 50% of the daytime labour force was engaged in service occupations. This compared to 31% in manufacturing and just fewer than 20% in building, public utilities, transport and communications. These employment patterns were given a further boost by the relaxation of planning laws and the rise of property speculation in the late 1950s and early 1960s. This produced a surge in new office building and contributed to the growth in London of relatively high-skilled service employment, including advertising.[7]

The association between the advertising industry and the commercial geography of the capital city was not a new phenomenon of the post-war years. The geographical concentration of the industry in London's West End and the lanes around Fleet Street towards the east of the city was well established and dated back to the establishment of the first recognizably modern service advertising agencies in the late nineteenth century.[8] While there were advertising agencies in Britain's other big cities, including regional offices of the big agencies, London was the unchallenged centre of advertising in the UK. This relationship was strengthened from the late 1950s as the industry underwent sustained growth on the back of rising advertising expenditure. This led to not only to an increase in advertising employment in the capital, but also to the arrival in London of a swathe of US-owned advertising agencies which established subsidiary offices in the city. Like the British agencies, these US-owned advertising agencies located their offices in the tightly packed spaces of London's business districts, close to not only the headquarters of the consumer goods manufacturers in central London, but also within touching distance of the national newspapers, TV production companies, film businesses, the studios of photographers, designers and the West End theatre. Advertising's post-war growth, while it had a broader national significance, was generated from within the specific spaces of London's commercial geography.

In this chapter, I explore some of the institutional developments within the advertising industry in the 1950s and 1960s and consider the shape of the agency sector that emerged from within a buoyant national advertising market and a booming cultural economy in London. This was a dynamic period of growth for the advertising industry and I reflect, in particular, on the key players who dominated the industry as it underwent expansion and on the social make-up of the individuals who shaped advertising during this period. Responding to growing domestic demand was not the only imperative for advertising agencies. Between 1958 and 1968, there was a massive expansion in the trade in industrial products between the developed capitalist economies. The US economy dominated its trading partners in this expansion and US firms exported, in particular, a host of consumer products to Europe. These included cars, kitchen appliances, washing machines, radio and TV sets, cameras and film, cosmetics, detergents, breakfast cereals, canned food, frozen food and cake mixes.[9] Advertising agencies responded to these developments in international trade by internationalizing their own operations. Alongside the quantitative expansion of the industry in Britain, it was the growing international reach of advertising agencies, including the growing presence of US agencies in London, which emerged as a further key feature of this period of institutional change and expansion.

The buoyancy of the London-based advertising industry was profoundly influenced by the spending decisions of the big advertisers in the consumer goods industries, including American-owned companies. Before turning to the institutional structure of the London-based advertising industry, I reflect in some detail on the advertising decisions of these advertisers and the overall pattern of advertising expenditure. Central to both was the way advertising was distributed across different advertising media. One of the key factors that influenced this distribution was the arrival of television advertising in 1955 with the creation of ITV. While it took a number of years for ITV to establish itself as a national service and for television to become a viable medium for targeting mass consumers, the arrival of ITV quickly transformed the market for advertising. By the early 1960s, faith in the power of the new medium had helped to elevate it to a central position in the business of commercial communication.

The market for advertising services

The recovery of domestic consumer markets and with them advertising expenditure was a notable feature of the British economy in the late 1950s and 1960s. Overall consumer expenditure returned to its pre-war level by 1950, though spending on key sectors like clothing and furniture remained below 1938 levels until 1953 when consumer expenditure across the board increased rapidly. By 1960 it was 27% higher than it had been a decade before.[10] Advertising expenditure broadly mirrored this growth in popular consumption. In the early 1950s, with austerity controls continuing to limit private-sector consumption, total advertising expenditure stood at about 1.4% of national income, considerably lower than the immediate pre-war level of 2.1%.[11] Expenditure on advertising, however, began to grow steadily from 1953 onwards and underwent a major expansion between 1956 and 1960. In fact, in the four years from 1956 it increased by nearly 50%.[12] By 1960 total advertising expenditure stood at 2.2% of the UK's national income, overtaking the levels seen before the war (Fig. 1).[13]

Advertising expenditure was dominated in this period by the manufacturers of mass-market consumer goods, especially groceries. In 1960, for example, the top twenty advertisers were made up of the manufacturers of detergents, washing powders, toiletries and confectionery, with cigarette manufacturers and oil and petrol companies also represented.[14] When these figures are broken down further into commodity groups, food advertising emerged as the biggest sector. Thus, just over 50% of all advertising expenditure went on food, with

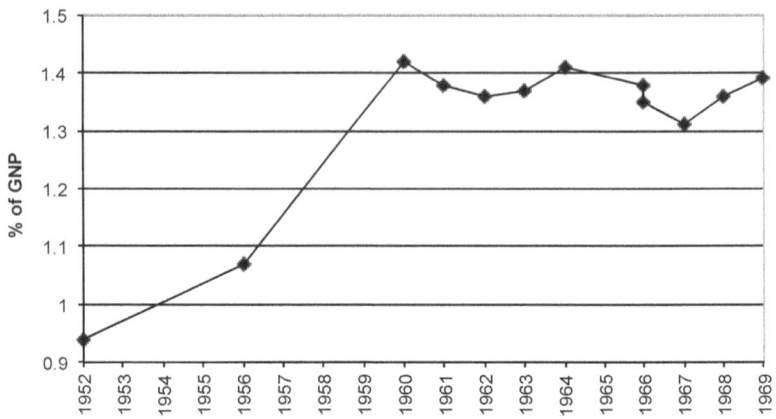

Total advertising expenditure as a percentage of GNP, 1952–69
Source: Advertising Association, *Advertising Expenditure 1960–73*,
London: Advertising Association, 1974

the largest percentage of this, just over 6%, going on chocolate advertising. Advertising for soaps, detergents, cleaners and scourers accounted for just over 29% of total advertising expenditure. Cars and commercial vehicles, by contrast, accounted for a mere 4% of the total advertising.[15] These patterns of expenditure remained more or less stable through the 1960s. The top spenders in 1967 confirmed the dominance of detergent and chocolate manufacturers (Fig. 2). Unilever, the Anglo-Dutch manufacturer of soap powders, detergents and margarines, was a heavy advertiser of its products. In 1960 it was Britain's biggest advertiser, spending £13.1m, well ahead of the second largest advertiser, the Beecham Group, which spent £6.3m. Behind them were two of the big confectionery manufacturers, Cadbury's (5th) and Rowntrees (7th), spending £3.2m and £2.8m, respectively.[16]

Advertising expenditure was principally spread across four media in the mid-1950s: national newspapers, mass circulation magazines, regional newspapers and outdoor advertising. The establishment of ITV added a fifth (and increasingly important) medium, television. TV advertising rose from 3.4% of total advertising expenditure in 1956 to 15.8% in 1960. The Advertising Association, in its review of advertising expenditure between 1960 and 1973, claimed that TV advertising had overtaken expenditure on national and London evening newspapers in 1960.[17] Other figures confirmed TV's relative rise. Figures for 1962 showed TV accounting for 29% of total advertising – the largest share for any one medium.[18] By 1967 TV advertising was worth £115m, well ahead of the £83m spent in national newspapers and the £47m

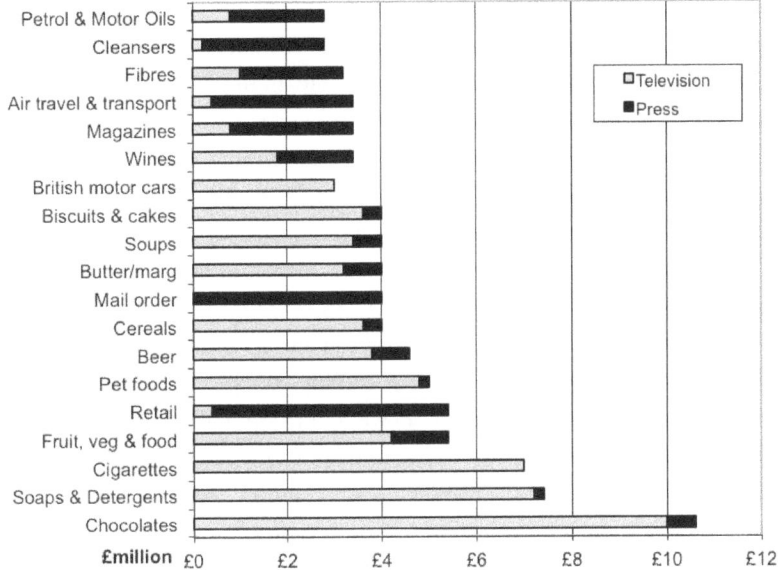

Advertising expenditure and product groups, 1967
Source: The Economist, 25 July 1968, p. 57

spent in magazines and periodicals.[19] One consequence of the overall growth in advertising between 1956 and 1966 was that the surge in expenditure on television advertising was generally absorbed by the overall growth in spending and did not detract significantly from expenditure on the press. In fact, advertising placed in national and regional newspapers increased in real terms between 1956 and 1960.[20] It was only towards the end of the 1960s, as overall

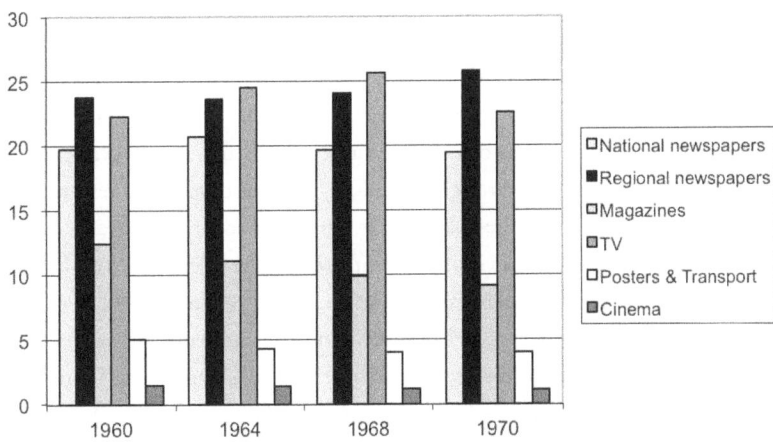

Advertising expenditure by media (as percentage of total spend), 1960–70
Source: Advertising Association, Advertising Expenditure 1960–73,
London: Advertising Association, 1974

advertising expenditure fell in more difficult economic circumstances, that press advertising expenditure dropped markedly (from £87m in 1966 to £83m in 1967), while TV advertising revenue continued to increase (Fig. 3).[21]

Unilever was one of the biggest users of TV advertising and among the three advertisers who dominated ITV from the mid-1950s, the others being Procter & Gamble and the Beecham Group. Between them they were responsible for a quarter of advertising expenditure on television.[22] In fact, Unilever was to be ITV's largest advertiser between 1955 and 1985. The company made clear its intent on the opening night of ITV. Of the 23 products advertised on Associated-Rediffusion that September evening, five were Unilever products. They included the first commercial shown on ITV, for Gibbs-SR toothpaste.[23] This commitment to television was made despite early reservations about ITV. The board of directors of Unilever's British company were initially cautious about the prospects for commercial television as an advertising medium. They noted in November 1954 that it was unlikely to be 'very profitable in the early stages' because of the small size of the audience for ITV. The directors suggested, however, that its experience in the United States encouraged the company to believe that it would be a valuable advertising medium in time.[24] As a result of this thinking, the company moved quickly to secure early bookings on the new service.[25]

Other marketing-orientated companies shared Unilever's view that it was important to invest in ITV in its early days to secure an advantageous position. Rowntree, the confectionery manufacturer, for example, took the decision in 1955 to invest heavily in TV. Its marketing and advertising committee felt that the company should be 'in from the beginning of TV advertising'.[26] The company divided its advertising resources between its many brands, beginning in November 1955 with TV advertising for Fruit Gums. By the end of 1957 half of its marketing budget was being spent on television and almost every one of its major brands was sold through television. This was despite the reservations that Rowntree had about the ability of its long-term advertising agents, JWT, to deal effectively with television. Rowntree's felt the agency lacked knowledge about TV and had limited experience of the medium.[27] As it turned out, Rowntree's concerns were ill-founded and the company viewed its early commercials as a great success, especially those for Kit Kat and Aero. From early 1958 it decided to concentrate its marketing through the medium of TV.[28] One particularly notable success was the launching of After Eight mints through television in 1961, a product that JWT had helped the company to develop and market. Tellingly, Rowntree even viewed the large costs of TV advertising as offering it a competitive advantage. As they confessed, the very expense of TV gave large businesses like itself advantages over smaller competitors.[29]

The Beecham Group took a similar view of television, seeing it as the best way of reaching the mass housewife audience.[30] Before the arrival of ITV, as Sir Ronald Halstead, chairman of the Beecham Group, recalled:

> mass audiences could be reached through the *News of the World*, the *Radio Times* and leading women's weeklies. But we discovered soon after the introduction of television [that] advertising in the new medium had far greater immediacy and impact. By 1960, the most popular ITV programmes were being seen by over 40% of all housewives, and that was at a time when only about half the households in Britain had a set capable of receiving ITV.[31]

Many different advertisers used ITV in its first decade and figures from the *Statistical Review of Independent Television* in May 1959, for example, recorded that 4,000 individual advertisers had used it up to that point.[32] As a group, however, British businesses were often reluctant to invest heavily in advertising (and not just TV advertising) because of the dominance of a product- and production-orientated ethos. This meant that few were strongly marketing-orientated. As the British Institute of Management argued in a survey from 1961, 'the trend towards implementing the marketing concept is scarcely perceptible in this country'. Products, it claimed, were produced on the basis of hunches or because the production and engineering departments were committed to them.[33] The Economics Research Unit within the Labour government of the late 1960s confirmed this view. Reflecting on its own proposed study of the economics of advertising, J. Jordon, one of the ERU's officials, suggested that the enquiry should focus on Unilever, Procter & Gamble and Beecham, firms that 'use fairly sophisticated techniques to determine and control advertising'. These firms stood out, for Jordon, from the majority of British companies in which there was 'a general lack of sophistication in … marketing procedures'.[34]

Being product- or production-orientated, of course, did not prevent companies from advertising, but it did generally mean a weaker commitment to it that often stemmed from a belief in the intrinsic qualities of the product. This attitude surfaced among the big multiple retailers. Commenting on the move of its advertising business to the advertising agency Colman Prentis Varley in 1965, a spokesmen for Marks & Spencer confessed, 'Our advertising expenditure is minute, most of it done locally, but it does represent a very small relative amount. This is part of the marketing policy of Marks & Spencer. We have always believed that goods sell themselves.'[35] In 1964 Marks & Spencer spent just £27,000 on its advertising (99% in the press), while other retailers in the clothing retail sector were also parsimonious with their advertising expenditure. Fenwick's, for example, spent only £50,000 (all in the press) and Richard Shops only a little more (£53,000), largely in the provincial press.[36]

The arrival of television could also reveal the limits of even committed advertisers. Speaking in October 1953 Lord Moyne, of the brewers Arthur Guinness, made it clear that, while the company had used advertising since 1928, he considered the 'existing channels entirely adequate and commercial television an unnecessary and extravagant extension'.[37] Similarly, senior figures at the US soup manufacturer Campbells were cautious about paying for television air time in the UK, and warned their advertising agents that they did not want 'to drive the soup business into the soap business' way of doing things – a reference to the large sums spent by the washing powder manufacturers.[38] Views such as these pointed to the particular reluctance of certain sectors of business to use television advertising as a key vehicle in their marketing strategies. Through the 1950s and 1960s brewers, multiple retailers, the fashion sector, the manufacturers of luxury goods and businesses in the travel and tourism industry and car manufacturers were among those sectors that were resistant to the selling power of television. The reason for this is hard to ascertain, but seemed to spring from the corporate cultures and sector-specific traditions of these companies.[39] It was also related to the perceived limitations of black-and-white TV as an advertising medium and the emphasis within ITV's scheduling upon the mass family audience. The US airline Pan Am, for example, used the press, posters and the trade press rather than TV. These media allowed it to better target its key market of high-class consumers and offered colour reproductions of adverts.[40] Similar thinking lay behind the reluctance of fashion advertisers, luxury goods companies and retailers to use TV. In the case of car manufacturers, their limited use of television as an advertising medium stemmed from an unofficial agreement between them to limit its use.[41] The effect of these differences across British (and international) business was to create a situation in which ITV was dominated by the advertisers of packaged goods aimed at the mass-market housewife. This gave a distinctive character and feel to British television advertising in the 1950s and 60s.

As I have already noted, despite TV's rise as an advertising medium, magazine, press and poster advertising continued to be important for advertisers through the 1950s and 1960s. Women's magazines, with circulations regularly reaching nearly three-and-a-half million readers, were an important vehicle for targeting female consumers. The launch of magazines aimed at young, single women and teenage girls through the late 1950s and 1960s further helped the printed media to maximize its value to advertisers.[42] The mass circulation daily papers also continued to deliver large readerships for advertisers. Despite the loss of several established papers in the 1950s, the biggest sellers – the *Daily Express* and the *Daily Mirror* – maintained large circulations.[43] Readerships of the quality press, especially the Sunday papers, grew strongly from the late 1950s. Press advertising was also given a fillip by the introduction of the *Sunday Times* colour supplement in 1962. This offered advertisers access to affluent middle-class readers through a colour medium. The *Sunday Times* magazine became, through the mid-to-late 1960s, an important vehicle for the selling of alcohol, de luxe toiletries and luxury goods (including expensive watches and high-class brands of cigarettes).[44] Innovations in design, typography and photography helped magazines to strengthen the appeal of print culture for advertisers.[45] In the 1960s a number British advertising agencies, most notably Collett Dickenson Pearce (CDP), gained a strong reputation for their press advertising, and the *Sunday Times* magazine almost became CDP's 'house journal'.[46]

Overall, then, the national press and magazines enjoyed continuing success as advertising media despite the arrival of TV and all advertising media benefited from the buoyant advertising market of the late 1950s and 1960s. What, however, was the state of the advertising industry that was buying advertising space from the media during this period? It is to the agency sector that I now turn.

The advertising industry

The advertising industry that emerged from the dislocations of the war and the years of post-war austerity still bore the shape that it had acquired in the inter-war years. The industry was made up of a plethora of weakly capitalized privately owned businesses that were geographically concentrated in and around central London. Many of the large agencies occupied properties in Mayfair and Knightsbridge through to Holborn, Tottenham Court Road and Euston Road, and in Fleet Street and its surrounding lanes. By the end of the 1960s these London-based agencies were conducting 90% of the advertising business done in Britain.[47] This concentration of the business of advertising within or adjacent to a small area of London's West End contrasted to the American advertising industry where, despite the importance of Madison Avenue as a key centre for advertising in New York, strong regional centres also existed, notably in Chicago, Detroit and Los Angeles. Together with New York, these three cities accounted for 80% of the agency business in the USA.[48] The majority of the large London-based advertising agencies were members of the Institute of Practitioners in Advertising (IPA), the industry's key professional body. Along with its sister organization, the Advertising Association (AA), the IPA represented the interests of the advertising industry, specifically service advertising agencies. The IPA also ran a series of advertising examinations to bolster advertising education and was strongly committed to raising the professional standing of advertising and its wider cultural legitimacy.[49] In 1966 the IPA estimated that its member agencies employed 90% of the probable 22,000 employees of all advertising agencies.[50] The figure for employment in the industry as a whole represented a post-war high, showing an increase from the 17,000 employed in 1957.[51] The IPA's member agencies represented just under half of all advertising agencies registered as private companies in Britain. Among its 272 member agencies, 19 were what the IPA classified as large agencies, 44 medium-sized and 209 small. Size, for the IPA, was determined by turnover: a large agency had an annual turnover of £4m or more, a medium-sized agency had a turnover of £1–4m, while small agencies operated on an annual turnover of less than £1m. This meant that, when compared to the large client companies that they worked for, even the big agencies were economically relatively weak organizations, with notably low net asset values and turnover. The massive Unilever Group of companies, for example, had a total turnover of nearly £2,000m in 1964, with pre-tax profits of £119m. The Cadbury's Group, though a smaller business, still had turnover of £84m in 1959.[52]

When classified by the size of their billings – the cost of the advertising that they placed for clients and a measure that broadly mirrored the figures for turnover – the agency rankings showed that the large advertising agencies dominated the business. In 1962 the top five agencies based on billings placed a quarter of all advertising and about half of all advertising was handled by the top 14 agencies.[53] This dominance by a small number of big players revealed the tendency towards concentration within the advertising industry, where size gave agencies competitive advantages. Big agencies were able to offer clients a large range of services and had more leverage in negotiating with the media. The fact that a large number of small agencies were also able to successfully trade, however, pointed to another distinctive feature of the business. This was its fissiparous character, fuelled by the relative ease with which agencies could be established, often as breakaways from established companies. The viability of new agency start-ups was facilitated by the tendency of large advertisers to split the advertising of their brands across a range of agencies. This was done to put some competitive pressure on each agency working for the client. It also had the effect of spreading advertising budgets more widely than might otherwise have been the case, despite the relative concentration of advertising expenditure. Imperial Tobacco, for example, used 14 separate agencies to handle the advertising of its brands.[54] Unilever also split its advertising across a group of agencies and Ford, when it reorganized its advertising business in 1966, divided its business between four agencies.[55]

Through the 1950s and 1960s the agency rankings were dominated by a dozen or so big agencies. These included the US-owned agencies J. Walter Thompson, Erwin Wasey Ruthrauff & Ryan, Young & Rubicam, Foote Cone Belding and McCann-Erickson, together with five big British agencies: London Press Exchange, S.H. Benson, Mather & Crowther, Colman Prentis Varley and W.S. Crawford. Many of these agencies bore the names of their founding partners and these individuals often remained powerful presences within the companies. Arthur Varley – or Colonel Arthur Noel Claude Varley, CBE, MIPA, to give him his full title – a founding partner of CPV, was one example of this type of influential personality. In the early 1960s Varley appeared 'as an amiable, slightly portly good-looking old Wykehamist with a pipe and a tweed suit'.[56] He was also known not only as a businessman, but also a shaman, 'a person who could arouse belief'.[57] Charismatic rather than bureaucratic authority, then, was a distinctive feature of these agencies.

Varley's public school and Oxbridge background – he had gone to Worcester College, Oxford, after leaving Winchester – was typical of agency bosses and the London-based industry was notable for its generally urbane and educated staff, particularly at the upper echelons. At the large IPA agencies 20% of staff came from public school and 1 in 10 of all employees of IPA member agencies were graduates.[58] This was at a time when only around 6% of the population attended public school and less than 7% of the population went to university.[59] The agency Robert Sharpe & Partners, well-known for its aggressive and somewhat arch self-promotion, was headed by three old Etonians, Mark Ramage, Oliver Knox and Christopher Murray, and was more explicit than most agencies in advertising in *The Times* for Cambridge graduates with first class degrees to join it.[60] The public school backgrounds of senior advertising managers was broadly representative of the social backgrounds of top managers in the rest of British industry in this period, and the concentration of graduates, including Oxbridge graduates, at the apex of advertising mirrored the educational provenance of Britain's industrial elites.[61] As Mike Roper suggests, a public school education was seen as a qualification for the owner-managers of British business, but as management became professionalized through the 1960s, graduates became more important.

Outside the senior management positions graduates also dominated the other professional jobs within agencies. This included the roles of account executive or representative, copywriter and market research staff. Specialist staff involved in the preparation of press and poster production and printing represented a notable proportion of the non-graduate employees. They were joined by other secondary-school entrants working in the TV, cinema, radio and film production departments.[62] Secretarial staff and office juniors, together with a range of ancillary roles, however, constituted the bulk of non-graduate employees and accounted for 40% of all staff working for IPA agencies.[63] Unsurprisingly, women were concentrated in these secretarial positions and accounted for 99% of all those employed in this role. Conversely, women were weakly represented in the key creative jobs, with only 20% of copywriters and 11% of artists being women. Among marketing services (including market research) women were significantly better represented and made up nearly half of those employed. A similar picture was in evidence for PR roles, where 48% of the staff were women.[64]

Employment in the industry grew through the late 1950s and 1960s and reached a post-war high point of 22,000 in 1966.[65] The buoyant period of growth for advertising employment coincided with important institutional developments. Central to these was the expansion of agencies into overseas markets, largely on the back of expanding world trade. Colonel Varley's agency, CPV, was a good example of this development. CPV established a number of international subsidiaries and overseas associates.[66] By the mid-1960s the company consisted of the two core British arms, Colman Prentis Varley Ltd and CPV (International) Ltd, together with five offices in Europe (including CPV Italiana, the biggest advertising agency in Italy), six offices in Latin America and the Caribbean and a contact office in New York. In addition, CPV worked with 75 associate agencies in 47 countries.[67] CPV's pattern of growth was centred upon two broad geographical areas – Europe, an increasingly important area for trade, and the Caribbean/Latin America region – and driven by the need to service the overseas advertising of its clients' businesses in these markets.

The London Press Exchange (LPE) also expanded its overseas operations in the post-war period for similar reasons to CPV. Just after the war it had established an international division and this formed the basis of a new subsidiary company, Intam, formed in 1948, which coordinated LPE's international advertising through a number of international offices and associate agencies. By the early 1960s this included branch offices in Johannesburg, Cape Town, Salisbury and Milan. Capturing LPE's ties with the sterling trade area and the former British colonies, the agency's staff magazine recurrently referred to the 'Intam commonwealth' or the 'LPE Empire'.[68] W.S. Crawford, one of the most important British agencies of the 1930s and still in the top twenty rankings based on billings in the early 1960s, had four overseas offices by 1963 (in Belgium, France, Holland and Pakistan), with associate offices in another 57 countries.[69] S.H. Benson, another venerable British agency and the most successful British agency of the 1960s, also had an international network of offices and associates. As with CPV, the agency was split between two parent companies, S.H. Benson Ltd and S.H. Benson International Ltd, with 19 wholly or partly owned subsidiary companies and 60 associated agencies in locations such as Bombay, Brisbane, Calcutta, Hong Kong, Lagos, Melbourne, Nairobi, Vancouver and Milan.[70] S.H. Benson was unusual, however, among the big British agencies in seeking to establish a significant presence in the USA. In 1948 it linked up with another British agency, Mather & Crowther, to jointly form a New York business, Benson & Mather New York. The agency was headed by David Ogilvy, the younger brother of Mather & Crowther's managing director, Francis Ogilvy. David Ogilvy would become the most celebrated advertising man of the 1960s, the British ad man who had made it big in the States.[71] The agency he ran opened its doors in September 1948 as Hewitt Ogilvy Benson & Mather, before shortening this to Ogilvy Benson Mather (OBM) in 1952 following the departure of one of the founding partners, Anderson Hewitt. In 1964 Mather & Crowther merged with OBM New York to form a new parent company, Ogilvy & Mather International.[72] O&M International was floated simultaneously on the Stock Exchange in London and Wall Street in New York in April 1966 and remained one of the largest international advertising agencies until it was bought by the British agency WPP in 1989.[73]

Expanding internationally into the USA, as Bensons and Mather & Crowther had done, was generally difficult for British agencies for a number of reasons. Pre-eminent among these was the size and financial muscle of US advertising agencies in their home market. Fuelled by US economic growth, high levels of advertising expenditure and the size of the American market, US agencies – especially the large multinationals – outstripped their British competitors. This imbalance not only served to make it difficult for British agencies to establish operations in the USA, but it also drove the reverse process – the expansion of American-owned agencies through acquisition into the British advertising industry. US agencies had first established a significant presence in Britain in the first quarter of the twentieth century when agencies like Dorlands, J. Walter Thompson, Erwin Rasey and McCann-Erickson established offices in London in order to service US clients in the British and continental markets.[74] Two further US agencies arrived in Britain between 1945 and 1948 – Young & Rubicam and Foote Cone Belding. Both, again, set up operations in London in order to conduct work for US clients (General Motors and Lockheed, respectively).[75]

It was the ending of exchange controls in 1958 and the removal in 1959 of import controls on dollar goods (such as domestic appliances, radios and TV sets) that gave a renewed spur to what became known in the industry as the 'American invasion' of British advertising.[76] Between 1957 and 1969 US agencies bought 32 British agencies. These included the acquisition of Lambe & Robinson by Benton & Bowles in October 1958, the takeover of Hobson Bates & Partners, an agency formed in 1955 as a breakaway of senior partners from CPV, by Ted Bates in 1959, the financial merger between W.S. Crawford and Dorlands in 1965 and the acquisition of LPE by Leo Burnett in 1969. By the end of the 1960s, six of the top ten advertising agencies in Britain were US-owned.[77] The 'American invasion' worked to reinforce the concentration of advertising services among the large agencies in Britain. It also served to make clear the links, evident since the inter-war years, between the growth of the advertising industry and the international expansion of world trade – especially that which was associated with US manufacturers. Britain benefited through the 1960s from investment by US manufacturers and it remained the single most important destination for foreign direct investment outside of Canada of these US companies.[78] It was these US investors from the consumer goods industries that also helped to drive the expansion of US advertising agencies into Britain.

Conclusion

The growing international character of the advertising industry through the 1960s formed one commercial logic that advertising agencies in Britain had to negotiate. One of the consequences of this development was the deepening of the strongly bifurcated structure of the industry in Britain, split between a small number of relatively big international agencies and a plethora of smaller private enterprises. The arrival of US-owned agencies formed part of this growing internationalization and they were central to how the advertising industry in Britain changed through the late 1950s and 1960s. American know-how, expertise and marketing ideas followed the arrival of US agencies to London. This built on the transfer of knowledge established from the 1920s with the arrival of the first wave of multinational US-owned agencies like J. Walter Thompson, Dorland and McCann-Erickson. If the growing internationalism of the advertising industry in Britain during the 1950s and 1960s helped to define a key dynamic of the industry during this period, then, as we have seen, it also remained an industry which was heavily concentrated in Britain within London's West End and the lanes around Fleet Street. The offices of advertising agencies nestled close to the head offices of British and international consumer goods manufacturers, the TV and film production companies and West End theatre in what amounted to a clustering of commercial expertise and commercial endeavour.

While the industry was part of a buoyant cultural economy in London, it also benefited from the growth of national advertising. The buoyancy of the advertising industry was, as we have seen, dependent upon the sharp increases in advertising expenditure which occurred from 1956 onwards. ITV's arrival and with it television advertising did much to stimulate demand for advertising, at least for the heaviest spenders among the client companies. It was the belief in the power and value of TV advertising among the big advertisers in the groceries market, including the giant washing powder manufacturers and the sweets and confectionery makers, which helped agency turnover to increase and the sector to grow. Television was important not just for the greater financial rewards that it offered advertising agencies, but also because it contributed to the advertising industry's growing visibility in the culture. Commercials not only grabbed the attention of advertisers, but also drew viewers into a new relationship with advertising. At the same time, for cultural critics, TV advertising stirred new anxieties about the advertising industry and its social influence. The presence of US advertising agencies in London also troubled the industry's opponents and cultural pessimists in general. This was a debate focused on the dangers of the 'Americanization' of British commerce and culture in which advertising agencies were seen as key vehicles for US commercial domination. In the next chapter I reflect on this debate and consider how one US-owned advertising agency in particular – J. Walter Thompson – responded to this critical attack upon American advertising.

Notes

1 *London Life*, 21 May 1966, pp. 6–9.
2 Thus, in April 1966, Michael Beaumann, an account executive at the agency Ogilvy & Mather, was photographed wearing a stylish grey suit and camel-coloured overcoat from Austin Reed's men's boutique 'Cue', while J. Walter Thompson copywriter Jill Neville posed elegantly in a maroon corduroy suit from fashionable boutique 'Top Gear' in May 1966. See also *London Life*, 2 April 1966, pp. 26–7; 18 August 1966, pp. 20–1; 4 June 1966, pp. 30–1; 21 May 1966, pp. 38–9.
3 *London Life*, 22 October 1965, p. 24; 17 December 1965, p. 34.
4 C. Booker, *The Neophiliacs: A Study of the Revolution in English Life in the 50s and 60s*, London: Collins, 1969, p. 24.
5 D. Sutherland, cited in F. Mort, *Capital Affairs: The Making of the Permissive Society*, New Haven and London: Yale University Press, 2010, p. 125.
6 Quant, cited in C. Breward, 'Clothing desire: the problem of the British fashion consumer c. 1955–1975', *Cultures of Consumption* working paper series, 7, 2004, p. 34.
7 C. Breward and D. Gilbert, 'Anticipation of the new urban cultural economy: fashion and the transformation of London's West End', in M. Hebler and C. Zimmermann (eds), *Creative Urban Milieus: Historical Perspectives in Culture, Economy and the City*, Frankfurt and New York: Campus Verlag, 2008, pp. 165–6.
8 'General Advertising Service Agents, consultants, etc.', in *Advertiser's Annual 1966*, London: Admark Publishing, 1966.
9 R. Pells, *Not Like Us: How Europeans Have Loved, Hated and Transformed American Culture since World War Two*, New York: Basic Books, 1997, p. 190; E. Hobsbawn, *Age of Extremes: The Short Twentieth Century*, London: Michael Joseph, 1994, pp. 258–69.
10 I. Zweiniger Bargielowska, *Austerity in Britain: Rationing Controls and Consumption, 1939–1955*, Oxford: Oxford University Press, 2000, pp. 54–6.
11 Advertising Association, *Advertising Expenditure*, London: Advertising Association, 1953, p. 9.
12 *The Times*, 19 December 1962, p. 5. 1960 was an exceptional year, with spending on advertising growing by 34%; *The Times*, 12 December 1963, p. 18.
13 *The Times*, 19 December 1962, p. 5; Advertising Association, *Advertising Expenditure 1960*, London: Advertising Association, 1962, p. 26. Expressed in slightly different terms as a percentage of GNP, advertising expenditure rose from 0.94% in 1952 to 1.42% in 1960. It then more or less stabilized at just under 1.4% of GNP for the rest of the 1960s; Advertising Association, *Advertising Expenditure 1960–73*, London: Advertising Association, 1974. While as a percentage of national income post-war advertising expenditure only just passed the 1938 figure, there was a big increase in GDP in the post-war period. The rate of growth was 40% higher between 1955 and 1973 than it had been between 1924 and 1937. See W.P. Howlett, 'The "Golden Age", 1955–1973', in P. Johnson (ed.), *Twentieth Century British History: Economic, Social and Cultural Change*, London: Longman, 1994, p. 320.

14 *The Times*, 18 August 1961, p. 13.
15 Advertising Association, *Advertising Expenditure 1960*, Table 38.
16 On the 'vital role' played by advertising in the company's growth, see *The Times*, 25 April 1958, p. 17, and 'Advertising', *Unilever House Magazine*, June/July 1958, pp. 7–8. See also The Monopolies Commission, *Household Detergents: A Report on the Supply of Household Detergents*, HMSO, 1966.
17 Advertising Association, *Advertising Expenditure 1960–73*.
18 *The Times*, 21 May 1964, p. v.
19 *The Times*, 24 January 1968, p. 19.
20 Advertising Association, *Advertising Expenditure 1960*.
21 *The Times*, 24 January 1968, p. 19.
22 B. Henry, 'The history', in B. Henry (ed.), *British Television Advertising: The First Thirty Years*, London: Ebury Press, 1986, pp. 100–1. This concentration of advertising paralleled the situation in the USA. In 1958 15 companies spent almost half of all network TV dollars and were responsible for almost a third of all spot advertising; L. Samuel, *Brought To You By: Post-war Television Advertising and the American Dream*, Austin: University of Texas Press, 2002, p. 119.
23 *Advertiser's Weekly*, 30 September 1955, p. 6.
24 *Unilever Directors' Conference*, 4 November 1954, Unilever Archives, Port Sunlight.
25 Ibid.
26 R. Fitzgerald, *Rowntree and the Marketing Revolution, 1862–1969*, Cambridge: Cambridge University Press, 1995, pp. 443–4.
27 Ibid., p. 444.
28 Ibid., pp. 444–67.
29 Ibid., p. 454.
30 Sir Ronald Halstead 'The effect of television on marketing', in B. Henry (ed.), *British Television Advertising: The First Thirty Years*, London: Ebury Press, 1986, p. 407.
31 Ibid.; Bird's Eye Foods, the frozen food manufacturer, was also a heavy user of television advertising and in the first quarter of 1964, for example, spent 92% of its total advertising budget on TV. Procter & Gamble similarly spent heavily on TV advertising for its washing powder brand Daz, spending 99% of budget on TV advertising in the same first quarter of 1964, compared to less than 1% on the press. Ford, by contrast, spent over 99% of its budget through its agency the London Press Exchange on press advertising in the same period, and less than 1% on television. *Statistical Review of Independent Television*, January–March 1964, pp. 79–134.
32 *Statistical Review of Independent Television*, May 1959, p. 4.
33 Cited in Fitzgerald, *Rowntree and the Marketing Revolution*, pp. 32–3.
34 Notes from J. Jordon, ERU, 17 May 1967, PRO BT 213/489.
35 *Advertiser's Weekly*, 15 October 1965, p. 5.
36 Richard Shops, memo from Lottie Winant to Account Team, 23 March 1966, JWT/HAT Box 326.
37 Cited in H.H. Wilson, *Pressure Group: The Campaign for Commercial Television*, New Brunswick: Rutgers University Press, 1961, p. 139.

38 Memo from Edward G. Wilson to Samuel Meek, 'Re: Campbell Soup – London', 28 March 1961, JWT/HAT, Box 638.
39 See R. Church and A. Godley (eds), *The Emergence of Modern Marketing*, London: Frank Cass, 2003.
40 Pan American Airways, JWT/HAT, Box 168.
41 T. Bell, 'The agency viewpoint 3', in B. Henry (ed.), *British Television Advertising: The First Thirty Years*, London: Ebury Press, 1986, p. 441.
42 *Woman*, the monthly magazine, had a circulation of 3,427,465 in the late 1950s and kept this into the 1960s. See *The Times*, 2 May 1957, p. 5; 2 October 1962, p. 11. *Honey* was launched in 1959, aimed at young, fashion-conscious women. *Advertiser's Weekly*, 4 December 1959, p. 10.
43 The *Daily Express* and *Daily Mirror* dominated the mass-market dailies and though the circulations of national newspapers peaked in 1951 and declined thereafter, in the early 1960s both the *Mirror* and the *Express* could still command circulations of nearly four-and-a-half million; *Report of the Royal Commission on the Press, 1961–2*, 1961–62 Cmnd. 1811, p. 26. The circulations of the quality Sunday papers rose from 1,174,000 in 1955 to 2,343,000 in 1961; ibid., p. 10.
44 R. Shaw, 'Sunday persuasion – the adverts', in R. Hoggart (ed.), *Your Sunday Paper*, London: University of London Press, 1967, pp. 95–108.
45 'Press vs TV, publishers unite', *The Times*, 27 June 1967, p. vi.
46 Interview by the author with David Puttnam, 2008.
47 205 of the 509 advertising agencies operating in 1961 were outside London, though some of these were regional offices of the large London-based agencies; *Advertiser's Annual 1966*; J. O'Connor, 'From minor to major key', in IPA, *Fifty Years of Growing Responsibility*, London: IPA, 1967, p. 13.
48 J. Crichton, 'A major influence on economic growth', in IPA, *Fifty Years of Growing Responsibility*, London: IPA, 1967, p. 16.
49 See S. Nixon, 'In pursuit of the professional ideal: advertising and the construction of commercial expertise in Britain 1953–64', in P. Jackson, M. Lowe, D. Miller and F. Mort (eds), *Commercial Cultures: Economies, Practices, Spaces*, Oxford: Berg, 2000, pp. 55–74; S. Schwarzkopf, 'Respectable persuaders, the advertising industry and British society 1900–39', unpublished PhD thesis, Birkbeck College, University of London, 2008.
50 IPA, *Agency Employment*, London: IPA, 1966, p. 10.
51 O'Connor, 'From minor to major key', p. 8.
52 *The Times*, 25 May 1959, p. 17; 8 April 1964, p. 19.
53 J. Tunstall, *The Advertising Man in London Advertising Agencies*, London: Chapman & Hall, 1964, p. 27.
54 Ibid., p. 27.
55 *Daily Telegraph*, 6 December 1966, p. 12.
56 J. Pearson and G. Turner, *The Persuasion Industry*, London: Eyre & Spottiswoode, 1965, p. 107.
57 Ibid., p. 108.
58 IPA, *Agency Employment*, 1966, p. 6.
59 The Public Schools Commission: first report, London: HMSO, 1968. A survey of

the Chamber of Commerce for London in 1964 which focused on young executives aged under 40 noted that 46% had been to public school, but only 23% to university; *The Times*, 3 September 1964, p. 15. R. Scase and P. Brown, *Higher Education and Corporate Realities*, Milton Keynes: Open University Press, 1994.
60 On Oliver Knox, see his obituary, *Daily Telegraph*, 19 July 2002, p. 25.
61 M. Roper, *Masculinity and the British Organisation Man*, Oxford: Oxford University Press, 1994, pp. 48, 53.
62 IPA, *Agency Employment*, 1966, p. 10.
63 Ibid.
64 Ibid., p. 12. On women in advertising, see 'Who are the gentle persuaders?', *The Times*, 13 April 1967, p. 7, and 'The gentle persuaders 2', *The Times*, 20 April 1967, p. 9.
65 IPA, *Agency Employment*, London: IPA, 1967, p. 8.
66 Associate offices were generally used to buy local media space and prepare the finished adverts for insertion in the media.
67 *Adam*, 2(1), 1964, p. 3.
68 *IAOTL* (*In and Out the Lane*), Christmas 1962 and spring 1961.
69 W.S. Crawford, Annual General Meeting, 30 March 1965, JWT/HAT.
70 *Kompass*, September 1962, p. 15, company advert.
71 On Ogilvy, see his *Confessions of an Advertising Man*, London: Mayflower Books, 1966 [1963].
72 S.H. Benson sold its stake in 1961.
73 S. Piggott, *OBM, A Celebration of 125 Years in Advertising*, London: Ogilvy Benson & Mather, 1975, pp. 43–63.
74 D. West, 'Multinational competition in the British advertising agency business 1936–87', *Business History Review*, 62(3), 1988, p. 471 n. 2.
75 Ibid., p. 414.
76 *The Times*, 4 November 1959, p. 12.
77 West, 'Multinational competition', p. 414.
78 Pells, *Not Like Us*, p. 145.

2

Apostle of Americanization? J. Walter Thompson, advertising and Anglo-American relations

In December 1960 Tom Sutton, the chief executive of J. Walter Thompson Company Ltd, London, wrote to his immediate superior Norman Strouse, chief executive of the parent company based in New York. Sutton's letter addressed the forthcoming competition for Ford's British car advertising business. While JWT's Detroit office had conducted car advertising for Ford in the USA since 1943 and the parent company handled most of Ford's worldwide advertising, in Britain the small British agency Rumble Crowther and Nicholson had directed Ford's advertising since 1946. Sutton's letter aired his concerns about the difficulties he thought JWT London faced in winning the business. These centred upon the perceived American-ness of JWT. As Sutton noted,

> On account of the overall political situation (take-over, anti-American feeling etc.) [Ford] may argue that it is the time to appoint a British agency. If this is so ... if *British* is the criteria of choice we qualify as well as anyone in London. We are a British agency in every sense of the word, although we are also proud of our American parentage ... JWT London has been the leader in the agency field – by size of billings – since 1950 without interruption; 3 members of Parliament, and one member of the House of Lords, are members of the London office staff; ... and the Company is giving its services (free of charge) to a number of organizations and institutions which are a part of British life (including The Duke of Edinburgh Annual Award; The Tate Gallery; St. Paul's Cathedral; The Royal Hospital).[1]

Sutton's assertion of the Britishness of the London office was, on first inspection, puzzling. Why should JWT London be so concerned to dissociate itself from its parent company in a competition for the business of what was, after all, a US multinational car manufacturer? Why did it matter that it wasn't a wholly British-owned company? Sutton's letter had been prompted in the first instance by the known views of Ford UK's advertising manager, Robert Adams.

Adams had declared that among the checklist of questions that he drew up when selecting any agency was 'the crunch question, to what extent is the agency felt to be American, felt to be British'.[2] In making the nationality of the agency central to its selection, Adams was acting under his own auspices. He was able to do so because Ford Detroit, like other international manufacturing companies in the mid-twentieth century, gave considerable operational discretion to its national subsidiaries to devise their own marketing campaigns.[3] In the case of Ford UK, this made particular sense since it manufactured a range of cars distinct from those produced in North America.[4] Given Adams' operational autonomy, JWT's head office in New York could exert little pressure on him through their connections with Ford's parent company in the States. Thus, Tom Sutton's fears were realized and it was to the wholly British owned agency, the London Press Exchange, that Robert Adams turned in order to take Ford UK's advertising into the 1960s.

The circumstances of the pitch for the Ford account and the glimpses given of the selection process by Sutton's letter and Adams' comments open up some larger questions. What drove the Ford man to make the national character of the agency he was choosing so central? And what else lay behind Tom Sutton's assertions about the ties that connected JWT London to its adopted country? In beginning to answer these questions it is clear that the calculations of both men were informed by a wider public debate about the apparent 'Americanization' of British commerce and culture that flourished through the 1950s and 1960s and that was fuelled by both the growth of American imports and the increased presence of US companies, including advertising agencies, with subsidiary operations in Britain.[5] For some contemporary commentators, these companies were an alien presence in the British commercial landscape and responsible for disseminating not only an American idiom of selling, but also American values.[6] For these critics, American commercial expansion threatened not only to overwhelm indigenous business and commerce, but also to transform the broader national culture and sensibilities of the British people.

This chapter explores how concern about the apparent 'Americanization' of British commerce played out within the world of London advertising. I take the case of JWT London and its relationship with its parent company in order to explore claims about US commercial domination. JWT is an instructive case because it was a classic example of an international advertising agency in the era of high American commercial expansion.[7] Yet the organization of its London office and the relations between London and New York reveal a picture of business practices that complicates assumptions about American commercial hegemony. JWT London was not the bold apostle of the American vision of its parent company. Rather, in the face of cultural differences between British and American consumers and the nationalism of sections of British business, it sought to soften rather than aggressively asserting the corporate identity and commercial ethos of its American parent. In this regard, JWT London, like other US companies before and since, worked to shed its American-ness and go native. To insist on this process of indigenization is not to deny the authority of US models of commercial life in this period. Rather it is to suggest that even within a US-owned company like J. Walter Thompson, American commercial influences took particular forms in Britain, and American domination over Europe was neither monolithic nor homogeneous nor irresistible.

JWT London: a jewel in the JWT crown?

J. Walter Thompson was a dominant player on the world advertising stage. With its head office occupying three and a half floors of the imposing Graybar building in central New York, it was the most successful of a group of four large agencies that dominated the US advertising industry in the post-war decades and had been the first to pass the $100m billings mark in 1947.[8] Between 1927 and 1930 it had spread into Europe, South America, New Zealand, Java and Canada.[9] In 1919 an independent JWT office was formed in London and this became the first building block in JWT's international expansion, with the London office conducting much of the company's work in continental Europe prior to the establishment of offices in Paris and Berlin in the 1920s. By 1933 the London office had acquired greater administrative and operational autonomy as a separate limited company with its own board of directors.[10] At this time, the office was based in Bush House (later to become the home of the BBC's World Service) near the Waldorf Hotel and the High Courts, but in 1945 it moved to 40 Berkeley Square in London's Mayfair. The signing of the lease on the building marked the beginning of a significant period in the history of the agency with JWT London acquiring its first all-British senior management team in 1946. Douglas Saunders, the first Englishman to work for JWT New York and one of the founding partners of the London company, was promoted to chief executive, with Bill Hinks, a media buyer who had joined the company in 1926, becoming chairman. Saunders and Hinks ran the agency together until 1959, steering JWT London through the immediate aftermath of the war and the difficult years of post-war austerity. By 1950 JWT London was the top agency in Britain, reaching number one in the rankings of agencies based on billings, and it stayed there for much of the next two decades.

JWT London became known during this period for the relatively high social standing of its professional and managerial staff. An internal report from 1963 shed light on the social make-up of Berkeley Square, revealing that 44% of its staff (excluding the directors of the company) hailed from AB social backgrounds, with 50% from C1 families. As the report commented, 'in terms of social grade the staff profile is wildly atypical [of consumers as a whole] and it is difficult to imagine any other type of organization that could combine such a high proportion of ABC1 employees'.[11] Another JWT London publication produced for new staff in 1967 emphasized the educational calibre of the London office, stating that 'of the 900 men and women who work [here], 118 are graduates. A list of their degrees reads like a University prospectus.'[12] While the educational and social provenance of its staff was consistent with the broader social make-up of London advertising agencies that I discussed in chapter one, JWT London was known for its urbane culture. The London office's film club, established in 1966 by the creative department, revealed the eclectic and culturally ambitious tastes of its members. It screened a mixture of French New Wave (including *Jules et Jim* and *400 Blows*), together with some popular Hollywood and older classics (like the Marx Brothers and W.C. Fields).[13] Agency insiders also drew attention to the stylishness of JWT staff. As Ursula Sedgwick, a senior figure in the agency involved in discussions to establish a fashion advisory panel, boasted, 'I believe that in JWT we have more decorative people, dressed more decoratively, than in almost any other building in the world.'[14] JWT London's reputation as a culturally sophisticated and 'classy agency' was further evident in the interior decoration of its reception at 40 Berkeley Square and in its 'impressively upholstered meeting rooms'.[15] Significantly, while the agency included staff with experience across JWT's international offices, by the 1950s there were few Americans employed. This represented something of a reversal of the pre-war situation when Sam Meek, a senior figure in the parent company, had headed an office with strong American representation at its upper echelons.

Even with an all-British management team and overwhelmingly British staff, however, JWT London was tied to the parent company in New York by clear forms of financial and organizational control. New York owned 50% of the London company's equity and possessed the majority of voting shares.[16] London was also required to seek formal approval from New York for the appointment of directors and associate directors, with headquarters also responsible for appointing the office's senior management. Formal links between New York and London were also maintained through visits by senior New York staff. Edward Wilson, Sam Meek's successor as head of the International Department, was one of the most frequent visitors.[17] Wilson's visits were one of the ways in which the department that he headed sought to assist, support and monitor 'local offices' like London and it was partly through the auspices of the International Department that JWT sought to disseminate a coherent and consistent marketing approach throughout its business empire.[18] The company often identified its approach to advertising with the homely epithet, the 'Thompson way'. JWT's senior managers had, from the early decades of the century, sought to codify a coherent and consistent approach to advertising and to set in place mechanisms across its national and international network of offices to ensure a consistency of service. JWT's reputation in the USA from the 1920s had been founded upon a 'scientific approach' to its clients' needs. The principles that informed this approach were documented in Thompson's 'Blue Book', at the heart of which was the T-square – the central marketing tool used to codify and export the Thompson way. The T-square sought to formalize the process of developing advertising, giving it rigour and a 'scientific basis' against more ad hoc approaches. It imposed upon copywriters and artists the discipline of addressing five central questions: 'What are we selling? To whom are we selling? Where are we selling? When are we selling? How are we selling?' As a company publication suggested, the ambition was to develop standardized practices which began by finding out 'the facts about the performance of a product in relation to people's needs and wants', before beginning the process of advertising development.[19] The approach to advertising codified in the T-square was rigorously imposed through all of JWT's offices, and Tom Rayfield, a copywriter at Berkeley Square, recalled that in the 1950s all of the London office staff received a laminated copy of it for their desks.[20]

The T-Square undoubtedly contributed to the distinctive house style of JWT advertising. The company gained a reputation in the world of American business for its extensive use of market research and for advertising that was typically built around a clear rational message to the consumer. The discipline of the T-Square certainly rooted the company's press and magazine advertising within the tradition of long-copy, 'reason why' advertising that dominated American marketing in the early-to-mid-twentieth century.[21] While this style of advertising may have been effective in winning the company business both at home and abroad, later commentators have been less enthralled by its communicative idioms. Victoria de Grazia, in a waspish but perceptive observation, suggested that JWT's press advertising was defined by its 'literate prolixity ... It was the master of the specious argument delivered with well-modulated rhetoric, the editorial voice castigating bad habits and enjoining new virtues, and the invidious comparison sweetened by a scientific factoid.'[22] The editorial style of JWT's press advertising, with its stress on guiding the consumer towards better tastes and social improvement, fitted well the form of long-copy persuasion. JWT frequently added testimonials to their long-copy advertisements. In these instances, the authoritative editorial voice was echoed by or taken over by a well-known face or person of substance. This was the case with the advertising that the agency produced for the American cosmetics company Cheeseborough-Ponds. In 1924 JWT New York ran the first in a long-running series of testimonial adverts featuring 'society ladies' testifying to how Ponds' cold creams helped them to keep their beauty.[23]

These techniques were important for JWT London's staff. In the 1930s, when Americans headed the creative department, they were an obvious and important creative resource. Such techniques remained influential into the post-war period, in part because of important continuities in JWT London's pre-war and post-war advertising business.[24] In addition, a number of significant international advertising accounts that were centrally run from the New York office provided a more direct conduit for the transmission of American advertising styles into Berkeley Square. The Pan American Airways account was the classic example. JWT New York worked closely with Pan Am's Long Island head office in running the worldwide advertising for the carrier. JWT London was sent proofs and layouts by the New York office that required minimal revision. In other cases, dollars were changed to pounds or small differences between US and British phrasing were made (like 'substitute "oil and cowboy country" for "oil and cattle country"').[25]

It wasn't only at the level of creative practices that the parent company sought to disseminate a consistent service across its network of subsidiary offices. When it came to management techniques and organizational strategy, it deployed other mechanisms for reproducing the 'Thompson way' at home and abroad. Important among these was the overseas posting of staff. Employees of the London office were among those encouraged to spend time immersed in the culture of the parent company.[26] This was seen as particularly important for senior managers, and the company noted that 'foreign managers should make extended visits to the US, probably at least every 2 or 3 years'.[27] The International Department played an active role in both supporting and coordinating these international postings.[28] In addition, the New York office could requisition staff and post them to other JWT offices across the world. This practice was not without its complications, however. Senior managers of the London office often experienced these requisitions as an imposition and felt they were disproportionately required to 'sacrifice' good people for the benefit of the parent company as a whole.[29] Tensions over this issue reveal much about how the two offices interacted and the way, in particular, that New York viewed its London subsidiary, for it is undoubtedly the case that London was required to make particular sacrifices for the parent company because of its role in the company's early twentieth-century expansion.[30] As such, the historical importance of the London office to the parent company continued to shape relations between New York and London through the post-war years.

It is also clear that the size and commercial success of the London office prompted New York to treat it rather differently from its other subsidiaries. Even in the difficult years of wartime restrictions Berkeley Square managed to sustain a functioning subsidiary and by the early 1960s the London office was a large and profitable company that dwarfed all the other international offices.[31] The size and commercial success of London, particularly the fact that most of its business was generated independently of the parent company, encouraged New York to grant it special privileges.[32] One of the most important of these concerned the company policy on handling potential conflicts of interest between international and local advertising business. From the 1920s JWT New York had pursued a strategy of international growth that prioritized the winning of large international advertising accounts. As with its early association with General Motors, JWT sought to represent international advertisers in all the markets in which they operated. This strategy required that subsidiary offices decline local advertising that might generate conflicts of interest with the big international advertisers. Problems of this sort certainly arose from time to time. A policy document produced for senior JWT managers in New York in 1945, for example, acknowledged this and sought to formalize how the company might deal with such issues. The document stated that potential 'conflicts of interest [such as 'those already creating problems like the Horlick's/Kraft issue and the Ford/GM situation'] … could be limited by sacrificing local business if an international account can be won'. What was striking, however, was the concession given to the London office within this policy. As the document went on to note,

> these policies should be applied generally to the company's international offices with one exception. The business of the London subsidiary will undoubtedly have to be developed under a somewhat different set of rules. London has been

getting enough volume ... to justify a strongly independent attitude by its management.[33]

The independence referred to by New York in this passage meant in practice that the London office had more room for manouevre in pursuing local business than most JWT subsidiaries. Senior managers at Berkeley Square used this relative autonomy in how they presented the company to potential clients. From the mid-1940s senior managers in London would often seek to strategically distance themselves from the parent company and emphasize the Britishness of the London office. Why did they feel the need to do this? And what did the parent company gain from allowing the London subsidiary to operate under a different set of rules from other offices? Both sets of responses were precipitated in the first instance by the impact on the commercial fortunes of the London office of what JWT New York itself identified as the 'nationalism' of sections of British business. This problem was spelt out clearly in the 1945 policy document. Having defined the greater independence granted to London, the report went on:

> This attitude is further stiffened by the nationalism of British business in general. Under the circumstances, any attempt to favour US clients with arbitrary priorities in the British market could soon bring a collapse of the parent company's hold there. Considering both its current volume and prospective expansion, the UK business is fully as important to JWT as any single domestic US client is likely to be ... However, put London on notice: that an over-riding priority in favour of American concerns will apply to the territories of existing offices outside the UK.[34]

The nationalism referred to in this extract was intimately bound up with anti-Americanism. In the next section I want to explore this phenomenon as it surfaced within the British advertising industry and reflect further on how it shaped the ways in which Berkeley Square softened the commercial traditions and approaches of its parent company.

The problem of Anti-Americanism

In the immediate post-war years there existed in Britain among sections of the political and cultural elites, businessmen and at a more popular level an assertive hostility to the products of 'American civilization'. Of course anti-Americanism was not new and, as Dick Hebdige among others has noted, since the 1930s there had been a strong current within elite culture in Britain that was hostile to America's industrial and cultural rise.[35] Anti-Americanism also co-existed with a more enthusiastic embrace of America's economic, intellectual and cultural output among both the popular and educated classes.[36] The young Malcolm Bradbury was representative of those energized by American culture. Visiting the United States in 1955 he claimed that 'America was where all that was freest and most novel came from: the best movies, the best clothes, the best ice-cream, the best gum, the best cars, the best comics, the best jazz, even the best books'.[37] The theatre director Richard Eyre, a teenager in the 1950s, made a similar confession. 'Like many of my generation', he suggested, 'I was a cultural Fifth Columnist … it wasn't just that America was something other, something not British, it was simply better than anything we had.'[38] Others were struck by America's affluence and the plethora of goods available, 'by the proud abundance of everything, at the shop windows, at the well dressed people, at the long queues of shining cars on the roads'.[39] Advertising practitioners were often drawn to make the same consumerist contrasts. Ashley Havinden, art director at the British agency W.S. Crawford, wrote to American friends following a visit to their home in Connecticut in December 1950 to thank them for their hospitality. His letter dwelt on the quality of their home and its 'magnificent kitchen and superb plumbing'. Referring to a forthcoming piece on his own home in rural Hertfordshire in the magazine *House and Garden*, he rather mournfully compared his friends' living standards with his own, suggesting that the feature 'may interest you to see how nicely you live in comparison to us'.[40] A rather differently placed practitioner, Peggy Bowden, an administrator at the agency London Press Exchange, revealed a similar sense of awe about the American way of life. She spent part of the autumn of 1966 on the Eastern seaboard and among her favourable impressions of the Boston area was the colossal size of its supermarkets and the 'giant' packets of detergents.[41]

The visible presence of American tourists and businesspeople in Britain, especially following the introduction of jet travel in 1958, together with the increase in the volume of US imports into Britain signalled an intensification of Anglo-American relations in the late 1950s. The arrival of US advertising agencies in London on an unprecedented scale was another manifestation of the growing impact of US commerce and culture. The latter development fed into already established concerns in the advertising trade press that dated back to the early 1950s of an 'American invasion' and trade commentators certainly became highly attuned from that point onwards to any signs of what Anthony Sampson called the 'American ballyhoo'.[42] In the first edition of the trade journal *Advertising Review*, published in the summer of 1954, for example, much of the content focused upon a defence of the superior quality of indigenous advertising techniques against those coming from America. The editorial praised what it described as the 'witty, typically English poster designs like Gilroy's successes for Guinness and Searl's Lemon Hart rum'.[43] Elsewhere in the same issue, E.C. MacKenzie, celebrating the life of the founder of the British agency W.S. Crawford, Sir William Crawford, was prompted to reflect on the limitations of American advertising. He noted: 'Transatlantic influences must be assessed. The virility and vulgarity of America are here in force. By vulgarity I mean the literal "of the people" fashion of appeal. The hit-em-for-six school. Absent in this quarter is any sense of the aesthetic responsibility, of leadership.'[44] Margaret Havinden, a copywriter at W.S. Crawford and wife of Ashley Havinden, also took to task American techniques of persuasion. She implored her readers: 'for goodness sake let us stop being pixilated by America. We are British people and we have our own forms of expression, and very good our best forms are. There is nothing in America to beat "Guinness is good for you" or the "This England" advertisements for Worthington.' She then went on to offer a checklist of appropriate techniques for selling to British women:

> give them facts, or if you tell them a story let it be solidly bedded in truth, and let it be human: we don't like exaggeration when it is done seriously. We like the moral to be pointed with a laugh ... Be inspiring – and don't think that Hollywood glamour is the only form of inspiration that women respond to.[45]

Prominent figures within British advertising also weighed into the debate. Reporting back on a trip to America in 1956, Lt. Col. Alan Wilkinson, president of the IPA, while encouraging his readers to visit the States, cautioned them against a too easy adoption of American practices. As he put it,

> Inevitably, an advertising man returning to these shores after so invigorating an experience ... brings back a mixed bag of impressions. Some of these, if he is wise, he will translate into practice. Other impressions, coloured as they must be by difference of tempo and idiom – to say nothing of economic contrasts between the two countries – he will store away among his other mental snapshots of an all-too-brief encounter with a lively, stimulating and friendly community of advertising men.[46]

If Wilkinson's comments included, along with his insistence on the enduring differences between British and American advertising, a more enthusiastic response to American salesmanship than that revealed by *Advertising Review*, other commentators saw in the 'American invasion' of British advertising more profound effects. Denis Caton, director of the agency Charles F. Higham Ltd, railed against the commercial and cultural impact of American agencies in

London. He saw signs of staff working for American-owned agencies infiltrating the IPA, claiming that 'America get the voice, the vote and a very large share of the IPA backing' and suggesting that American agencies used their luxurious offices and 'lots of smooth talk' to seduce British advertisers into giving them their business. The effect of this was that American agencies exerted growing influence over British advertising. It was these agencies, he asserted, 'who are largely responsible for the shocking prostitution of the television screen on which the British public is assumed to have an average IQ equal to a child of 10'.[47] The journalists Pearson and Turner were more precise in their observations of the way American-style advertising was making its presence felt in Britain. They singled out Hobson Bates and Partners (HBP), the agency formed by the takeover of John Hobson and Partners by Ted Bates, the fifth largest US agency, in 1959 as the prime vehicle for this. HBP, they claimed, was the 'one doctrinally correct USP agency in London'.[48] USP (unique selling proposition) advertising represented an approach formalized by Ted Bates' chief executive, Rosser Reeves. For Reeves, advertising had to be based upon promoting a distinct product benefit to the consumer. This benefit should be unique and in turn should form the basis of the advertising.[49] In effect, Reeves sought to address the consumer as a rational purchaser who could be persuaded by the clearly demonstrable advantages of the product. There was no need, for Reeves, to seek out the unconscious desires or motivations of the consumer. Once identified, the unique selling proposition could be ruthlessly hammered home in 'hard sell' advertising.

There was, of course, a question about how new or specifically American this technique really was. As Pearson and Turner conceded, prior to the takeover of John Hobson and Partners by Ted Bates, the agency had used a classic USP line for a cough treatment that ran 'It calms the nerves that make you cough.'[50] After the takeover, they advertised Cadbury's Bournvita with the less strident 'Helps you relax the natural way'. Perceptions, nonetheless, were important, and the increased presence of US-owned agencies in London by the early 1960s undoubtedly touched on the sensitive issue of Britain's post-war economic decline and highlighted again the commercial power of the US. As we have seen, from 1959 onwards, following the ending of restrictions on dollar imports, American agencies moved aggressively to acquire British advertising agencies.[51] The increased presence and visibility of American agencies through the 1960s formed part of a significant structural transformation of British advertising that was associated with the concomitant spread of (typically) US-owned multinational manufacturing companies into Europe.[52] It was these companies that

US advertising agencies typically serviced. JWT's own early twentieth-century expansion into Europe had been paradigmatic in this respect. It had initially opened its European offices in an arrangement with General Motors to service the car manufacturer wherever it had manufacturing plants.[53]

Differences between the British and American advertising industries and, in particular, the economic conditions in which each was operating in its home markets further served to underscore the gap between the economic fortunes of the two countries and to make Anglo-American relations a sensitive issue for protagonists in and around the British advertising industry. In the US, total advertising expenditure had doubled from $2.9bn in 1945 to $5.7bn in 1950 and between 1950 and 1959 gross advertising expenditure increased by 75%.[54] The 1950s saw a huge growth, in particular, in the advertising of that icon of affluence, the automobile, with Coca-Cola the only non-car advertiser represented in the top ten of advertisers by billings through the decade.[55] In the United States, JWT allied itself strongly with growing affluence. The company produced a series of corporate adverts that urged advertisers to take full advantage of the opportunities offered by higher levels of consumer spending. In the adverts, JWT positioned itself as an experienced and authoritative pilot which could steer the ships of commerce into the warm and deep waters of prosperity. The adverts speak volumes for the company's confidence at this time, but they also reveal the 'advanced' standards of American commercial life compared to the landscape of commerce in Britain.[56] As we saw in chapter one, in the UK advertising expenditure remained at relatively low levels between 1945 and 1956, and it wasn't until 1960 that it began to rise steeply.[57] Wartime restrictions on newsprint, which had seen most popular daily papers drastically reduced in size from 24 to four pages and Sunday papers reduced to 6–8 pages, were not finally lifted until 1959 and this worked to limit the available advertising space in the dominant advertising medium of the time. The policy of the post-war Labour chancellor, Stafford Cripps, to reduce levels of domestic consumption and stimulate, in its place, production for export included a short-lived policy to restrict advertising expenditure in 1948/9, while the continuation of product rationing until 1954 more effectively worked to suppress advertising expenditure until the turn of the decade.[58]

Some sense of the difficulties faced by JWT London during the first post-war decade of austerity can be discerned from the fact that New York was sending food and clothing parcels to London office staff until 1953.[59] It was in this context, and amid concerns about American commercial power, that JWT sought to emphasize its indigenous credentials to prospective clients and to play on the contemporary impulses towards commercial nationalism. One episode captured this particularly clearly. It concerned JWT London's ambitions to work with the British carrier BOAC and the parent company's decision to overrule this.

JWT London: on being a British agency

In February 1945 Bill Hinks, chairman of JWT London, visited the New York office to consult Sam Meek, a senior figure in the parent company, about a potential conflict of interest that he perceived might exist between the Pan American Airways business held in New York and JWT London's relationship with the British air carrier British Overseas Airways Corporation (BOAC). JWT London had held the BOAC advertising business since 1938 and the agency was seeking to develop its relationship with BOAC following approaches from the company. Hinks sent a cablegram back to his colleagues in London on 20 February reassuring them that he had reached a general understanding with New York that Pan Am had no objections in principle to their association with BOAC as long as they did not compete with it on the North Atlantic routes. After Hinks' return to London, however, Pan Am's view of the matter began to change. Between March and May 1945 they made it clear to JWT New York that they had a desire to work with the company across all its international markets. This made JWT London's association with BOAC potentially more problematic. JWT London gradually became aware of Pan Am's rethink and it precipitated a series of intense cablegrams between London and New York. This exchange became increasingly fraught during the course of the summer and autumn of 1945 and tensions between the two offices were heightened by Meek's handling of the situation. He kept both JWT London and, through them, BOAC, waiting for a definitive decision and news that he had visited London during this period without meeting colleagues in the London office prompted an angry telegram from Hinks and his chief executive, Douglas Saunders. Appealing over Meek's head to the co-owner of the company, Stanley Resor, they claimed:

> This account [BOAC] vital to us and whole company STOP … All here have been through much since 1939 and have struggled desperately to keep business going and we cannot build proper cooperation unless all there are made to feel that it works both ways STOP.[60]

While this cablegram asserted the importance of the BOAC business to the commercial viability of the London office, senior managers in London produced a detailed statement documenting the reasons why New York should allow it to pursue its relationship with BOAC. In setting out these arguments, JWT London aligned itself with Britain's commercial and military interests in the reconfigured post-war world order. The document argued that Britain's success in overseas air transport was vital to its security and was a major factor in maintaining its balance of trade in competition with America. For the document's authors, air transport was a particularly powerful symbol of a nation's prestige and standing in the world. It was, they claimed, 'the most obvious and tangible symbol both of the survival of Empire and of her rivalry with the US ... For all these reasons BOAC will be a completely unique advertising account.'[61]

The rousing defence of an independent national airline made in the document and the company's desire to identify itself with this project was then woven into a commercial argument about the necessity of developing a distinct identity separate from the American parent company. This played upon the themes of popular anti-Americanism and currents of commercial nationalism within British business:

> If we now were selected, in effect by the British government itself, to act as its counsel both within and without the Empire for one of its most vital post-war efforts, this should be the most convincing proof we have ever been able to give our clients that they are unassailable in employing us. [Before the war] many people felt that our [JWT London] leadership was due mainly to 'un-English' qualities such as aggressiveness, ruthlessness, sensationalism. This feeling was fed by our highly competitive tactics in certain campaigns and by our service of a number of patent medicines. It was fed further by the actions of other 'American' agencies, most which have gradually come to combine the worst features (in British eyes) of the American and native agency ... In addition to these un-English qualities, we were universally thought of being, in fact, foreign. Though there was some professional prestige in our American origin, it was a specific bar, in some of the highest business circles, to unique leadership such as JWT America enjoys. This was not solely a matter of nationalistic feeling. Between the wars, Britain had a rough time economically and politically; and there was considerable reason behind the feeling not only that we, but also that many of our clients, represented a foreign invasion and a further threat to the British position.[62]

JWT London's desire to be allowed to develop its own identity distinct from the parent company and to position itself as a British agency guided by national economic interests was powerfully made in this statement. Despite the fact that the office did, in the end, submit to New York's authority, it continued to bridle at the loss of the BOAC business and the way, it felt, this implicitly affected its standing among business opinion in Britain. The depth of feelings aroused by the episode were evident when, seven years later, in a communication with Pan Am's advertising manager in London which was copied to New York, JWT London rather pointedly suggested that Pan Am should make something of its decision to buy British Comet jets. Its letter noted that

> a gesture of this sort from the world's leading international airline, recognising a major success in Britain's struggle for a competitive position in the post-war world, would be taken as good sportsmanship by a people to whom sportsmanship means a great deal. It would, we feel, do much to counteract the natural loyalty Britons feel for their national carrier, BOAC, and increase their good will to its friendly competitor, Pan American.[63]

The underlying tensions generated by the dispute with the New York office over BOAC also surfaced in the rather acerbic observation made by J.R. Keith, London's representative on the Pan Am account, about the advertising that New York was producing for Pan Am's trans-Atlantic routes. Invoking the modernity of Britain's Comet jets, Keith scoffed at the use of a propeller plane in a New York produced advert. As he put it, 'the piece of art work showing the nose of a plane is the sort of thing which airlines were running 4 or 5 years ago'.[64]

In the exchanges between London and New York over the Pan Am/BOAC accounts that saw JWT London emphasizing its indigenous credentials, just as it would do in 1960 with the Ford pitch, it is clear that the intention was to register its closeness to market conditions in Britain and thus to establish for existing and potential British clients that it was not simply the appendage of an American company. It is notable, however, that even amid these moves by London's senior managers to separate the agency in the public mind from any associations of American-ness, JWT New York could privately still encourage its subsidiary to remind potential American clients that it had strong ties with the parent company in the States. Thus, for example, in the late summer of 1957 Sam Meek wrote to Sandy Mitchell-Innes, one of the directors at Berkeley Square, offering advice on how JWT London might persuade Campbell's of New Jersey, the soup and fruit juice manufacturer, to hire JWT London as their British agents. Meek suggested that London should stress two things: '1) our background in television and the fact that our people in London have been to Hollywood; 2) our broad public relations set up.'[65] Meek here, then, was encouraging London to emphasize its familiarity with American television advertising and even American-style entertainment ('Hollywood'), as well as the techniques of PR, at this time relatively underdeveloped in Britain. It is not clear whether Mitchell-Innes took Meek's advice, but London duly acquired the British advertising business of Campbell's in the autumn of 1957.[66]

Contact of this sort between New York and its London subsidiary confirmed the important connections that existed between the London and New York offices. However, this should not lead us to conclude that the moves made by the London office to emphasize its Britishness were merely a presentational exercise and fully explainable as such. While some contemporary commentators, like Anthony Sampson, may have picked up on the self-conscious nature of Berkeley Square's desire to be seen as an indigenous agency, its size and commercial success, together with the fact that most of its business was generated from clients won independently of New York, gave some substance to JWT London's assertion that it was fully integrated within the British advertising industry.[67] We have already seen in the dispute between JWT London and its New York parent over the BOAC account that senior managers at Berkeley Square, as well as staff lower down the company hierarchy, could feel moved to identify strongly with Britain's economic and military fortunes. Moreover, the composition of its staff and the social character of agency life embedded JWT London in the cultural life of the capital and the wider national scene. It is worth pausing to reflect on this point as it offers clues as to how JWT London softened its American-ness. For example, the agency enjoyed links with high society and the political classes in the 1950s and 1960s. Peter Ward, brother of Stephen, the society osteopath and chief victim of the Profumo affair, worked for the agency in the personnel department and Bill Hinks had used his brother's services. Mark Birley, who worked in the art department, was a well-known socialite and established Annabel's, an up-market nightclub that catered for minor royals and other notables.[68] Robin Douglas-Home, a copywriter at the agency and part of the Douglas-Home family that had produced prime ministers and playwrights, was also close to high society, being both a friend of Princess Margaret and involved in a high-profile romantic liaison with Princess Margaretha of Sweden in 1956.[69] More prosaically, John Rodgers was one of three MPs who worked for the agency. Rodgers was Conservative MP for Sevenoaks and an under-secretary in Macmillan's government, as well as being associated with the Campaign for Commercial Television.

The agency went to considerable trouble to consolidate these relationships with influential social actors. As the 1960s progressed, this included the pursuit of contacts within the newly important world of entertainment and the new cultural establishment. The agency's 'creative lunches' and 'V.I.P. meetings', which ran through 1963–64, were two of the vehicles it used to foster these connections. Derrick Cawston, the JWT staffer charged with running the 'V.I.P. meetings', made it clear that their purpose was to ensure that JWT was 'a force in the land in the same way as the Monarchy, the Church, Parliament, ICI or the Beatles are a force in the land'.[70] Speakers at the VIP meetings included the Beatles' manager Brian Epstein in April 1964, while the political journalist Anthony Sampson, the pop artist Peter Blake and the editor of *Queen* magazine Jocelyn Stevens were among those who attended the 'creative lunches' at JWT London's offices.[71] A further sense of the connections JWT was hoping to form is also evident in the list of proposed speakers at the 'creative lunches' in 1964. These included cultural critic Richard Hoggart, *World in Action* producer Tim Hewat, impresario Lew Grade, hairdresser Vidal Sassoon and fashion designer Mary Quant, as well as the comedian Benny Hill and Coronation Street writers speaking 'on how to set a scene'.

It is clear that these forums were designed to ensure that JWT enjoyed proximity with the new cultural 'establishment' and through this remained close to trends within British popular culture. While this was an ambition any agency would have been likely to pursue in order to ensure that its advertising connected to key consumer aspirations, JWT London was well placed to open up lines of communication with the cultural movers and shakers. Its decision to hire as a consultant its former employee, Robin Douglas-Home, was an instructive case in point.[72] Douglas-Home had worked for the company in the 1950s while pursuing an alternative career as a Mayfair cocktail pianist by night.[73] By the early 1960s he was known as an accomplished photographer and journalist. He also worked as a weekly columnist on the *Daily Express*, a role that included reviewing pop records for the paper. Douglas-Home claimed that his position at the *Express* gave him access to 'general trends amongst the "pace-setters"'.[74] He was also a contributing editor to American *Vogue* and an associate editor of English *Vogue*. These jobs placed him at the heart of the world of fashion and close to photographers, designers and models, especially, he noted, 'the unknown, up-and comings'.[75] JWT London was keen for Robin Douglas-Home to use his connections with the worlds of fashion and entertainment for the benefit of itself and its clients. As Dermot Wilson, in charge of liaising between the creative department and Douglas-Home, conceded in a letter to his colleagues 'Robin has a particular gift for being "with it"'.[76]

Connections of this sort were important to JWT's embedding in the culture of London life and the wider national scene. They undoubtedly contributed to the distinctiveness of the advertising that JWT London produced through the 1960s. Much of the company's press and poster advertising through the 1950s had drawn strongly upon the traditions of the parent company, adapting the commercial idioms of US advertising to a British context. The work that it

For this pen you'll gladly put aside your others!

It's the New Parker "51" with the exclusive Aero-metric Ink System

INSIDE...THIS SILVERY SHEATH WITH PLI-GLASS RESERVOIR

TO OWN it is to prize it! For New "51" captivates heart and hand. Beautiful, precise... it's the choice of discriminating people everywhere. Only New "51" offers the new, better way to draw in, store, safeguard, and release ink—the *Aero-metric Ink System*. It brings true writing satisfaction.

The New 51's 14K gold point, gliding silently on a Plathenium tip, makes words come easy. Ink meters into a skip-free line. Your hand seems to have new skill. Blotters are passé. New "51" *writes dry* with Superchrome ink. It can use other inks, too.

You'll want to write on and on! And you *can*. New "51" holds more ink. The reservoir is *bigger*. Made of *Pli-glass*, it has a 30-year life expectancy. (No rubber parts!)

Filling is faster, easier. The ink level is *visible*.

Visit your Parker dealer. Try the New "51". See why it has led so many to discard other pens. 8 colors. Lustraloy or gold-filled caps. Pens, $13.50 up. Pen and pencil sets, $19.75 up. The Parker Pen Company, Janesville, Wis., U. S. A.; Toronto, Canada.

OTHER NEW PARKER PENS

NEW PARKER "51" SPECIAL—$10.00. Typical "51" beauty and superb writing precision.
NEW PARKER "21"—$5.00. Smart styling and fine-pen features at a popular price.
NEW PARKETTE—$3.00. Economy coupled with genuine quality and new writing ease.
NEW PARKER MAGNETIX PEN SETS—$8.75 to $75.00. Distinctive beauty for desk or table.

NOTE: No F. E. tax on pens listed above

BETTY MacDONALD

Author of The Egg and I, *the hilarious tale that set all America to laughing. "I've had at least a hundred pens," writes Betty MacDonald. "But with this New '51' the search is over. My new '51' writes like a dream. And it makes perfectly beautiful autographs in my new book* Anybody Can Do anything.*"*

Copr. 1951 by The Parker Pen Company

New Parker "51"
World's most wanted pen... writes dry with wet ink!

Jack Hawkins gave his wife a Parker '51' for her birthday

Not everyone realizes that Jack Hawkins' recent film triumphs were preceded by many successful, if less spectacular, years on the stage. He met his wife Doreen (they have two sons) in India during the war, when she was on an ENSA tour and he was serving in South East Asia Command. His sensational successes "The Cruel Sea," "Malta Story," and "The Intruder" are now followed by "The Seekers" (J. Arthur Rank Organisation release)—filmed in New Zealand. For her birthday, he gave his wife a Parker '51'.

CONTEMPORARY ELEGANCE—
and an ink system far ahead of any other

To people who are accustomed to the best of everything, no other writing instrument but a New Parker '51' is really acceptable.

Its design is both elegant and practical; it is truly graceful in the best contemporary manner. What is more, the New Parker '51' is mechanically far ahead of any other pen, since its Aero-metric Ink System draws up, stores, and releases ink in a unique way — setting new standards of reliable writing.

As a special gift for a particular occasion, anyone would be honoured to receive a Parker '51.' Buy one for yourself, and you will have a constant, treasured companion.

Choice of four colours, and eight different nib grades to suit every hand. With Rolled Gold Cap, now only 105/-; with Lustraloy cap 82/3.

'51' PEN AND PENCIL SET
with Rolled Gold caps — £7.18.6 — Pencil alone 52/6
with Lustraloy caps — £6.4.0 — Pencil alone 40/10

OTHER FAMOUS PARKER MODELS
Senior Duofold pen 43/- | Victory pen 30/11
New Duofold pen 37/11 | Slimfold pen 23/11
Pencil to match all four pens 20/5
Presentation cases available for all pen and pencil sets

new Parker '51'
The world's most wanted pen
GIVEN AND USED BY FAMOUS PEOPLE

THE PARKER PEN COMPANY LIMITED · BUSH HOUSE · LONDON · W.C.2

3831-1 K&C Parker Pen (Colour) Good Housekeeping July, 1954 10×7½

Final Proof A13097

Parker Pens, JWT London, 1954

produced for Parker Pens was a case in point (Figs. 4 and 5). JWT London ran a campaign for Parker in the British press between 1951 and 1955 which closely followed the style of the American advertising produced by JWT Chicago. It was based upon the same testimonial advertising approach and echoed the layouts of the US advertisements, including their focus upon impeccably drawn hand(s) holding the Parker pen. Rather than use well-known US writers, the British adverts cast British film stars to testify to the qualities of the pens. These were the kind of prominent people that the agency's research suggested would appeal to British consumers, stars whose 'gift giving would be acknowledged as being in the best taste by all sections of the population'. Through casting and the rephrasing of the advertising copy JWT London subtly reworked the American advertising, while staying within the approach developed in Chicago.

By the 1960s, however, JWT London's advertising for Parker Pens reflected less its dependence on its parent company and more its own confident and independent outlook and approach. JWT London had won back the Parker business in 1963, following its loss of the account in 1955 in the wake of disagreements between Parker and JWT in America. JWT Chicago did not regain the account there until 1968. The new campaign produced by Berkeley Square, which begin in March 1966, was designed to offer an 'avant garde image for the mass market'.[77] The adverts used the established testimonial form, but reworked it by using not celebrities but apparently real people or at least recognizable social types. These included a vicar, a schoolboy and two versions of the 'dolly bird', replete with heavy eye make-up (though both characters were married women). *Round the Square*, JWT London's house magazine, described the women as '"Mrs Dolly Blonde" and "Mrs Gionconda Smile"'.[78] The copy was quirky and used humour to play on established social conventions and mores. Thus, the headline for the advert featuring 'Mrs Dolly Blonde' (Fig. 6) broke the taboo of speaking openly about divorce, even making a joke out it, with its bold declaration 'O.K., I said, Divorce Me!' These adverts were sharply different from the sedate and respectful style of the 1950s advertising and showed the way the agency was seeking to connect with some of the social changes unfolding in 1960s Britain and the broader shifts in the iconography of (especially) femininity associated with 'Swinging London' in adjacent media, like the colour supplements.

These latter influences were also evident in JWT London's work for the womenswear chain Richard Shops in 1966. Its press campaign drew strongly on the style of London's 'new wave' fashion photography and the new fashion cultures of the mid-to-late 1960s. The campaign focused on 'Gaby', the quintessential 1960s 'Single Girl' or 'dolly bird' (Figs. 7 and 8). It precisely followed the representational conventions associated with the depiction of this social type pioneered in the photography of David Bailey and Brian Duffy by showing Gaby 'shot outside, often walking or running', to use Hilary Radner's description of the fashion photography of the 'Single Girl'.[79] The

Parker Pens, JWT London, 1966

adverts were aimed at the 16–40-year-old market who were 'basically fashionable without being too kooky'. *Round the Square* waxed lyrical about the campaign. Displaying a precise awareness of the cultural influences on the adverts, it purred, 'The backgrounds against which the girls appear ... suggest Antonioni's heroines on the run ... busy city centres with furtive cars; lamp lit corners of Embassy'd squares. A very clever campaign, for clever clothes.' The reference to Antonioni was telling. Not only would he define the image of the 1960s fashion photographer with his film *Blow-Up* (released 1966), but

Richard Shops, JWT London, 1966

his film making had been an influence on exponents of 'new wave' fashion photography like Bailey.[80]

A draft script for another Richard Shops advert from December 1966 continued this positioning of the campaign around the 'Single Girl'. Describing the casting of the model for the advert, the script suggested she 'will be interesting rather than smooth in a Françoise Hardy sort of way. The sequence should have the feeling that the Julie Christie street scene had in Billy Liar.'[81] Françoise Hardy was the gamine French singer/actress whose quirky style

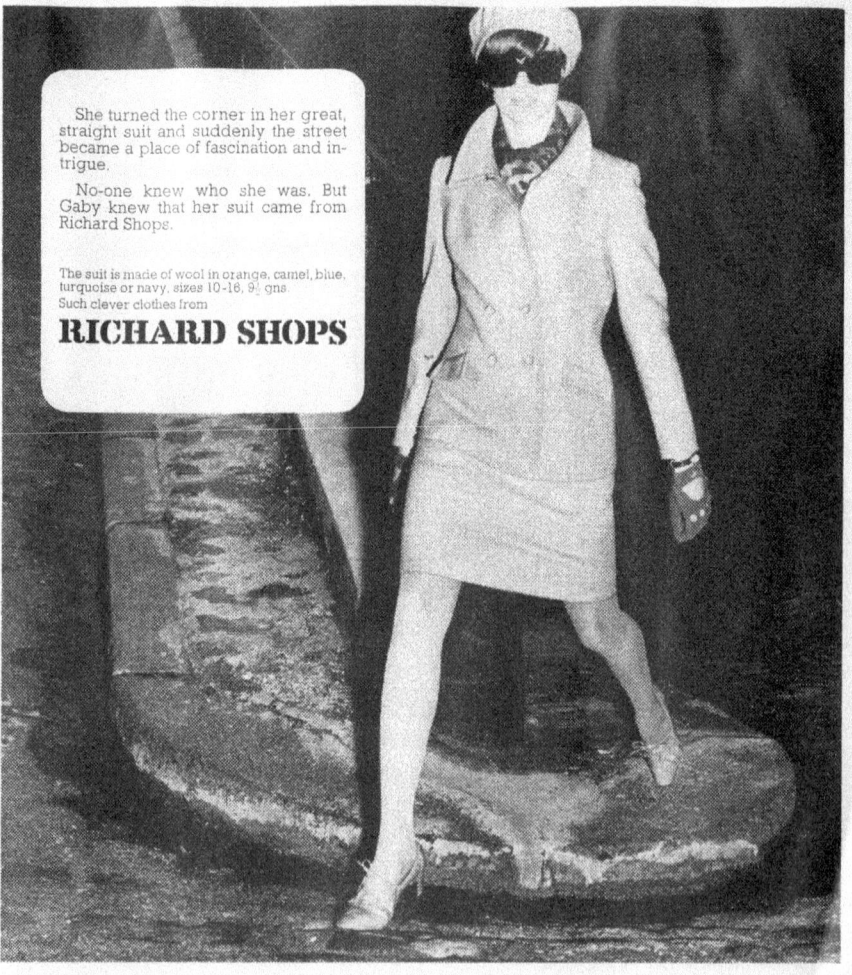

Richard Shops, JWT London, 1966

mixed androgynous clothing and pouting Gallic beauty. The Julie Christie character, Liz, in the 1963 film *Billy Liar* expressed a new kind of mobility and freedom for young single women. In the 'street scene' alluded to, Liz swings her handbag in a moment of unselfconscious confidence and enjoyment.[82] The invocation of these exemplars of new femininity by the JWT account team made clear, like the earlier references to 'new wave' fashion photography and Antonioni, the cultural resources that they were drawing on; resources from British and French/Italian cinema and London fashion photography. Advertising like this revealed much about the independent path taken by the London office as it translated, reworked and ultimately reinvented the commercial idioms of its parent company.[83]

Conclusion

I've ended by describing the distinctive commercial style of some of JWT London's advertising which emerged in accounts like those of Parker Pens and Richard Shops by the 1960s. This advertising was the product of an agency that was increasingly able, through the post-war period, to establish an identity distinct from the parent company on the back of its commercial success at winning business independently of the New York office. This commercial independence was reinforced by the ability of the agency to forge links with the local metropolitan and the wider national political and cultural scene. Its ties with society and the political classes embedded it in British society, helping to soften its American-ness. In fact, it was the elite backgrounds of key JWT staff which enabled it to forge such a strong British identity. It was an agency staffed by individuals, especially at the upper echelons, who were well connected with Britain's political and cultural elite, not an agency led by American outsiders.

While these moves to emphasize its independence as a company had initially been precipitated by the wider climate of concern about the 'Americanization' of British commerce and had been shaped by a strategic positioning of the London office as a British company, it has been my contention that there was a more substantial, if incomplete, process of indigenization going on that underpinned these transformations. Certainly, while the organizational and creative practices of the company continued to be shaped by relations with its parent company, by the 1960s JWT London was producing advertising that was both different from that generated in America and rooted in a world of distinctively British cultural references. As de Grazia has noted, increasingly through the post-war period US goods stopped outwardly proclaiming their American-ness and went native. The example of JWT London suggests that it wasn't just goods that did this, but also US companies. We might speculate that business travellers from Britain to America in the late 1960s, on finding a JWT office in America, could have been prompted to echo the sentiments of Britons in the 1940s exclaiming to their American hosts on seeing the familiar frontage of Woolworth's, 'Oh, you have Woolworth's in the United States, as well!'[84]

The story of JWT London, then, is one that tells us something about the way models of US commerce went native in the UK. Understanding and documenting this process of commercial syncretism is a big part of the story of how US commercial authority was negotiated in Britain. In the next chapter I explore these processes in relation to the techniques of market research.

Notes

1 Tom Sutton, letter to Norman Strouse, 16 December 1960, Edward G. Wilson papers, JWT/Duke, Box 8 (emphasis in original).
2 Memo Tom Sutton to Hinks, Mitchell-Innes and Curling, 20 October 1963, JWT/HAT, Box 495. Pearson and Turner discuss the Ford account in J. Pearson and G. Turner, *The Persuasion Industry*, London: Eyre & Spottiswoode, 1965, p. 21.
3 The Anglo-Dutch consumer goods manufacturer Unilever was a strong exponent of this philosophy. See G. Jones, 'Control, performance and knowledge transfers in large multinationals: Unilever in the United States, 1945–80', *Business History Review*, 76, 2002, pp. 435–78.
4 J. Zeitlin and G. Herrigel (eds), *Americanization and its Limits: Reworking US Technology and Management in Post-war Europe and Japan*, Oxford: Oxford University Press, 2000.
5 US investment in Britain had climbed to $6bn by 1967 and through the 1960s Britain became the most important destination for US capital outside Canada. Between 1958 and 1963, 1,000 US companies set up operations or formed subsidiaries in Britain; R. Pells, *Not Like Us: How Europeans Have Loved, Hated and Transformed American Culture since World War Two*, New York: Basic Books, 1997, p. 190.
6 See Francis Williams' book *The American Invasion* (London: Anthony Blond, 1962), together with Richard Hoggart's *The Uses of Literacy* (Harmondsworth: Penguin Books, 1957), as two classic examples. Dennis Potter produced two polemical accounts of social change in 1950s Britain that also invoked the spectre of growing American cultural influence. See D. Potter, *The Changing Forest*, London: Secker & Warburg, 1962, and *The Glittering Coffin*, London: Gollancz, 1960. The debate on the introduction of commercial television was also strong shaped by concerns about the 'Americanization' of Britain. See chapters four and seven.
7 Victoria de Grazia devotes a long chapter to JWT's expansion into Europe in the early twentieth century, though she tellingly has little to say about the London

office, focusing more on JWT's experiences in Germany and France. See V. de Grazia, *Irresistible Empire: America's Advance Through Twentieth Century Europe*, Cambridge, MA, and London: The Belknap Press of Harvard University Press, 2005, pp. 226–83.
8 S. Fox, *The Mirror Makers: A History of American Advertising and its Creators*, New York: Morrow, 1984, p. 173.
9 JWT offices, 1951–60, n.d., Edward G. Wilson papers, JWT/Duke, Box 8.
10 JWT offices, 1951–60, n.d., Edward G. Wilson papers, JWT/Duke; International Organization, July 1953, Edward G. Wilson papers, JWT/Duke, Box 8. The London company's board of directors included two Americans, one of whom was the chairman, Rae Smith.
11 Office Panel, 1963, JWT/HAT, Box 578; 40 Berkeley Square, JWT London, 1967, JWT/HAT, Box 578.
12 Office Panel, 1963, JWT/HAT, Box 578; 40 Berkeley Square, JWT London, 1967, JWT/HAT, Box 578.
13 Office Panel, 1963, JWT/HAT, Box 578; 40 Berkeley Square, JWT London, 1967, JWT/HAT, Box 578; memo, Creative Department, 17/8/66, JWT/HAT, Box 605. It also noted that the 'age profile is heavily biased towards the youngest age groups with two thirds aged under 35 years compared with one third of the general population'.
14 Memo from Ursula Sedgwick to Denis Lanigan, Fashion Accounts, 25 November 1966, JWT/HAT, Box 243.
15 P. Yeo, 'Reflections on an agency', unpublished manuscript, n.d., p. 6, JWT/HAT.
16 Organization – London office, 27 May 1959, Edward G. Wilson papers, JWT/Duke, Box 9; letter from Andrew Sinclair to Ed Wilson, 1 June 1961, Edward G. Wilson papers, JWT/Duke, Box 9.
17 In the first 11 months of his tenure in 1954, for example, he crossed the Atlantic eight times.
18 Established in 1931, the International Department also helped to plan and execute advertising campaigns in international media and provide local offices with artwork and materials for campaigns, as well as distributing JWT research, marketing methods and ways of working and training for personnel in international offices.
19 'Early days of BMRB', unsigned 1964 paper in the Sidney R. Bernstein Collection, JWT/HAT, Box 238. On the T-square, see D. West, 'From T-square to T-plan: the London office of the J. Walter Thompson advertising agency 1919–70', *Business History*, 19(2), 1987, pp. 199–217.
20 T. Rayfield, *Fifty in Forty: The Unofficial History of JWT London, 1945–95*, privately published, 1996. The T-square method of developing advertising was not the only mechanism through which JWT New York sought to standardize and regulate advertising practices across its international operations. In 1942 the company introduced a system of review boards in its New York office and these were subsequently extended to overseas offices. The review boards consisted of senior staff in the agency and represented a way, as the 1956 review board procedure document put it, of furnishing 'the maximum amount of company experience ... that can be brought to bear on the basic planning of each account'. In practice this meant

ensuring that the account team responsible for particular client campaigns had followed the procedures codified in the T-square and thus had developed a sound marketing proposition before expensive production was undertaken. In addition the board sought to give a certain consistency and house style to JWT's advertising. If, on occasions, internal memos revealed that JWT's leading figures worried that this might produce 'safe, dull advertising', they reassured themselves that this would be offset by the general 'maintenance of creative standards' across the agency. Edward G. Wilson files, JWT/Duke, Box 10.

21 So widely used by American agencies was this style of persuasion that Victoria de Grazia has suggested that it came to carry connotations of American-ness when transposed to Europe by JWT and other American agencies in the inter-war years. De Grazia, *Irresistible Empire*, pp. 237–8.

22 Ibid., pp. 37–8.

23 The testimonial as a promotional form had its roots in late nineteenth-century and early twentieth-century American Protestant culture. As Jackson Lears has suggestively argued, testimonials represented a secular appropriation of the narrative of the conversion experience. Rather than confessing their relief from suffering caused by sin, advertising testimonials documented the relief from more profane sources of distress offered by consumer goods. J. Lears, *Fables of Abundance: A Cultural History of American Advertising*, New York: Basic Books, 1994, p. 143.

24 A good example of this was the advertising produced for the malted drink manufacturer, Horlicks. The Horlicks' account was one of Berkeley Square's most celebrated and longest running campaigns. The business had been acquired in 1934 and was one of a number of significant British accounts that helped the London office to establish itself in the inter-war period.

25 Pan American Airways, file dated 8 June 1962, JWT/HAT, Box 537.

26 For example, Denis Lanigan, later to become the chairman of JWT London, spent a year in New York working on the Stripe toothpaste account in 1959. Tom Rayfield, one of London's best copywriters, spent a year in the US in 1966, and there were many other examples. *J. Walter Thompson Company News*, 10 August 1953; 7 October 1966; *Round the Square*, June 1956; September 1960; Edward G. Wilson papers, JWT/Duke, Box 10.

27 'The International Operations of J. Walter Thompson Co. Ltd, Analysis of an expanding venture with policy recommendations', 15 December 1945, p. 9, Edward G. Wilson papers, JWT/Duke, Box 8.

28 Letter from Edward G. Wilson to six US admen in foreign offices, 31 March 1965, Edward G. Wilson papers, JWT/Duke, Box 9.

29 Letter to Douglas Saunders from Sam Meek, 2 November 1959, Sam Meek papers, JWT/Duke, Box 2.

30 Between 1957 and 1959, JWT London helped to train staff in the Paris office, C.E. Hultquist, 'Americans in Paris: J. Walter Thompson company in France 1927–68', *Enterprise & Society*, 4(3), 2003, p. 494.

31 India was the next biggest with 544 staff, though the majority of its 25 international offices had under 100 staff. International Offices, January 1962, Edward G. Wilson papers, JWT/Duke, Box 1.

32 83% of JWT London's clients had been built up independently, with only 17% of its turnover coming from clients shared with the New York office. Tom Sutton, letter to Norman Strouse, 16 December 1960, Edward G. Wilson papers, JWT/Duke, Box 8.
33 'The International Operations of J. Walter Thompson Co. Ltd, Analysis of an expanding venture with policy recommendations', 15 December 1945, p. 15, Edward G. Wilson papers, JWT/Duke, Box 8.
34 Ibid.
35 D. Hebdige, 'Towards a cartography of taste 1935–62', in D. Hebdige, *Hiding in the Light*, London: Comedia, 1988, pp. 45–76; D. Le Mahieu, *A Culture of Democracy: Mass Communication and the Cultivated Mind in Britain between the Wars*, Oxford: Clarendon Press, 1988.
36 Hoggart, *The Uses of Literacy*. See also P. Gurney, 'The battle for the consumer in post-war Britain', *Journal of Modern History*, 77, 2005, pp. 970–5; L. Black, *The Political Culture of the Left in Affluent Britain, 1951–64*, Basingstoke: Palgrave Macmillan, 2003, chapters 4 and 5.
37 M. Bradbury, *Dangerous Pilgrimages: Trans-Atlantic Mythologies and the Novel*, London: Secker & Warburg, 1995, p. 164.
38 R. Eyre, cited in P. Hennessy, *Having It So Good: Britain in the Fifties*, Harmondsworth: Penguin Books, 2007, p. 16.
39 Pells, *Not Like Us*, p. 164.
40 Letter to Lester and Dorothy Beall, 19 December 1950, Ashley Havinden Archives, National Galleries of Scotland, Edinburgh, Box GMA A39/1/253.
41 'Peggy in North America', *IAOTL* (*In and Out the Lane*), 1966, pp. 41–2
42 Pearson and Turner, *The Persuasion Industry*, p. 95; A. Sampson, *Anatomy of Britain Today*, London: Hodder & Stoughton, 1962, p. 362.
43 *Advertising Review*, 1(1), 1954, p. 1.
44 Ibid., p. 8.
45 Ibid., pp. 54–5.
46 *Institute Information*, 3(9), 1956, p. 6.
47 'British advertising is big American business', *Advertiser's Weekly*, 23 February 1962, p. 20; see also 'Brunning makes attack on American influence, research like a religious sect', *Advertiser's Weekly*, 11 March 1960, p.1.
48 Pearson and Turner, *The Persuasion Industry*, p. 146.
49 Ibid.
50 Ibid., p. 147.
51 'The new challenge', *Advertiser's Weekly*, 6 November 1959, p. 16; 'You British have nothing to fear from US invasion', *Advertiser's Weekly*, 13 May 1960, p. 82; 'New style Anglo-American tie-up', *Advertiser's Weekly*, 15 July 1960, p. 5; 'Second wave', *Advertiser's Weekly*, 17 July 1964, p. 24; 'The creative revolution', *Advertiser's Weekly*, 8 April 1966, p. 32; 'Why Madison Avenue moved in', *The Times*, 26 June 1969, p. 25.
52 The top British agencies by billings were London Press Exchange, Colman Prentis Varley and S.H. Benson. On US ownership, see D. West, 'Multinational competition in the British advertising agency business 1936–87', *Business History Review*, 62(3), 1988, p. 475; Sampson, *Anatomy of Britain*, p. 632.

53 G. Jones and F. Bostock, 'US multinationals in British manufacturing before 1962', *Business History Review*, 70, 1996, pp. 207–56.
54 Fox, *The Mirror Makers*, p. 173.
55 Ibid.
56 See JWT's corporate adverts in *Printer's Ink*, 1 February 1957; *Advertising Age*, April and June 1958.
57 T. Nevett, *Advertising in Britain: A History*, London: Collins, 1982, p. 177.
58 *Advertiser's Weekly*, 20 November 1947, pp. 360–1; 4 December 1947, pp. 463–8.
59 Rayfield, *Fifty in Forty*, p. 12.
60 Saunders and Hinks to New York, 5 July 1945, JWT/HAT, Box 537.
61 'Notes on negotiations that have so far taken place between JWT London and JWT New York', August 1945, JWT/HAT, Box 537.
62 Ibid.
63 'Pan American World Airways Incorporated Purchase of de Havilland Comets, proposed advertising in Britain', JWT London, October 1952, JWT/HAT, Box 537.
64 Letter to D. Dougherty from J.R. Keith, 14 December 1953, JWT/HAT, Box 537.
65 Letter from Sam Meek to Sandy Mitchell-Innes, 23 September 1957, JWT/HAT, Box 537.
66 Guidance of this sort from New York revealed important continuities between the pre-war and post-war practices followed within the company as a whole in developing overseas business. It echoed, in particular, the tone of a publication produced by JWT London for potential American clients. This had emphasized, not obscured, the company's American-ness. As a 1937 publication put it, 'JWT Co Ltd offers a complete American-type advertising and marketing service ... A number of its staff, in key positions, are Americans, and nearly every important executive has had American experience or training. Through constant interchange of personnel with its parent company in America, it is always in touch with the latest developments in American advertising and marketing methods.'
67 One symbol of this was Douglas Saunders' appointment to the top position in the IPA, the British advertising industry's corporate body. He served as president in 1958.
68 Yeo, 'Reflections on an agency', n.d., pp. 28, 29, JWT/HAT. Annabel's opened two doors away from JWT London's office at 44 Berkeley Square in 1963. It was named after Birley's then wife, Lady Annabel Goldsmith.
69 Robin Douglas-Home was the membership secretary of the Playboy Club in 1966, see *The Times*, 23 April 1966, p. 11; *The Times*, 3 March 1958, p. 14. His father was the younger brother of Sir Alec Douglas-Home, the Tory prime minister. His uncle, William, was a minor playwright. His younger brother, Charles, became editor of *The Times* in 1982.
70 Letter from Derrick Cawston to Tom Sutton, 14 April 1964, JWT/HAT, Box 238.
71 Letter from Edward Booth-Clibborn to Dermot Wilson, 9 August 1963; letter from Edward Booth-Clibborn to Violet Skeates, 9 July 1963; letter from Edward Booth-Clibborn to Chris Higham, 29 September 1964; letter from Edward Booth-Clibborn to J. Bullmore, 11 November 1964; letter from Don Michel to Edward Booth-Clibborn, 18 December 1964; JWT/HAT, Box 238.

72 JWT London also approached Liz Smith, fashion editor of the *Observer* colour supplement, as fashion adviser for JWT. See letter from Terri Hamaton to Norman Philip, 25 October 1968, JWT/HAT, Box 238.
73 *The Times*, 16 October 1968, p. 12.
74 Recorded in letter from Dermot Wilson to the Creative Department, 28 April 1964, JWT/HAT, Box 628.
75 Ibid.
76 Ibid.
77 *Round The Square*, March 1966, p. 1
78 *Round The Square*, March 1966, p. 5.
79 H. Radner, 'On the move, fashion photography and the Single Girl in the 1960s', in S. Bruzzi and P. Church Gibson (eds), *Fashion Cultures: Theories, Explorations and Analyses*, London: Routledge, 2000, p. 129.
80 Ibid.
81 'Fashion for real', draft script, December 1966, JWT/HAT, Box 326.
82 See P. Church Gibson, 'From up north to up west? London on screen 1965–67', *The London Journal*, 31(1), June 2006, p. 85.
83 London's growing self-assurance was further evidenced by its bold move to revise the T-square. Under the direction of Stephen King, a leading researcher at JWT London, the office proposed that Sam Meek's original formula be redesigned and renamed the T-plan. As West has argued, what was significant about this shift to the T-plan was that it moved the development of advertising away from its reliance on a rather mechanical use of market research towards an approach that sought to identify the desired response that was sought in the consumer and to develop advertising that stimulated this. As the company itself put it, the aim was to 'establish what the target group of consumers should notice in the brand, should believe about it and feel towards it'. 'JWT London, history', JWT/HAT, Box 15, p. 12.
84 Quoted in J. Winship, 'Culture of restraint: the British chain store 1920–39', in P. Jackson, M. Lowe, D. Miller and F. Mort (eds), *Commercial Cultures: Economies, Practices, Spaces*, Oxford: Berg, 2000, p. 16.

3

Understanding ordinary women: consumer research and the mass-market housewife

In May 1959 J. Walter Thompson's head office placed a corporate advertisement in the pages of *Fortune* magazine (Fig. 9). The advert depicted a young modern housewife standing amid a towering array of groceries spread out on her kitchen table. She held in her hands an official-looking booklet in which she noted down the goods that she had bought. The advert promoted JWT's consumer panel, a market research survey that drew upon the contributions of 5,000 housewives and their daily purchases of a range of domestic groceries. For JWT, the consumer panel revealed a detailed picture of how 'America actually bought by region, age, education, income and race' and the company promoted it as an indispensable service to clients that could help them to market their goods more effectively.

The advertisement is telling in a number of ways. It speaks volumes for JWT's commercial confidence in the 1950s as one of the largest US advertising agencies, with the resources to offer its clients access to an extensive programme of market research as part of the service that it offered. The consumer panel itself also tells us something about the agency's commercial ethos and, in particular, its commitment to market research as central to the 'science of selling'. JWT had a well-established reputation in the US for its attention to market research and this formed part of a highly formalized conception of advertising production. This approach set it apart from its more 'creatively' driven competitors during the late 1950s and 1960s.[1] JWT, however, was not alone in using market research and the *Fortune* advert is indicative of a more general growth in its use by advertising agencies across the trans-Atlantic world in the post-war period, a growth that included its expansion in Britain.[2]

The *Fortune* advert is striking in other ways. Echoing an ideal repeated across consumer advertising and on the pages of women's magazines, the advert fixed the consumer as the housewife, the lynchpin of domestic consumption. While

'A remarkably accurate marketing tool', JWT, 1959

there were other social types and groups who were addressed as consumers across commercial culture, it says much about the attention on women as the 'choosers and spenders' of the household budget that it was the figure of the ordinary housewife that JWT chose to single out in its consumer purchasing panel.[3] 'Mrs Housewife', however, was not as self-evident a figure as the iterative power of the ideal implied. In Britain, she was the product of intersecting social forces. Central to these was the decline in women's participation in the labour market in the immediate post-war decades. This created a situation in which approximately two-thirds of all women aged between 20 and 64 were full-time housewives by the early 1950s.[4] This situation was encouraged by policy makers, with the system of tax allowances, benefits and national insurance all promoting the idea of a dependent wife within a stable nuclear family.[5] Educationalists from the mid-1940s also sought to entrench the idea that being a wife and mother was the primary 'career' for women, with both the Norwood Report (1943) and the Crowther Report (1959) arguing that girls' secondary education should be focused upon this expectation of their future domestic duties.[6] Child psychologists like Winnicott and Bowlby gave additional intellectual weight to the idea that women's key social responsibility was as a full-time mother who took exclusive care of the developing child. Demographic trends supported the emphasis of experts on women's domestic and familial responsibilities. By the early 1960s women were marrying younger and having children earlier than they had before the war. In the early 1960s, 60% of women aged between 20 and 24 were married and most had their children in the early to mid-20s.[7] The image of the full-time housewife as a young married mother was rooted in these demographic shifts. At the same time there was a convergence in the domestic duties undertaken by middle-class and working-class women, fuelled by the relative decline of domestic service after 1945. By the early 1960s there were only 200,000 residential domestic workers, down from a figure of 2 million in 1931.[8] The rise of the 'servantless home' for middle-class families brought the domestic experience of middle-class and working-class women closer together through the 1950s and 1960s as they shouldered similar domestic duties.[9]

Within this context of demographic and policy-driven change, commercial practitioners like the manufacturers of domestic technologies and commodities, architects and evangelists in women's magazines played a key role in elaborating the role of Mrs Housewife.[10] Market research, however, was also crucial in the 'assembling' of this consumer subject. It played an important linking role within the various interventions into domestic living through helping to consolidate the figure of the average housewife as a knowable social type upon whom manufacturers and advertisers could act. It is the knowledge generated by market research about the housewife that this chapter sets out to explore. Specifically, the chapter reflects on the ways in which market research in Britain helped produce understandings of and information about the 'mass housewife' in the 1950s and 1960s. It does this through considering the market research used and generated by JWT London, focusing on three key client accounts – those for the Pin-Up home perm, Brillo soap pads and Oxo cubes – together with the agency's non-product-specific research. The chapter aims to show how JWT sought to understand the ordinary housewife and her consumption habits.

In exploring the agency's approach to the 'mass-market' housewife, the chapter draws on recent sociological arguments about advertising and market research that have conceptualized these commercial practices as technologies or socio-technical devices for 'making-up' the consumer; that is, devices for formatting and framing consumer dispositions. In particular, I draw on the arguments of Nicholas Rose and Peter Miller.[11] In an influential essay, they foregrounded the role played by market research in shaping the relationships formed between consumers and commodities. In particular they documented the influence of ideas of the human personality and techniques of group discussion derived from the psychological sciences. They claimed that these research techniques worked to draw out and render instrumentalizable the inner motivations of consumers. In other words, they contended that market researchers sought to forge connections between consumers' desires and specific goods by forcing these feelings into the open in the research encounter. Miller and Rose described this process as 'mobilizing' the consumer': that is, 'affiliating … needs with particular products' and 'simultaneously making up the commodity and assembling the little rituals of everyday life that give that commodity meaning and value'.[12] Out of this process, they argued, comes 'an unprecedented and meticulous cartography' of everyday life and consumption through the technology of market research.[13]

Miller and Rose's conception of the capacity of market research to 'mobilize' the consumer and their vivid sense of the 'meticulous cartography' of consumption that it helps to generate are instructive ideas in making sense of the role played by consumer research in the promotional economy. In particular, they enable us to grasp the way market research opens up the practical uses, symbolic dimensions and emotional dynamics of everyday goods in the lives of consumers. In exploring the use made of market research by JWT London, however, this chapter also seeks to revise certain aspects of Miller and Rose's thesis while continuing to draw on their broad insights. I propose a more differentiated sense of the various marketing and market research paradigms that were used by advertising agencies. Post-war market research in Britain was alive with controversies about the best way to measure markets, define consumers and understand consumption. This disputation and struggle for professional leadership among differently constituted practitioners disappears in Miller and Rose's essay. Moreover, they occlude these intellectual and practical debates by privileging the influence of the psychological sciences upon market research. In doing so, they effectively rehearse an argument, evident in both contemporary post-war accounts of advertising and in more recent scholarship, that post-war market research was subject to growing sophistication under the influence of the psychological sciences. The evidence developed in this chapter suggests that JWT London used different ways of measuring markets, apprehending the consumer and understanding the use of goods by consumers. This certainly included the application of forms of psychological knowledge, but the agency's overall approach to consumers and consumer markets reveals that these were neither the only nor necessarily the most important forms of research. In this regard, JWT London was broadly typical of British advertising and market research. This should prompt us to qualify those claims that see Freudian thought as triggering some kind of 'Copernican turn' in marketing in this period.[14]

The chapter also seeks to bring a more international and specifically trans-Atlantic dimension to the understanding of post-war market research than is the case in Miller and Rose's essay. One notable feature of post-war market research in Britain was the influence of commercial techniques first formulated in the United States, including applied psychological knowledge. Like many other aspects of advertising in the 1950s and 1960s, market research moved in an eastward direction across the Atlantic. US advertising agencies and market research companies dominated this movement and their actions were underpinned by the investment of US manufacturing companies in Britain and by the initiatives of government departments on both sides of the Atlantic that sought to facilitate the transfer of commercial know-how from the US to Britain. JWT London's parent company was an important player in this world and through its offices on both sides of the Atlantic it helped to disseminate research methods and techniques first pioneered in the USA. These US-derived techniques formed a visible presence within post-war British market research and constituted a key point of reference for British-based practitioners. Of course, this influence was neither totalizing nor did it go unchallenged. Staff at JWT's London office, like colleagues elsewhere in British advertising, selectively appropriated and reworked elements of US market research, frequently combining it with more indigenous traditions of social research. Nonetheless, even as they rejected elements of 'American' approaches to consumers, they still had to reckon with their intellectual authority and commercial force in this period.

J. Walter Thompson and the role of market research

An agency trained to watch consumer behaviour with this degree of concentration is probably as close to shifts of mood and attitudes among ordinary people as any group in Britain.[15]

Published in a booklet for its new staff, JWT London's confident claim about its expertise in understanding consumer behaviour followed a reference to the £1.5m that it had spent on consumer research for its clients in the previous ten years. In fact, in introducing the agency to its new members, JWT London foregrounded its status as an exponent of well-researched advertising. This self-positioning echoed that of its parent company in the US where, from the early part of the twentieth century, it had been known for its pioneering studies of consumer behaviour and for the weight it placed on 'scientific' studies of the consumer in the development of advertising. The JWT consumer purchasing panel was prominent in this commitment to consumer research and was introduced in 1927 to assist one of JWT's major clients, Ponds, the cosmetic manufacturer. The relationship with Ponds was also important in stimulating the agency to undertake its first 'depth interviews' with consumers in 1948. These sought to 'probe the motives underlying cosmetic usage and the attitudes attendant to this usage' by encouraging respondents to 'reach down' into their experiences and pull out the 'connective links which motivates [their] behaviour'.[16] The consumer purchasing panel and 'depth interviews' were part of an extensive range of approaches to the study of consumer behaviour used by the parent company. These included studies of basic economic and population trends, media analysis of press and broadcast audiences, analysis of the client's own sales data and of total market and competitive sales trends and motivation surveys that attempt 'to develop the "why" of consumer habits and attitudes, copy testing before the advert appears and after it has run'.[17]

The London office of JWT followed the lead of its parent and made extensive use of market research.[18] While some of this research was undertaken by JWT London's marketing department, the agency also used the services of a subsidiary company, the British Market Research Bureau (BMRB), to conduct market research for its clients as well as for businesses that didn't advertise with the agency.[19] By the 1950s BMRB was one of the three largest research companies in the UK and employed 150 full-time staff. These included 25 university-trained research executives, most of whom were graduates in economics, statistics or psychology.[20] The research conducted by the agency and by BMRB was broadly representative of the paradigms of consumer research being undertaken in Britain in the 1950s and 1960s. This included the use of official statistics, together with surveys produced by the agency.[21] The two most important were retail audit research and consumer purchasing panels. Retail audit research used a representative panel of shops drawn from the Census of Distribution and weekly figures on the sales of a selected range of goods were collected. From this, researchers could generate evidence on the current size of particular markets and track any trends in sales. Consumer purchasing panels, like the one used by JWT's parent company in the US, typically consisted of approximately 2,000 households who reported on a regular basis the various purchases they had made of selected branded goods. The CPPs produced data not only on the volume of purchases, but also on which households were buying the goods.[22]

Across this range of research, markets and consumers were rarely defined as a homogeneous mass, but rather demographic categories were used to classify consumers. The most important were the well-known demographic categories of class or occupational description.[23] These occupational descriptions of the population were complemented by attention to the importance of age as a key indicator of purchasing behaviour and hence market description. Much of the impetus for this attention to age was driven by commercial interest in the growing youth market.[24] While JWT London was not heavily involved in selling to teenagers, its market research did engage with the idea of segmenting consumers by stages of the life cycle and it used this technique, as we will see later, in study the mass-market housewife. Perhaps the most significant wider development in market research with which JWT and BMRB engaged in the 1950s and 1960s was motivation research. This had its immediate roots in American commerce, though it was the product of European émigrés to the US. Its most celebrated exponent was the Austrian-born Ernest Dichter. Dichter's central ambition was to explain not what consumers bought, but why they bought, and his approach offered a radically different paradigm for understanding and segmenting consumers. Dichter deployed in-depth interviews with consumers in order to understand the symbolic meaning of goods and the deeper psychological needs they might serve. His Freudian approach not only introduced a thicker idea of human subjectivity into market research, but also worked to segment consumers less by social class or sex or age (though these categories were often still part of his consumer research) than by psychological disposition. Thus, in early research conducted in the late 1940s into the consumption of home appliances, Dichter developed a three-fold classification of women: the 'career women' who disliked domesticity and hated housework; the 'pure housewife' who identified so strongly with her role as guardian of the home that she was anxious about the role played by home appliances and expressed hostility towards them because they undermined her role; and the 'balanced woman' who was the most fulfilled emotionally because she knew she was capable of both housework and career.[25] Later Dichter recast his conception of the 'balanced woman' as the kind who could be encouraged to see housework as an arena of creativity in which she could 'use at home all the faculties she would display in an outside career'.[26]

Dichter's conception of these psychological categories was informed by his own highly positive view of consumer society. As Daniel Horowitz has suggested, Dichter saw the whole process of market research as therapeutic for the consumer and not only useful for the selling of goods. In fact, Dichter was driven by a wholly positive conception of the private pleasures of consumption and saw his work as contributing to the unblocking of feelings of guilt about consumption within the population that derived from the puritan culture of self-restraint.[27] Dichter argued that the central aim of advertising was to give the customer permission to 'enjoy his life freely' and 'to demonstrate that he is right in surrounding himself with products that enrich his life and give him pleasure'.[28] It was the attention to the psychological segmentation of consumer types, rather than his therapeutic model of consumption, that gave Dichter's work much of its appeal, though in Britain his approach was by no means uncontroversial. Dichter established an office in London in 1957, though the business was slow to grow.[29] By the early 1960s Dichter's UK operation was only contributing between 3% and 5% of the parent company's international turnover.[30] Dichter complained to journalists that Britain remained the 'most puritanical country in the world' and that British consumers were resistant to expressing themselves through goods despite growing affluence.[31] British market researchers and advertising agencies were also publicly critical of motivation research. The IPA cautioned against a doctrinal applications of motivation research, suggesting that 'motivation research … is part of a co-operative enterprise, not a separate entity governed by laws peculiar to itself and proceeding to its own esoteric and isolated conclusions'.[32] Mark Abrams, director of Research Services Ltd, went further in suggesting that market researchers had 'no future as "engineers of consent" assembling and reshuffling a known spectrum of unconscious desires'.[33]

JWT's parent company was not the most psycho-dynamically orientated, though it did use forms of motivation research in the US. In the UK, BMRB established a group under one of its senior researchers, Norman Philip, in 1957 to look into the use of the technique. This group included the four psychologists employed by the company, among them Pamela Vince who had recently worked on a study of the child viewer and television led by Hilde Himmeleweit for the Nuffield Foundation.[34] BMRB insiders claimed that JWT's approach to psychological motivations was distanced from the more 'flamboyant Freudian versions'.[35] Moreover, senior figures within BMRB and JWT London were critical of the universal claims of motivation research. John Treasure, former head of BMRB and JWT London's chairman, claimed that continuing cultural differences militated against the exclusive use of motivation research. As he put it, 'it may well be that basic motivations are the same in all countries. However, national habits, traditions and attitudes still differ widely and are a vital factor in … marketing.'[36] The pull of motivation research within JWT London was evident, however, when, three years after Treasure's article, another senior staffer within the company circulated a memo that voiced concerns about the need for the agency to develop more research of this sort. As the memo noted, JWT London was 'fantastically deficient about the basic information about consumers, about attitudes and motivations particularly'.[37] This led to a recommendation that the London office should develop 'new methods of defining the population in terms of personality groups and more refined user groups'.[38] Dichter himself visited JWT London in 1965 and met four account teams, including those for Brillo and Persil, to see what assistance he could offer.[39] During his visit, Dichter found an agency with a number of trained psychologists and those interested in consumer motivations, but also an agency that was committed to other kinds of qualitative consumer research as well as quantitative surveys. The pragmatic mixture of approaches to the problem of consumer behaviour ran right back through much of JWT London's post-war consumer studies and campaign planning and was strongly present in the research on ordinary women. It was notably evident in their work in the late 1940s and early 1950s for the Pin-Up home perm account. It is to this account that I now want to turn to look in more detail at some of JWT's consumer research.

Pin-Up home perm

Pin-Up home perm was launched by the American company Pepsodent in 1946, though it was not promoted nationally in Britain until 1948 (Fig. 10). At the time of the first promotion, JWT London estimated, with data drawn from retail audits and consumer purchasing panels, that 73% of British women were potential buyers of home perms, which gave a potential market of 11 million women for Pepsodent's product. However, there was an immediate problem for JWT in that 9 million of these women were already users of salon perms. JWT's principal aim, then, was to convert as many salon permers to home permers as possible.[40]

In January 1950 BMRB undertook research to ascertain the characteristics of existing home perm users. It expressed the results in demographic terms, identifying the particular age and class grouping most likely to use a home perm. The research revealed the preponderance of young and youngish working-class women among the consumers of the product: 30% of home permers were under 24 years old and 50% were aged 25–39. Sixty per cent of all home perm users were from social class D, 35% from class C, with only 5% being from social class A or B. This research complemented earlier studies by BMRB which had sought to investigate women's hair doing and shampooing habits. For example, an extensive set of qualitative interviews were undertaken in August and October 1948 in which 4,144 women were spoken to about their hair-care habits.[41]

This interest in hair-care habits was central to a further qualitative study undertaken in 1950.

'Pin-Up', JWT London, 1950

This research was conducted not by BMRB but by the Tavistock Institute of Human Relations (TIHR).[42] Pepsodent approached TIHR to assist it in understanding more about the users of home perms. Thus, in January 1950 TIHR began a ten-month study on the Pin-Up perm. The report produced by TIHR was pioneering in that it offered a psycho-dynamically orientated approach to consumer behaviour at a time when psychology had a limited presence in market research in Britain. The scope and ambition of the report was evident in its methods and title. It used group discussion and non-directive interviews to explore the 'attitudes of women towards their hair'.[43]

The report started from the observation that attaining a good appearance was central to fulfilling the adult feminine role. This required the acquisition of the skills and social judgements necessary for making and maintaining a good appearance. The report noted that the contemporary ideal of good appearance included the valorization of wavy or curly hair – waviness was associated with softness, naturalness, smoothness and shininess. Straight hair, by contrast, was seen as masculine or childish. Moreover, the authors of the report argued that curly or wavy hair was recognized as a way of expressing female sexual maturity.[44] Alongside the detailing of this cultural ideal, TIHR sought to reflect on women's psychological relationship to their hair and hair doing. They argued that hair doing satisfied the obsessional needs of women and that it stemmed from a wish to control untidy hair – to put hair in order. At the same time, hair doing involved destructive and reparative tendencies. Washing hair was seen as a destructive act in which hair lost its shape and so was a process that was often postponed. However, the restoration of the hairstyle could, conversely, offer women pleasure – the pleasure of making good the shape. Other anxieties could also surface around hair care. These included aggressive feelings about the routine of hair drying that the authors saw as a legacy of the child's dependency on her mother in the early years of hair care. As they put it, 'unconscious difficulties in the daughter-mother relationship persist in adult attitudes towards hair doing'.[45]

Complementing their exploration of the psychology of hair, the authors of the report detailed some of the sociological aspects of home perming. In so doing they delved into the habits of use already associated with home perms. The most notable observation concerned a distinction between three kinds of home-perming culture. The first of these revolved around what the report called 'gatekeeper groups'. These centred on women who had certain hairdressing skills and who assisted others in doing their hair. As the report noted, the 'gatekeeper' role satisfied social as well as creative needs for these women through hairdressing. The second home-perming culture involved 'solos', women who had the same skills as 'gatekeepers' but who had not collected a group around them. Finally, there was the 'two-person relationship', in which friends or relations offered each other mutual support with the problem of home perming and who again lacked the desire to control expressed by 'gatekeepers'.

Cutting across these different ways of doing home perms, TIHR found recurring problems with the product among its various users which were working to limit its use. Among these was the guilt that came from asking hairdressers to cut their hair in preparation for the home perm (the hair had to be tapered for the perm to work properly), concerns about the unpleasant smell of the lotion and the length of time taken to process the perm, including the preparation of curling the hair and waiting for the lotion to work. In addition, women expressed disappointment about the fact that home perms did not last as long as those done in a salon and required more upkeep in the form of weekly washing and overnight curling to keep the hair in good shape.[46]

TIHR's report was discussed by JWT staff, the client and Miss Hurstfield of TIHR at a meeting held at Park Royal, Pepsodent's UK head office, on 15 November 1950. It was later circulated among the relevant staff within the advertising agency. Their response revealed some resistance to the approach adopted by the Tavistock. Michael Stern, JWT's representative on the account, for example, confessed that he couldn't find a 'single new contribution' in the research, insisting that it said nothing that they had not already thought of or discovered 'in a quantitative way using normal consumer research'.[47] The small sample – and its psychological focus – concerned Stern. As he put it, 'by its very nature an enquiry of this sort can do no more than throw up ideas for further investigation and discussion, since, however deep the probing of the psychologists, the statistical inadequacy of a sample of 80 still prevents us from drawing any definite conclusions'.[48] Rather instrumentally, Stern proposed that the research should be used to support some of 'our views previously rejected by the client', notably the disadvantages of promoting overnight processing, and other than that 'we should encourage the client to forget it the best he can'.[49] A more positive response was offered by Mr Silvester, Stern's colleague. While he too began by confirming that the report 'brings us nothing new – but does confirm our thinking on a number of points', Silvester went on to suggest that TIHR's finding that the time home perming took was a deterrent to its use was a helpful observation. He proposed that Pepsodent should try and speed up the process.[50] What was also notable about Silvester's comments was that he was drawn, like the Tavistock researchers, into the world of women's hair care and all its paraphernalia and rituals. Thus, he proposed that the company should offer instructions on how to achieve the best results after the perm. This meant advising women not only on 'shampooing, but also how to set their hair at night, the use of hairnets and the importance of general regular brushing etc.'.[51] Despite intellectual reservations about the research methods of the Tavistock Institute, then, at least one key member of the JWT team was drawn on to the terrain of the intimate rituals of hair doing documented by the report, even as he downplayed the psychological understandings that it had privileged.

Brillo pads

An interest in domestic routine and the place of commodities in the performance of the role of the adult woman was also evident in JWT's work for the US soap pad manufacturer, Brillo. In the research produced for the company, JWT London again used a range of ways of understanding the consumer. In this case, however, the agency was notably more open to psychological approaches. Brillo's steel wool cleaning pads impregnated with detergent were promoted in the UK by JWT from the late 1950s. In a booklet produced by the agency for Brillo sales staff, JWT emphasized its interest in what it called 'Mrs Brillo Consumer'. Mrs Brillo Consumer was part of the 15 million households in Britain who had shaped a 'consumer revolution'. This was a revolution in domestic consumption expressed through the purchasing of electric and gas cookers, furniture, washing machines, fridges and television sets.[52] Alongside this increased purchasing power came more leisure, including travel abroad. The result was 'easier, more comfortable lives'. It was into this world of what the booklet called the 'new British home' that Brillo entered and offered the housewife the possibility of new levels of hygiene and greater speed in the performance of domestic tasks. The report was notable for how it represented Mrs Brillo Consumer. Using caricature, she was counterposed to the old housewife, round and prematurely aged and weighed down by a heavy, iron pan. Next to her, Mrs Brillo Consumer was an embodiment of the new, modern housewife: taller, slimmer, neater, replete with a contemporary perm and benefiting from having bright, shiny pans.

JWT's research for the account built on this positioning of Mrs Brillo Consumer and focused on the routines of domestic life that the pads were designed to alleviate. This led JWT to reflect on the problem of washing up and how it could understand the satisfactions, as well as the drudgery, of washing up for housewives. JWT captured the fundamental problem of washing up in a 1965 memo: 'washing up, when it comes to utensils, is a nasty chore and the primary need is for something which will get it done easier and faster and in the less objectionable way'.[53] The agency realized that in promoting Brillo to meet this function it had to insert the pads into women's domestic routines and care was needed not to over-promote their use. As they put it, 'once a week, on Sunday after the main meal, is the time for a real blast at the pots and pans. Ask them to do it every day and, regardless of the miraculous qualities of the product, you are asking them to take on extra work.'[54]

With these reservations in mind, JWT sought to link the product with certain social and psychological aspects of washing the pots. This meant picking up on the pride women felt in having done the washing up and produced clean pots. While evidence from research suggested that 'pots and pans are not objects of admiration and many housewives don't expect them to be shining', nevertheless it was felt that housewives did reveal pleasure, as well as practical satisfaction, from getting the pots washed. As they noted, 'there is something in Dichter's observation that washing up can be a source of some perverted enjoyment in anticipation of meals to come or whatever'.[55]

The symbolism of 'shine' also surfaced in JWT's deliberations, despite the view that most women did not expect their pots to glisten. Shine, JWT argued, was evidence of better cleaning and could be linked with hygiene to reinforce its value as a sought-after property that Brillo could deliver. The copy strategy for 1965 certainly picked up on this thinking. Playing on consumer anxieties, JWT proposed to suggest that dull pans could be dangerous. As the memo noted, '[dull pans] are a threat to health. Only a pan so clean it shines can give the housewife the assurance that every particle of food has been removed.' The strategy, then, was to 'sell the shine that only Brillo can deliver'.[56] In a meeting with Dichter just prior to this strategy being formulated, the account team reflected in a 'brainstorming' session on 'surfaces'. Handwritten notes made by the team reveal some of the themes they were considering. Thus, there is the observation that certain surfaces 'need nourishing and feeding'; 'stainless steel gives you away, but aluminium doesn't'; 'some surfaces I can neglect, others betray me'; 'the pleasure in polishing, the caress of material things'; 'wipe on, wipe off satisfaction'.[57]

These impromptu attempts to map the psychological and symbolic dimensions stimulated by surfaces, including the surface of pans, offered ways for the agency to connect Brillo to the values and desires of its potential consumers

– and added something to the documenting of the routines of washing up that other research conducted by the agency had also revealed. This preoccupation with the social and symbolic dimension of goods was also evident in the research undertaken for Oxo cubes. For this account, the agency used research that described the consumer in demographic and psychological terms, as well as bringing to bear a sociological analysis to the problem of selling Oxo cubes.

Oxo cubes

Oxo, the processed beef supplement, was one of JWT's more celebrated advertising accounts. JWT had won the account in the late 1950s and was charged with countering Oxo's falling sales and perceptions that the product was bought by poor people and poor cooks. To this end, JWT sought to give the product a new, youthful image and upgrade the product socially. As a memo from 1962 spelt out, the early television advertising had sought to show that 'modern, capable, nice people used Oxo' – people like Katie and her husband Philip, the stars of the commercials.[58] The advertising also emphasized the role Oxo could play in good meat cooking (notably, pies and casseroles) and that the product was not a substitute food, but rather a supplement to beef in particular. To this end, JWT promoted the idea, as the 1962 memo reminded the account team, that 'Oxo is the mark of a good housewife'.[59] Being a good housewife meant providing tasty food for your husband in the first instance and the early advertising captured this with the slogan, 'Oxo gives a meal man appeal'.

As JWT continued to work on the advertising of Oxo through the 1960s, various kinds of market research were undertaken to track consumer sales and shifts within the target market. In the summer of 1963 the agency reviewed the account and looked ahead. It recognized that five successful years of advertising had helped to make 'Oxo respectable to use'. Phase two, it argued, had to supply housewives with more justification for its continued use. The 'new thought' focused on gravy and was expressed in the following way: 'It's the gravy that gives the flavour to the meat, it's the Oxo that gives the flavour to the gravy.'[60] This formulation stemmed from a BMRB survey produced in 1963 called 'The Gravymakers'. The report offered detailed information on the type of women who bought Oxo. Firstly, it claimed that, as an established brand, Oxo had been tried by 90% of all households, with the majority (74%) currently using it.[61] Expressing these figures for use in class terms, the research suggested that usage 'tends to be strongest amongst CDE class housewives and weakest in the AB classes'.[62] Glossing this evidence, the account team noted that 'we recommend that Oxo promotion should have, broadly speaking, an appeal to the mass housewife market (94% of UK housewives fall into the CDE class)'.[63]

Alongside the class-based descriptions of the market, 'The Gravymakers' study identified consumers by the frequency of use – what it called the 'light users', 'the heavy users' and 'the non-users'. 'Heavy users' were consumers buying at the rate of three or more cubes per week. The aim of the advertising, then, was to convert as many as possible of the 'light users' into 'heavy users'. It was the reflections on gravy itself, however, that were perhaps the most interesting aspect of the report. Here 'The Gravymakers' sought to draw out the attitudes housewives had towards gravy and the symbolic importance of the preparation of gravy to the successful fulfilment of the housewife role. It noted that 93% of women claimed to use meat juices at least sometimes in their gravy (across all classes). This use of meat juices stemmed from the perception that juices were 'the essence of the meat' and highly regarded by housewives as a nutritious gravy constituent.[64] Seventy-four per cent of all housewives also emphasized that they liked their gravy to be 'beefy-flavoured' and there was also a general emphasis on the use of vegetable water when making gravy because it was seen as a further source of 'goodness' and taste. Glossing these findings, the report suggested that 'housewives believe that gravy plays a key role in meat cooking. Gravy to the British is not unlike tea; its making is an important function that the whole family influences.'[65]

The agency recognized, however, that family life, women's expectations and domestic routine were not static. JWT's researching of the Oxo account was preoccupied in the early 1960s with the transformations that were taking place in social life and eating habits. The nature of these transformations and what they might mean for the promotion of Oxo prompted the agency on to the terrain of sociological analysis. As a memo from July 1963 noted, while 'Katie' might have been ahead of most of Oxo's consumers in 1958, now there was a danger that she was being left behind (Fig. 11). It conceded, 'She is no longer setting a pattern of living that is envied. All the exciting new things that have happened to young women in society – holidays abroad, theatre outings, mad new clothes, promotion for husband, a new car etc somehow have passed her by, while she has been preparing cosy meals at the stove for Philip.'[66]

These concerns encouraged JWT to propose that Oxo develop a new range of flavours so that the product 'is more in line with future trends in people's needs and desires in flavouring products'. These included more 'subtle' or 'spicy' flavours and the creation of variants of Oxo to be used with light or dark meats. Thought was also put into the style of the pack. The report prepared by the account team asked if the pack design needed 'greater sophistication? More sensual pleasure? Nearer to cooking in feeling? More modern typography?'[67] Further market research was undertaken to test this range of propositions. The

Open on C.U. of transparent
jug of near boiling water.
Super: LIFE WITH KATIE.
Cube suspended above jug.

Fade super as Golden Oxo
cube plops down into jug
from top of frame.

Silver spoon comes into
frame.and stirs stock.

Cut to C.U. of pack, with
one loose cube. Spoon is
laid down beside it.

Cut to M.S. of Katie at
central unit of kitchen.
She is stirring half made
gravy in enamelled roasting
pan. She picks up jug of
stock.

Cut to C.U. as Katie starts
to pour Golden Oxo stock
into gravy, stirring as she
does so.

Cut to Philip, who has
appeared, coming towards
the food.

Cut to C.U. as Philip takes
spoon of gravy and tastes it.

Cut back to Katie as she puts
spoon down on working surface,
and picks up pack.

Cut to C.U. of pack in her
hand. Pan with pack as she
turns to put it away.

Cut as Katie's hand puts
pack down on shelf of herb
rack on her kitchen wall,
alongside standard Oxo pack.

II   'Oxo', JWT London

research was notable for way it sought to differentiate between housewives in terms of their attitudes to cooking, highlighting a key group of women it called 'experimentalist cooks' whose needs were not being met by existing Oxo products. These 'experimentalist cooks', whom it loosely defined as those who used recipes to make their own dishes, felt that existing mass-market products, including Oxo, were unsubtle in their flavours (being synthetic), lacked body and did not come in a wide enough range of flavours to match the variety of their cooking.

The classification of an attitude group of housewives, the 'experimentalist cooks', had developed out of conversations between Oxo and JWT over the perceived limitations of demographic breakdowns within market research. As L.W. Hore, Oxo's general brand manager, noted in 1966 in a letter to JWT's marketing department, 'As you know we have discussed the inconsistency of existing demographic breakdowns … and in various ad hoc surveys endeavoured to discriminate between "experimental/sophisticated" housewives and other.'[68] Both Oxo and JWT were interested in the 'psychological groupings' produced by the research company Attwoods, which had segmented housewives into five groups. These consisted of 'conscientiousness', 'economy conscious', 'conservatism in brand choice', 'traditionalism in housework' and 'willingness to experiment in shopping'.[69] J.R. Stonehewer, of Attwoods, suggested that three of these categories – 'conscientiousness', 'economy conscious', 'conservatism in brand choice' – might be most appropriate for understanding Oxo consumers.[70] Such an understanding, however, ran counter to the ambition of JWT London to promote the association of Oxo with socially progressive housewives. And it was to the 'experimental cooks' that JWT looked in its market research for 1967.[71]

The new housewife

An interest in those women more open to the acquisition of new ideas and consumption habits in the fulfilment of the housewife role and the factors that might both support and contain their embrace of new patterns of living was evident in a major study of new housewives produced by BMRB in 1967. The report, titled 'The New Housewife', drew upon research conducted in the autumn of 1964 and the spring of 1965. It represented an important synthesis of the client-specific research that JWT London had been conducting since the late 1940s on the 'mass housewife' and drew upon the considerable experience acquired by the agency and BMRB in researching into these consumers.

To this end, the research combined a strong class analysis of housewives with attention to life cycle classifications and a developed sociology of family and kinship structures. The report was written by Mollie Tarrant, a consultant researcher for both JWT and BMRB. Tarrant was relatively well known as she had been one of Mass Observation's most active fieldworkers in the Second World War and was later the managing director of Mass Observation as it moved into the field of commercial market research in the 1950s. The 'New Housewife' report began by noting that it had been prompted in part by the notable increase in the number of new housewives over the previous decade. This was an increase caused by the general expansion of the population and by the fact that many women were marrying younger. It further suggested that these young married women accounted for a significant proportion of consumer expenditure. The reason for this was clear:

> These young women have set up home for the first time and face a lifetime of running it. They have new and wide responsibilities – for the daily diet, for the upkeep of the home and the miscellany of purchases that sustain it; for children, for the family's health; for entertainment, and for many other things. Some of them, 48% of married women aged between 16–34, work outside as well as inside the home; and young women and young housewives, experimenting and adapting at each stage of their lives, are important arbiters of the future.[72]

In opening up the 'attitudes and behaviour' of the new housewife, the report was concerned centrally with how established habits and ideas were changed or reworked by young women as they experienced transformations in their life situation through marriage and the setting up of their own home. In exploring these changes, the report signalled the explanatory value of the concept of stages of the life cycle. Life cycle was important, it contended, because 'habits were trimmed to meet the demands of life situations' and this 'trimming' of habits had a significant bearing on consumption.[73]

As well as life cycle, the report sought to locate the new housewife in a broader social context. This meant, in the first instance, the ways in which social class might shape the housewife's consuming habits. The report also sought, rather innovatively, to understand the community relations and kinship structures in which the new housewife lived. It suggested that these social relations, and the values bound up with them, were in a particularly fluid state, with the geographical and social mobility of the post-war years having served to recast them. In particular, 'increased social and consumer opportunity' was throwing up new challenges and opportunities for young housewives. One consequence for young working-class housewives was the possibility of a more middle-class lifestyle as older patterns of working-class life were disrupted by the decline of the extended family and the availability of labour-saving devices that combined to bring middle-class and working-class homes closer together.[74]

The report was especially interested in the changing form of working-class family and community life and the effect of these relationships on the take-up of new domestic habits and routines. These community and kinship ties were central to understanding, in particular, the role of tradition in inhibiting the take-up of new habits at a stage of life when change was most likely. As the report suggested, '[our interest in social groups] underlines our interest in social interaction and social dependencies, since it is in situations like those of early marriage when group loyalties are confirmed or in the process of reformation that we might expect a higher potential for change'.[75] To this end, the report was interested in the continuing role of the young housewife's mother in the transmission of 'backward looking tendencies' and in restricting the development of new habits and ideas. It sought to explore the mother/daughter relationship by, firstly, drawing upon sociological understandings of the form of 'matrilocality' evident in working-class communities, that is, the tendency of young working-class women to live close to their mother. Noting that one-third of young housewives lived within walking distance of 'mum', the report cited supporting evidence of this fact from Willmott and Young's *Family and Kinship in Bethnal Green*. Thus,

> Peter Willmott and Michael Young have given detailed accounts of the way marriage often begins in the maternal home and is afterwards sustained and highly influenced by mother–daughter relationships and close kinship ties. If 'Mum' lives near or is easily reached, she has more opportunity to 'teach' her, and geographical proximity is one obvious measure of potential influence.[76]

This influence could be both positive and negative. Mum was there to offer advice and companionship, but there might also be conflicts with Mum over the young wife's independence and her performance of the housewife role. This influence was explored by documenting the 'pattern of dependency' between mothers and daughter. The report suggested that there were ten distinct groupings among its sample that revealed marked patterns of divergence between women in their feelings and attitudes towards this dependency. These included 'Rejecting mothers with dependent daughters' (11%): 'they want their daughters to live further away, but the daughters want to be near so they can get advice quickly'; 'mutual rejectors' (8%), 'both Mum and daughter think the daughter should live further away so she can be independent'; and 'Mutually sociable or affectionate (3%) – they want to be near because they enjoy each other's company'.[77]

The report drew from these classifications pointers to how these familial ties might shape the openness of housewives to acquiring new habits and routines. This theme was later explored by asking the same groups of women about their attitudes towards the housewife role and the broader idea of 'home-centredness'; that is, the wider view of domesticity and the organization of home life. Again the aim was to show how these attitudes might shape purchasing decisions, especially of food and major household items. The report revealed evidence of identification by many women with the homemaker role. This included the stated views of the majority that they liked housework, with two-fifths of the new housewives being what it called 'housework enthusiasts'. The report was appropriately sceptical about this finding, suggesting, 'What we almost certainly have here are the socially conditioned and generalised responses, to be accepted with reservation … More, housewives qua housewives have reputations to maintain and can hardly be expected to undermine them.'[78] The report did seek to disaggregate the responses of housewives' to their social role and it noted how, amid the generalized enthusiasm for housewifery, some domestic tasks were less favoured than others. These included cleaning and dusting, bed-making and washing up, whereas cooking and preparing meals and shopping (especially for clothes) were popular activities. Most striking, however, were the report's claims about the way class differences shaped the identification with and performance of the housewife role. As it noted,

> We have a very clear picture of the newly married working-class housewife's enthusiasm for housework, of her relatively greater interest compared with the middle class housewife in all household jobs bar cooking and preparing meals, of her more emphatic involvement in and more conservative reactions to the whole idea of housework, and of her 'better' training before marriage.[79]

The young housewives' approach to homemaking typically followed that of their mothers and there was a tendency to seek to replicate their parents' example of running a home. The report noted, however, that purchasing decisions concerning convenience products were shaped by two central preoccupations – whether the commodity added to the pleasures of already enjoyed tasks or whether it helped overcome some of the dislike of boring or distasteful jobs. An important ambition of the research here was to assess how well disposed housewives were to convenience products and domestic aids and whether they experienced these as a threat to their role and prestige as providers of a clean and comfortable house. Echoing Dichter's US study of thirty years earlier, the report produced a classification of housewives based on an attitude scale in order to draw out the degree of identification women had with the housewife role and, therefore, the extent to which they saw household aids as assisting them in that role or undermining their status. From this it produced a general observation that most of its new housewives felt that they had enlarged opportunities in domestic life compared to their mothers. These were opportunities fostered by the availability of frozen and convenience foods, more choice, the availability of washing machines, detergents and washing up liquids and the existence of better and more hygienic packaging.[80] The young women it interviewed, then, especially those in the early years of marriage, emerged from the report as strongly identifying with the image of the modern housewife and as seeing this role as a progressive development from the experiences of an earlier pre-affluence generation of women.

Conclusion

The 'New Housewife' report's long and detailed study of the sociology of young married women was a striking piece of research given its attention to the community and kinship relations that shaped individual consumption. If such an approach acknowledged the family relationships and social dependencies upon which the ideal of the individual consumer rested, its approach to the study of consumer behaviour was entirely consistent in other ways with a dominant principle of post-war market research. This was the concern to detail and capture *new* consumer habits. Like much contemporary sociology, post-war market researchers were riveted by aspects of social and cultural change and principally interested in established patterns of life only in as much as they inhibited this change and formed barriers to new consumption. Certainly in its studies of the mass-market housewife, JWT London and BMRB were concerned to attend to the points where commodity use met social change. Clearly the pace of post-war social change, especially in relation to the transformation in class-cultural patterns of consumption, encouraged market researchers to look to the innovations in the social use of goods.

Advertising agencies and their clients sought to understand these innovations in order to promote the consumption of their products. In the case of JWT London this was particularly true in relation to a whole range of groceries and domestic products that centred upon ordinary womanhood and contemporary ideals of femininity. Products like those discussed here – home perms, processed food and cleaning aids – offered women new kinds of convenience, comfort and cleanliness that were integral to the 'revolution' in domestic consumption associated with the new post-war household. They also generated new work for women. The market research registered this aspect of women's lives. It most often did so in neutral language and emphasized the pleasures as well as the pains of housework, cooking and the maintenance of a good appearance. The recognition within market research of some of the social and psychological dilemmas thrown up by the world of domestic goods for women was part of its more general attempt to understand the world of mass consumption. This amounted to an analysis, often quite sophisticated, which was designed to capture the banal domestic routines and habits of consumers. It led market researchers into an immersion in the lives of ordinary women and threw up at times startling juxtapositions. In the case of JWT London, this meant scenarios in which advertising men working for an urbane, West End London agency grappled with the intimate details of ordinary women's hair care, cooking and pot washing.

This endeavour involved the deployment of a range of different ways of measuring consumer markets and apprehending consumers. Psychological models of the human personality and psychologically derived techniques of research undoubtedly offered researchers some of the most imaginative and insightful ways of exploring how consumers experienced the world of goods. Researchers at BMRB and staff at JWT became more open to these approaches as the 1960s progressed. These were not the only ways these practitioners understood the consumer and consumer markets. As we have seen, sociological analysis, together with forms of economic measurement, were equally important and were deployed in order to assist in the entanglement of consumers with specific goods. In fact, by exploring the pragmatic deployment of these divergent kinds of research practice it is possible to see how market research sought to facilitate the stitching of consumers into particular kinds of consumption practices. It did so by seeking to understand the connections that existed between commodities and the habits, routines and inner motivations of consumers. This was a process that involved both technical and representational practices in an attempt to manage the commercial relations between advertisers and consumers.

The market research examined here undoubtedly sought to 'make-up' its target groups as certain kinds of consumers; indeed, as certain kinds of women. The 'mobilizing' of these consumer dispositions and attributes, however, was an act of forging connections between consumer practices and desires and specific commodities and not a constitution of these dispositions *ex nihilo*. If, as Miller and Rose suggest, consumers emerged as a highly problematic entity in post-war market research, this was at least partly because they brought to the moment of exchange and the use of goods sedimented dispositions and values, together with a deeper range of subjective attributes. Market researchers were strongly drawn to these aspects of consumers' subjectivities and it was often the emotions and feelings of the consumer that advertising agencies themselves sought to arouse and stimulate. While we might question some of the detail of the analysis, particularly the versions of psychoanalysis used by researchers, such an endeavour is one from which sociologists and historians of consumer society might learn. Certainly, the attention from sociologists to the socio-technical devices of consumption, productive though it is, does work with a deliberately 'thin' conception of the human material upon which the devices of the market work. Finding ways of researching the subjectivity of consumers – their conscious and unconscious feelings, the human relationships in which they are set – would enrich our understanding of the world of goods and the human attributes, capacities and relationships shaped in and through them.[81]

On a different tack, attending to the subjectivity of consumers reminds us that market research is only one part of a larger set of practice and devices through which consumers are linked to goods. The attempts to draw out certain responses from consumers by advertising agencies increasingly depended through the 1950s and 1960s on the technology of television and the cultural form of the TV commercial. The arts of modern living promoted by television commercials, including those aimed at the mass housewife, required the use of not just market research, but of the communicative idioms of television itself. How these idioms were invented is a question that I address in the next chapter.

Notes

1 On the 'creative revolution' in US advertising of the late 1950s and 1960s see S. Fox, *The Mirror Makers: A History of American Advertising and its Creators*, New York: Morrow, 1984. The New York agency Doyle Dane Bernbach was the most celebrated 'creative agency'. For a fascinating comparison of the ethos of its guiding spirit Bill Bernbach with that of other leading figures in US advertising, including David Ogilvy, see D. Higgins (ed.), *The Art of Writing Advertising*, Lincolnwood, IL: NTC Business Books, 1965.

2 On market research in Britain, see M. Abrams, *Social Surveys and Social Action*, London: Heinemann, 1951; 'Post-war boom in market research', *The Times*, 27 April 1960, p. 18; 'Rapid expansion of market research interviewing', *The Times*, 27 April 1962, p. 6; 'Research to make guessing easier', *The Times*, 18 October 1962, p.

x; Letter, *The Times*, 4 December 1950, p. 7; 'Market research, an image problem', *The Times*, 22 May 1968, p. 27; 'Market research', *The Times*, 16 September 1965, p. vii. The Market Research Society was formed in 1949. Membership grew to 273 members in 1956 and to 1,746 by 1966. J.A.P. Treasure estimated that in 1966 market research business was 'about four times as big as it was in 1956'; J. Treasure, 'Market research in Britain', *Commentary*, 8(3), 1966, p. 136; I. Blythe, *The Making of an Industry: The Market Research Society 1946–86*, London: Market Research Society, 2005. On the use of surveys for understanding the 'mass population' in America, see S.E. Igo, *The Average American: Surveys, Citizens and the Making of a Mass Public*, Cambridge, MA: Harvard University Press, 2007.

3 *The Times* estimated that the housewife accounted for 90% of money spent on food and household goods. 'The housewife – a sitting target', *The Times*, 18 October 1962, p. vii; 'The women's market', *Advertiser's Weekly*, 15 January 1960, pp. 24–34; 'Selling to women', *Advertiser's Weekly*, 8 January 1960, p. 40; 'Young homemakers', *Advertiser's Weekly*, 20 April 1962, p. 3; J. Walter Thompson, *Shopping in Suburbia*, London: JWT, 1962.

4 I. Zweiniger Bargeilowska, *Austerity in Britain: Rationing Controls and Consumption, 1939–1955*, Oxford: Oxford University Press, 2000, p. 103; L. Davidoff, M. Doolittle, J. Fink and K. Holden, *The Family Story: Blood, Contract and Intimacy, 1830–1960*, London: Longman, 1999, pp. 185–220.

5 Ibid.

6 P. Summerfield, 'Women in Britain since 1945, companionate marriage and the double burden', in J. Obelkovich and P. Catterall (eds), *Understanding Post-war British Society*, London: Routledge, 1994, p. 61.

7 R.M. Smith, 'Elements of demographic change in Britain', in J. Obelkovich and P. Catterall (eds), *Understanding Post-war British Society*, London: Routledge, 1994, pp. 22–8.

8 Some sense of the relative decline of domestic service is documented by Selina Todd. She notes that in 1921 domestic service was the largest employer of women under 25 in the UK, but by 1951 only 5% of these women were in service, the remainder having moved into clerical work and retailing; S. Todd, *Young Women, Work and Family in England, 1918–1950*, Oxford: Oxford University Press, 2005, p. 33.

9 J. Gershuny, cited in Zweiniger Bargeilowska, *Austerity in Britain*, p. 108.

10 On the role of women's magazines, see J. Winship, *Inside Women's Magazines*, London: Pandora, 1987. See also M. Glucksmann, *Women Assemble: Women Workers and the New Industries in Inter-war Britain*, London: Routledge, 1990. For a compelling account of the French experience, particularly in relation to the role played by women's magazines, see K. Ross, *Fast Cars, Clean Bodies: Decolonization and the Reordering of French Culture*, Cambridge, MA: MIT Press, 1995. The classic work on the North American experience is S. Strasser, *Never Done: A History of American Housework*, New York: Pantheon Books, 1982.

11 See also the work of Michel Callon and his co-authors on the material devices of consumption for a similar approach to the 'making up' of the consumer. In particular, M. Callon, C. Meadal and V. Rabeharisoa, 'The economy of qualities', *Economy*

& *Society*, 13(2), 2002, pp. 194–217; M. Callon, Y. Milo and F. Muniesa (eds), *Market Devices*, Oxford: Blackwell, 2007; M. Callon and F. Muniesa, 'Peripheral vision: economic markets as calculative collective devices', *Organization Studies*, 26(8), 2005, pp. 1229–50.
12 P. Miller and N. Rose, 'Mobilising the consumer, assembling the subject of consumption', *Theory, Culture & Society*, 14(1), 1997, p. 4.
13 Ibid.
14 A. Arvidsson, 'The therapy of consumption, motivation research and the new Italian housewife, 1958–62', *Journal of Material Culture*, 5(3), 2000, p. 254.
15 J. Walter Thompson, *40 Berkeley Square*, London: JWT, 1967, pp. 3–4.
16 'To all offices, a summary of development of the company's research in consumer behaviour', Howard Henderson, 21 February 1957, Edward G. Wilson papers, JWT/Duke, Box 6. See also 'Forecasting the demand for consumer durables', 1967; 'Market research and the retailer', 1967, Edward G. Wilson papers, JWT/Duke, Box 31.
17 'To all offices, a summary of development of the company's research in consumer behaviour', Howard Henderson, 21 February 1957, Edward G. Wilson papers, JWT/Duke, Box 6.
18 In the inter-war years JWT London had been unusual among British advertising agencies in conducting market research surveys. One of its earliest was for Sun Maid raisins and consisted of interviews with 200 customers and 60 dealers. JWT London also undertook work for Ponds and Kraft in the inter-war years and in 1936 worked on a readership survey of the *Daily Herald*. See Abrams, *Social Surveys and Social Action*.
19 Formed in 1933, BMRB was tied to JWT London by shared board membership and there was some movement of staff between the two companies. Of particular note was the role played by BMRB in supplying JWT London with two of its prominent post-war chief executives. These were Tom Sutton and John Treasure, influential CEOs who had worked for BMRB before climbing to the top management position within the parent company. This influence of BMRB men within the upper echelons of JWT London further helped to consolidate the importance of studies of consumer behaviour within the agency. See 'Early Days of BMRB', JWT London, 1964, Edward G. Wilson papers, JWT/ Duke, Box 2.
20 JWT & BMRB, December 1957, Edward G. Wilson papers, JWT/Duke, Box 2. Market research in Britain was dominated by practitioners with a background in economics and statistics. For example, many of the members of the Market Research Society had degrees in economics and allied studies from the London School of Economics. On the 'LSE factor', see Blythe, *The Making of an Industry*, p. 35.
21 The Census of Population, the Census of Distribution and the National Income Blue Book were used by market researchers to estimate the size of consumer markets. For example, the Registrar General's Census of Population was used to forecast the number of young married couples likely to be setting up home over a 10–20 year period and manufacturers of furniture, to take one instance, could be guided on how to plan their production.

22 There were two other important forms of research: media surveys of television audiences and newspaper and magazine readerships. Agencies also pre-tested ads on consumers, especially to help them select between different 'copy solutions'.
23 Blythe, *The Making of an Industry*, pp. 213–15; M. Abrams, *Education, Social Class and Newspaper Reading*, London: IPA, 1963, p. 4.
24 Mark Abrams' study of the teenager consumer, published in 1959, was the best-known example of this approach (*The Teenage Consumer*, London: London Press Exchange, 1959), though other researchers sought to survey the youth market and drew attention less to the teenager than the 'young married' or 'young homemakers'. See *Advertiser's Weekly*, 20 April 1962, p. 6; 12 February 1960, pp. 31, 32; 21 February 1958, pp. 23, 26; 23 January 1959, pp. 31, 32. Abrams' arguments focused on the way age was becoming a more reliable social category than class for explaining consumer behaviour and he supplemented the use of age segmentations of consumers with the idea of stages of the life cycle. As he put it, 'under conditions of increasing general prosperity, the social study of society in class terms is less and less illuminating. And its place is taken by differences related to age and stages in the family lifecycle'; Abrams, *Advertiser's Weekly*, 3 July 1964, p. 21.
25 D. Horowitz, *Anxieties of Affluence: Critiques of American Consumer Culture 1939–1979*, Cambridge, MA: University of Massachusetts Press, 2003, p. 57.
26 Ibid.
27 Ibid., p. 56.
28 *Advertiser's Weekly*, 8 November 1957, pp. 22, 24.
29 The office was in Victoria Street, London. See *Advertiser's Weekly*, 13 September 1957, p. 11; 'Pioneer of motive research', *The Times*, 14 April 1959, p. 7.
30 J. Pearson and G. Turner, *The Persuasion Industry*, London: Eyre & Spottiswoode, 1965, p. 175.
31 Ibid., p. 176.
32 IPA, *Motivation Research*, London: IPA, 1960, p. 5.
33 For the debate on motivation research in Britain, see 'Motivation research today', *Advertiser's Weekly*, 25 March 1960, pp. 22, 24; 'The bases for creative advertising research', *Advertiser's Weekly*, 19 August 1960, pp. 20, 22; 'The sins of motivation research', *Advertiser's Weekly*, 10 July 1964, pp. 22, 24; 'Motivation research today 3', *Advertiser's Weekly*, 9 September 1960, pp. 48–52; *The Times*, 17 April 1959, p. 15; 22 April 1959, p. 5; 'Contribution from some personality theories to market research', *Commentary*, 3, 1960, pp. 1–15. Harry Henry, head of research at the US-owned agency McCann-Erickson, developed a version of motivation research that was distinct from Dichter's techniques. See H. Henry, *Motivation Research: Its Practices and Uses for Advertising*, London: Crosby Lockwood & Son, 1958, and *Motivation Research and the TV Commercial*, London: ATV Series, 1959. For evidence of some of the studies Dichter produced for British clients, see S. Schwarzkopf, '"Culture" and the limits of innovations in marketing: Ernest Dichter, motivation studies and psychological consumer research in Britain, 1950s–70s', *Management and Organisational History*, 2(3), 2007, pp. 219–36.
34 See H. Himmelweit, A.N. Oppenheim and P. Vince, *Television and the Child*, Oxford: Oxford University Press, 1958.

35 J.S. Downham, *BMRB International: The First Sixty Years*, London: BMRB International, 1995, p. 95.
36 J. Treasure, 'American marketing in Britain', *The Grocer*, 8 July 1961, p. 41.
37 'A JWT programme for advertising research', JWT London, 1964, JWT/HAT, Box 579.
38 Ibid.
39 Memo from Noel Bews to Brillo account team, 1 February 1965, JWT/HAT, Box 113.
40 JWT Comprehensive Review, 1948–54, p. 5, JWT/HAT, Box 650; Pin-Up Research Summary, 1954, JWT/HAT, Box 650.
41 JWT Comprehensive Review, 1948–54, p. 5, JWT/HAT, Box 650.
42 TIHR had been formed in 1947 and sought to apply psychoanalytical concepts to the study of groups and organizational life.
43 TIHR, 'An appraisal of the attitudes of women towards their hair', 11 November 1950, doc. no. 262, JWT/HAT, Box 650.
44 Ibid., pp. 1–2.
45 Ibid., pp. 5–7.
46 Ibid., pp. 8–9.
47 Pin-Up, Tavistock Institute Final Report, Memorandum to Mr Silvester from Michael Stern, 26 January 1951, JWT/HAT, Box 650.
48 Ibid.
49 Ibid.
50 Tavistock Institute Report, from R. Silvester to Mr Mitchell-Innes cc Mr Stern, 26 February 1951, JWT/HAT, Box 650.
51 Ibid.
52 On the 'revolution' in domestic technologies, see S. Bowden and A. Offer, 'The technological revolution that never was: gender, class and the diffusion of household appliances in interwar England', in V. de Grazia and E. Furlough (eds), *The Sex of Things: Gender and Consumption in Historical Perspective*, Berkeley and Los Angeles: University of California Press, 1996, pp. 244–74.
53 Brillo: components of the advertising, from John O'Keefe to Daniel Curling and Sir John Rogers, 3 December 1965, JWT/HAT, Box 443.
54 Ibid.
55 Ibid.
56 Copy Strategy, 1965, JWT/HAT, Box 113.
57 Ibid.
58 Oxo cubes, 1962/3 Summary, JWT/HAT, Box 323.
59 Ibid.
60 Oxo overall plan, 4 July 1963, JWT/HAT, Box 323.
61 Oxo cubes – promotions Recommendations, February 1964, JWT/HAT, Box 323.
62 Oxo overall plan, 4 July 1963, JWT/HAT, Box 323.
63 Oxo cubes – promotions Recommendations, February 1964, JWT/HAT, Box 323.
64 Oxo overall plan, 4 July 1963, JWT/HAT, Box 323.
65 Ibid.
66 Ibid.

67 Oxo Ltd development work on gravy products, suggested programme, 1967, JWT/HAT, Box 323.
68 Letter from L.W. Hore, General Brand Manager, Oxo Ltd to Andrew Wilson, 22 April 1966, JWT/HAT, Box 323.
69 Letter from J.R. Stonehewer (Attwoods Statistics) to L.W. Hore, 18 April 1966, JWT/HAT, Box 323.
70 Ibid.
71 Oxo Ltd development work on gravy products, marketing plan, 1967/8, JWT/HAT, Box 323. On 'progressive cooks' see *The Times*, 18 October 1962, p. vii.
72 BMRB, *The New Housewife*, London: BMRB, 1967, p. 1.
73 Ibid., p. 2.
74 Ibid., p. 7.
75 Ibid., p. 22
76 Ibid., p. 22.
77 Ibid., pp. 33–4.
78 Ibid., p. 49.
79 Ibid., p. 58.
80 Ibid., p. 78.
81 For a discussion of what the study of 'subjectivity' might entail, see L. Roper, *Oedipus and the Devil: Witchcraft, Sexuality and Religion in Early Modern Europe*, London: Routledge, 1994, and M. Roper, 'Slipping out of view: subjectivity and emotion in gender history', *History Workshop Journal*, 59(1), 2005, pp. 57–72.

4

'A challenge both alarming and alluring': the birth of television advertising

On the opening night of independent television in the north of England in May 1956, Granada Television broadcast a 60-second commercial for Persil washing powder produced by JWT London. It featured Ruth Dunning, the actress well known for playing Mrs Grove in the BBC's family serial, *The Grove Family*, as an on-screen presenter.[1] Filmed in medium long shot, Dunning was shown standing by a table in a drawing room. In the homely yet authoritative style of a Crown Film Unit documentary she welcomed the arrival of ITV and offered the broadcaster the advertiser's salutations. Dunning then introduced the children from Persil's press advertising. As she acknowledged to the audience watching, they were probably familiar with these characters 'but here they are on television for the first time'. The commercial then cut from her live-action presentation to an animation of the Persil children. The animation was whimsical and simple in its narrative, with two girls shown sitting on a bench. One of them becomes caught up in a large soap bubble which they were playing with. Spinning around inside it, her dress is transformed. Gently dropping out of the bubble as it dissipates, she emerges in a strikingly white-looking dress. In contrast, her companion's dress remains a dull white. A male voice-over, provided by actor Michael Sanders, drew the commercial to a close with the phrase, 'Persil washes whiter – which means cleaner' as a shot of the Persil pack was held on the screen.

The gentle tone of the commercial and its restrained selling message were consistent with many others that were shown during ITV's first years of operation. It was a tone that had been set on the first night of commercial television in the London area in September 1955. As *The Times* noted in its review of that evening's fare on Associated-Rediffusion, the advertising agencies, like the programme contractor, had 'passed its first evening's test with a good measure of professional accomplishment'. The advertisements, in particular, had resisted the temptation to indulge more vulgar commercial impulses. Of them *The Times* suggested, 'offensive would be too strong a word by far for these comic little interruptions of entertainment', though the editorial did warn that before long 'a thick skin of resistance to them was likely to be needed'.[2] The *Daily Telegraph* made a similar observation, suggesting that the 'advertisements were throughout fairly unobtrusive and in reasonable taste. They did not break awkwardly into the programmes.' American newspaper correspondents in London, there to witness the opening of the new service, also praised the 'restraint' and 'brevity' of the advertising. Only the *Daily Express*, a vocal opponent of ITV, was hostile. It suggested the 'advertisements were irksome when the novelty had gone'.[3]

These observations on the 'restraint' and tasteful nature of the commercials made by most newspaper critics, and the gentle tone of the Persil advert with which I began, beg some larger questions. How are we to explain the qualities and style of the first commercials seen on British television? What factors bore upon the way that advertising agencies shaped them? What do these early commercials tell us about the attitude of agencies and the advertising industry in general towards the new medium? And what role did comparisons with US advertising play in these developments? The latter is important since the reference to the 'restrained' qualities of the adverts implicitly invited a contrast with the supposedly brasher styles of US television advertising which had been established prior to the launch of ITV.

In addressing these questions, this chapter seeks, firstly, to revise a prevalent assumption made by contemporary commentators that advertising agencies were enthusiastic advocates of the new medium.[4] Writers like the journalist Clive Jenkins, for example, reviewing the campaign for the second channel, answered his own question – 'Who wanted commercial TV?' – with the emphatic answer, 'It was the advertising agencies'.[5] Similarly, Christopher Mayhew, Labour MP for Woolwich East and vocal opponent of ITV, claimed that the instigators of the new service were a 'tiny number of active and influential advertisers, advertising agents and radio manufacturing firms'.[6] Mayhew singled out J. Walter Thompson as the most assertive proponent of commercial TV and the most aggressive agitator for the commercialization of British broadcasting. Even H.H. Wilson, in his more measured assessment of the campaign for commercial TV, saw advertising agencies, especially those with American owners, as an important part of the 'soufflé of interests' that had cohered around the parliamentary campaign to break the BBC's monopoly.[7] As Wilson himself acknowledged, however, there were important divisions between advertising agencies over the introduction of ITV. As a poll in the trade paper, *Advertiser's Weekly*, from September 1953 revealed, 44% of advertising agencies were opposed to commercial television and only 46% thought it would benefit advertising as a whole.[8] Other agencies, like the leading British agency Colman Prentis Varley, predicted that it would remain a largely peripheral form of advertising for the foreseeable future, while the London Press Exchange similarly decided to take a 'wait and see' approach.[9] And on the eve of the passage of the Television Act in 1954, an industry insider claimed that a majority of the members of the IPA were opposed to the introduction of commercial TV by a ratio of 4:1.[10] Rather than being a driving force behind the introduction of commercial TV, then, a significant proportion of advertising agencies were reluctant converts and walked backwards into the new world of TV advertising. If advertising agencies did, over time, come to terms with television and accommodate it into their practices, this was not because the majority of them were great advocates of it from the outset.

In understanding how advertising agencies responded to the challenges and opportunities of television, this chapter argues – and this is my second contention – that in the early-to-mid-1950s agencies looked towards the more 'advanced' world of US advertising, television and film making in order to adapt to the new medium. As in other areas of agency practice, American advertising was an important resource for agencies in Britain in relation to the medium of television. They looked towards the US for staff who could understand television and for representational techniques and practices they could draw on in developing commercials in Britain. At the same time, American television advertising also represented a system of advertising and 'sponsored' television which practitioners sought to define British television advertising against.[11] If American influences helped smooth the transition to the new system of television advertising, then what emerged was not simply a copy of US advertising. US techniques were adapted, revised and combined with more local cultural resources, both in terms of personnel and representational practices, that helped to shape a distinctive tradition of British television advertising, one that was differentiated from the dominant approaches of US advertising while drawing upon its example.

Advertising agencies, ITV and TV advertising

The introduction of commercial television under the 1954 Television Act was one of the most important pieces of cultural policy of the post-war years. The public debate about its introduction was preoccupied, for good reason, with the possible effects of advertising on the new service.[12] Certainly in the extensive parliamentary and extra-parliamentary lobbying which preceded and accompanied the passage of the Television Act through Parliament, the nature of the form of commercial subsidy that would underpin the new service generated sustained debate. In the course of these discussions the advertising industry was subject to intense scrutiny. For industry insiders much of this debate was ill-informed. As the *Journal of the Advertising Association*, the IPA's sister organization, complained, the Commons debates were marred by the 'mass of intellectual snobbery and prejudice' towards advertising.[13] Much of the focus of this 'snobbery' and 'prejudice' hinged on fears that an American-style system of sponsored television and radio was to be introduced into Britain. Such concerns touched deep chords within the political classes and educated opinion. Since the 1930s there had been fears among these groups that British culture and society was under threat from the growing commercial and cultural power of the United States. As I noted earlier, this potent anxiety was revivified in the immediate post-war decades. In the debate about the introduction of commercial television, US-sponsored television and US advertising were a constant point of reference. Critics like the Conservative MP Beverley Baxter, a close friend of the press magnate Lord Beaverbrook, feared that 'sponsored broadcasting' meant 'exposure to the terrorization of the mass suggestion of advertising'.[14] Even supporters of commercial television, in their desire to distance themselves from concerns about the US model, rehearsed ideas critical of American advertising. For example, Selwyn Lloyd, the Tory backbencher who was a key protagonist in the moves to break the BBC's broadcasting monopoly, suggested, following a visit to the USA in 1950, that 'much of the advertisement matter is boring, repetitive and rather offensive to British ears'.[15] Like the AA, the IPA was agitated that the debate about commercial television was simply serving to offer an opportunity for critics of advertising to attack the industry and that fears of 'Americanization' were having a detrimental effect upon the industry's reputation. As the leader article in the Institute's members' newsletter noted in August 1953, the lobbying around commercial television had enabled critics to assert that the power given to advertisers under a new broadcasting system was likely to 'lower standards and debase morals'.[16] In a speech at the Mansion House a month later, Hubert Oughton, the IPA's president, complained that there was an assumption among 'opponents of sponsored television that advertising will automatically degrade the decencies of family life'.[17] The IPA sought to deflect these charges by proposing that were a commercial broadcasting service to be introduced it should not follow the US model of programme sponsorship, but be developed along 'common-sense British lines'.[18] The IPA fleshed out this idea in a statement issued with the Incorporated Society of British Advertisers (ISBA), the organization representing British advertisers. Their joint publication, *Television, the Viewer and the Advertiser*, set out the case for what it called 'competitive television'.[19] Taking care to differentiate this from the US system of sponsored television, the IPA and ISBA proposed a form of commercial subsidy of television in which the programme stations would have sole responsibility for 'producing programmes and creating the audience'.[20] Advertisers would be allowed to insert their advertisements in the programmes in ways negotiated between the programme companies and advertisers. This model of television advertising was explicitly designed to mimic the form of press advertising. As the pamphlet spelt out, 'not only would programme content be free from the direct influence of advertisers', but also 'the purchasing of time on a competitive television station will be broadly analogous to the purchase of space in a newspaper'.[21]

The promotion by the IPA and ISBA of this model of commercial television revealed much about the concerns of their respective members about the likely costs of producing 'sponsored' programmes, particularly in the face of an established and powerful broadcaster like the BBC. Both agencies and advertisers feared that only a few advertisers would be able to afford to sponsor programmes of more than 15 minutes duration on a continuing basis.[22] Agencies were also resistant to the idea of 'becoming impresarios' who would be responsible for producing the television programmes, as happened in the US system of sponsored television.[23] As I have already noted, agency opinion was also notably divided on the issue of commercial television. Many of the IPA's member agencies feared that its introduction would favour the biggest agencies, particularly those, as one anonymous agency chief put it, 'that had an American parent company'.[24] The IPA took an increasingly low-key position in the debate on the introduction of commercial television. This stemmed not only from the divisions among its own members, but also because it feared that if it contributed to a high-profile campaign this would further deepen the criticisms of the advertising industry being generated by parliamentary debate on 'sponsored television'. The organization was, thus, conspicuously absent from the key lobbying group formed to press for a second commercial channel, the Popular Television Association.[25]

Despite its low-key approach, the IPA did continue to quietly press the case for a 'publishing style' form of subsidy for any new commercial television channel. It met with some success in this regard. When the Postmaster General eventually expressed the government's view in the White Paper on the second channel, it closely corresponded to the model proposed by the IPA and ISBA.[26] Other forces, however, were also at work shaping this framework for the new ITV service and it would be wrong to overplay the IPA's influence. Certainly, prominent individuals in the campaign for commercial television, like the Conservative MP Charles Orr-Ewing, had argued as early as 1951 that 'a compromise between public service monopoly at the one extreme and the free competitive system of the USA at the other extreme' represented the best model for commercial broadcasting in Britain.[27] The political compromises that shaped the Television Act (1954) placed great emphasis on the requirement to prevent the direct influence of advertisers over programme content and to ensure that the form of commercial subsidy of ITV did not undermine its public-service obligations.[28] These concerns, legally enshrined in the Act, directly led to the banning of 'sponsored broadcasting' and the creation of the 'spot advert' as the principal form of commercial subsidy for the new ITA network. Under the terms of the Television Act, spot adverts were required to be clearly separated from the surrounding programmes. In addition they were only to be placed between programmes or within 'natural breaks' in programmes.[29] In the early years of the service, these spots were sold to advertisers in one-minute, 30-second and 15-second slots, with the pricing structure designed to make shorter spots relatively more expensive. As demand for television air time grew, the 30-second spot became the favoured norm. The number of minutes of advertising that it was permissible to broadcast in any hour was set at an average of six minutes by the Television Act so as not to interrupt programmes and mar the viewing experience, problems that were seen to be a feature of the US system of sponsored television. With the main weekday broadcast hours restricted to three blocks of transmission – 10.30a.m.–12.30p.m., 5p.m.–6p.m. and 7.15p.m.–10.30p.m. – television advertising took up no more than 10% of the broadcasting day.[30] This arrangement remained relatively stable, save for the eradication of the 'toddlers' truce' in February 1957 that allowed broadcasting between 6p.m. and 7p.m., until the reorganization of ITV in 1968 and the switchover to colour in 1969.[31]

Despite its reluctance to openly campaign for commercial television, the IPA did seek to protect the interests of its member agencies in the development of the second channel. From early in 1955 it established negotiations with the ITV companies and their representative organization, the Television Programme Companies Association (later renamed the Independent Television Contractors Association [ITCA]) over the way in which advertising agencies would be remunerated for the buying of television air time. These negotiations centred upon the creation of a system of recognition agreements which would allow those agents or advertisers buying time on ITV to receive a commission on that purchase.[32] This sought to mirror the commission system already established for press, poster and cinema advertising. Developing a similar national system of recognition for television was important for the IPA in order to protect service advertising agencies from competition from other kinds of providers of TV advertising. Rumours that companies such as the Co-operative Wholesale Society and the Rank organization had been offered recognition by ITV companies particularly troubled the IPA.[33] The IPA was also concerned about the prospect of what it described as 'specialist television agencies' emerging and winning recognition from the commercial TV companies.[34] Despite these problems through the late 1950s, the IPA did have some success in securing the privileged position of its member agencies in its negotiations and by the early 1960s a recognition agreement was in place between the IPA and the ITCA.[35] Significantly, the recognition agreement issued by the ITCA, building on the precedent established by the early ITV companies, gave a commission rate of 15% on gross advertising expenditure. This was higher than the rate given by national newspapers and periodicals, making TV a more lucrative medium for advertising agencies. In response to this, as the ITV network grew and television became a viable medium for national advertising, at least one of the national newspaper publishers increased its commission rate in 1963.[36] The success of the IPA's negotiations with the ITCA helped its member agencies to effectively monopolize the originating and placing of TV advertising, with recognized agencies conducting 94% of the business of TV advertising by the early 1960s. This was even higher than the 81% they conducted for national newspapers.[37]

Advertising agencies prepare

While the IPA was involved in technical negotiations with the ITV companies over the form of remuneration for its members, individual advertising agencies actively began to prepare for the coming of television advertising. One response from these agencies was to look towards the more 'advanced' world of US advertising, television and film making for staff who could understand

12 Duncan Ross, Dorland advert, 1954

the new medium. As early as January 1953 the US agency Young & Rubicam had transferred a senior official, A.O. Buckingham, from its New York to its London office in preparation for the arrival of commercial television.[38] In

October 1954 Lambe & Robinson, a medium-sized British agency, trumpeted its hiring of Henry Hull – director of TV and radio at the NY agency Calkins & Holden – to manage its new TV department.[39] The London office of the US agency McCann-Erickson was another which moved to prepare in advance for the coming of ITV. In 1955 it hired two experienced film men – Barry Baron from Warner Brothers and John Reed, an animations director from Walt Disney – to contribute to its newly created Television Operations Board.[40] This sense of advertising agencies in Britain looking towards America for personnel who might understand the new medium was reinforced by the advertising trade press, which was peppered during the run-up to ITV's launch and in the first years of ITV with tutorials from US ad men on how to master the new medium. This included a long extract from American advertising man Harry Wayne McMahan's 1955 book *The Television Commercial* on the pitfalls of the new medium and how to use it to sell effectively.[41] McMahan's ideas were clearly well regarded. Seven years after the launch of ITV, in May 1962, he visited the London offices of JWT to advise its creative department on the best US TV advertising and continued to visit for the next three years. As Jeremy Bullmore, head of JWT's creative department reminded the company's directors, 'McMahan was perhaps the world's leading expert on the TV commercial'.[42]

US ad men were not the only influence, however, upon the new TV departments of advertising agencies in London. They were often joined by recruits from another, more local source – the BBC. Though they may have lacked direct advertising experience, BBC staff did have knowledge of working in TV or radio and a familiarity with the technologies and techniques of broadcast media. This seems to have been the reason behind their recruitment by agencies. Thus, alongside its American recruits, McCann-Erickson's TV Operations Board included the BBC radio script editor Larry Grayton and BBC TV's musical director Eric Robinson.[43] The agency Charles F. Higham made a similar move and hired former BBC writer and TV documentary producer Robert Barr for its new TV advertising company, while Dorlands hired Duncan Ross, a BBC TV producer (Fig. 12).[44] Peter Marsh, who started the agency Allen Brady and Marsh in 1965, worked as a writer and producer in the BBC documentary film unit before being hired to establish the television department of the agency Osborne & Peacock in 1957.[45] Some of these appointments were rather opportunistic and short lived. Eric Robinson soon returned to the BBC and his entry in *Who's Who* makes no reference to his sojourn in advertising. Duncan Ross's tenure was equally brief, though

Dorlands did try and replace him with Peter Dimmock, an influential figure in the BBC's coverage of sport.[46] What these appointments revealed, however, was the need for advertising agencies to look, in the first instance, outside the world of British advertising for personnel to smooth the transition to TV advertising.

The London office of JWT, identified, as we have seen, by some contemporary commentators as a powerful lobbyist in favour of the introduction of commercial television, was relatively unprepared for commercial TV. In 1954 it produced a number of what it called 'filmlets' and made two 15-second cinema films for Persil with the French cartoonist, André Sarrut, in preparation for commercial TV.[47] This experimentation was guided by staff sent from New York whose job it was to induct their London colleagues into the techniques of TV advertising. Throughout the 1950s staff were also sent from London to spend time in New York to learn from US TV advertising techniques. The parent company was certainly very experienced in television. It was an established producer of advertising and sponsored programmes on US television and had invested heavily in staff and technical resources. The latter included the creation of a television workshop complete with a fully equipped studio, television camera, 16mm sound motion-picture camera and closed-circuit television viewing facilities (Fig. 13). The television workshop was designed to allow clients to test out new ideas for advertising 'under actual telecast conditions' before they spent large sums of money on a campaign.[48]

Jeremy Bullmore, recruited as a trainee copywriter at JWT London in 1954, remembered the adverts they were shown by US colleagues and their own early attempts to get to grips with television. As he recalled,

> One of the first scripts I was shown was for Wisdom. It starred several talking toothbrushes and ran for three minutes. I thought it a miracle of economy. We knew that making films for TV was different from making films for the cinema, so we back-projected our experiments onto a small, waist-high screen with a plywood frame around it.[49]

Clearly JWT London's typically British amateurism was at some remove from the professionalism of its parent company at this stage! Bullmore's recruitment was itself revealing about the lack of television experience within the agency. He had appeared in a BBC television broadcast of Oxford University's Variety Show and JWT's head of art, George Butler, having seen the programme, invited Bullmore for an interview. This was on the assumption that, since he had been on television, he must know something about it.[50]

The problem for JWT London, as for other large established agencies, was knowing how to integrate the new function into their existing organizational

'A challenge both alarming and alluring': the birth of television advertising

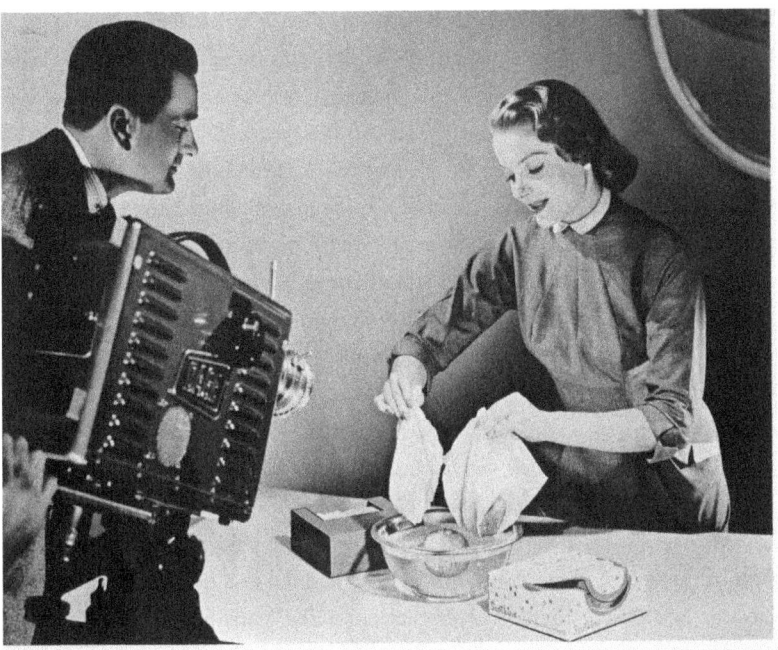

The Workshop found the Scotkin apple dunking test was convincing, easy to see, and familiar enough to appeal to any housewife

After 25 experiments—the *perfect* demonstration . . .

- Scotkins—the new paper napkins developed by the Scott Paper Company—are strong even when wet. How could this "wet strength" be demonstrated most dramatically on television?

  Twenty-five experiments were made on a "live" camera in the Television Workshop —all viewed *under actual telecast condi-*

tions on sets in the office. Finally, the famous "apple dunking" test was selected. Dramatic—but not a stunt—it was the perfect way to demonstrate "wet strength."

Finding the most dramatic way to demonstrate the qualities of your product — *before* investing in costly production time—is another way the Workshop serves you.

JWT television workshop, 1956

structures. Some agencies, like Charles F. Higham and the London Press Exchange, created separate companies in which TV was placed.[51] Others, like McCann-Erickson, established discrete departments within the agency. This was the approach taken by JWT London. It created a new television department headed by one its senior representatives, Michael Patmore. It was Patmore who hired the well-known radio correspondent Stanley Maxted to run the department, along with James Archibald from the film company

Rank.⁵² The head of art, George Butler, however, felt that television ought to belong to his department and it was Butler who hired Keith Ewart, a stills photographer, to be a television director and to oversee an experimental television unit in the art department.⁵³ This tension between the art and television departments was exacerbated by the fact that the majority of Butler's staff in the art department were not interested in the new medium. The editorial and plan department (the copy department) was also staffed by individuals generally unenthusiastic about television and committed to the disciplines of the press and posters.⁵⁴ Their views echoed wider divisions within the advertising industry between those practitioners formed by an earlier advertising culture centred upon the press and posters and the new world of TV. Even as TV grew in importance, there remained powerful voices within the advertising industry who championed the virtues of the older advertising order. Ashley Havinden, a member of the board of directors of Crawfords, bemoaned the influence of TV on advertising in 1964. Havinden, who had made his reputation in the 1930s, suggested that television had led to a declining role for 'the creative advertising man'. The emphasis on the 'convincing realism' of TV advertising had 'sadly warped' the 'creative arts of the layout man and the poster designer'. 'In too much British advertising', he opined, 'there is now a sameness of expression.'⁵⁵ Havinden's views were echoed by the Design and Art Directors Association (D&AD). Established in 1962 to promote good design and publicity in advertising and to improve graphic design standards, D&AD's project was clearly stimulated by a concern to protect the arts of design and art direction in the face of TV's growing dominance. The first annuals of work that D&AD produced made clear its antipathy to TV. While the first D&AD annual, from 1964, included sections on editorial design, consumer magazines, poster design, package design, book jackets and paperback covers, point of sale, trademarks and stationery and applied graphic design, TV only figured in a category with cinema. More than that, the entry for 'Advertising and Graphic Design in TV and Cinema: Section 1 TV commercials' appeared on page 104 of the 111-page annual. A similar pattern occurred in the D&AD annuals for the remainder of the 1960s, though TV's presence did increase markedly in the final annual of the 1960s, the annual for 1969 giving 13 pages to TV.⁵⁶

The organizational tensions within JWT London over the location of television advertising persisted until the agency reorganized its art, copy and television departments in 1961 by creating a single creative department. Within this new department the demands of TV advertising also prompted the agency to reorganize how its key creative staff, copywriters and art directors or visualizers worked. They did this in a way which broke with the system that had evolved in the first half of the twentieth century when press and poster advertising dominated. Reflecting on these changes in 1965, Jeremy Bullmore, who became head of the creative department in 1963, explained why the reorganization had been necessary and the implications this had for creative staff:

> Television made us re-assess ... the relationship between copy and art ... When print is your main medium, you can operate a system in which you have a copywriter and an art director sitting in different rooms. When we tried to apply the same situation to television, we discovered that there was a great gap between the writer and producer, or the art director, and that very bad commercials were being written simply because there was no liaison between the component parts. Three years ago we made it a self-contained, integrated group.[57]

The agency was also forced to establish new functions within its creative services department. While this continued to include art buyers, packaging and display staff and proofreaders, by the early 1960s it also included five TV producers who liaised with outside production companies, TV casting staff, people dealing with TV contracts and TV facilities. The agencies media department was also transformed by the arrival of TV. In 1962 it included 14 staff buying air time from the ITV companies, alongside three buying space in newspapers, one film buyer and three outdoor media people.[58] In short, dealing with TV came to occupy more and more staff within the agency and to outstrip the servicing of all other media creative services.

If organizational changes were an important part of how advertising agencies like JWT London adapted to the arrival of TV, then piecing together the form of the commercials themselves was also a complex process. Even more so than the reworking of organizational structures, this process revealed the influence of American advertising practices. It is to the representational practices that I want to turn in the next section.

Developing the genres of TV advertising

Advertising agencies drew upon a number of guiding principles in the first years of TV advertising in developing the form of the spot advert. One of the most important concerned the emphasis that agencies placed on liveness and immediacy. This concern reflected a deeper preoccupation with liveness within television production that had been first established in the 1930s.[59] A commitment to recording live on to film was also encouraged by the costs of videotape and by the fact that the trade unions representing members in the commercials production and film-processing industries resisted its introduction even as the cost of videotape fell in price.[60] The investment in liveness in TV adverts was often allied to the demonstration of products in use, a technique that formed one dominant early approach to the selling of goods through television. For many of the early experts on TV advertising it was television's ability to demonstrate product use and to depict this with a degree of verisimilitude that was its strongest card as a medium. As Harry Wayne McMahan suggested, 'live action is the most believable technique because it is human, personal experience itself. Seeing is believing.'[61] Demonstration-style ads could deploy a number of techniques, including before and after simulations of what the use of the product could achieve. Typically a male narrator or voice-over (MVO in the trade jargon) would identify a problem (like 'mouth odour' or 'perspiration') and then show how the product offered a solution, one that was either unique to the product or achieved through unique ingredients ('hexachlorophene' for the antiseptic mouthwash in Signal toothpaste, or the real jewellers' polish contained in Brillo soap pads, for example).[62] The demonstration of the product in use could also introduce viewers to possible applications of the product. Thus, Kraft's Cheese Whiz was sold in a live-action spot in which a young housewife illustrated, in didactic fashion, different uses of the product.[63] Other demonstration spots involved a stronger 'reason why' style of advertising. Thus, New Blue Vim, the cleaning powder, was sold in terms of the '5 ways to better cleaning' that it could offer: 'smooth and kind', 'spring-like perfume', 'kills germs' and so on. Live-action demonstrations could also use a repeated slogan that summed up the value of the product ('Cookeen – Real Fat' or, more musically, 'It's Nice to Know, You're Nice to Know' for Roxena soap).

Another important technique that was deployed in the early period of TV advertising involved on-screen presenters bringing news about the product or specific promotions to viewers. These could take the form of a newsflash, with a male authority figure sitting behind a desk, newsreader style, or moving through a scene telling viewers the good news. OMO, the washing powder, made regular use of the disc jockey Alan Freeman, whose relaxed, informal style carried the good news to viewers about the product and the injunction to buy or participate in a promotion. Sometimes a documentary format was used as the setting for the presenter's didactic message. These documentary adverts typically introduced viewers to the complex and highly modern techniques used to produce the product, with the emphasis on science and modernity. In an advert for Persil washing powder, Jane Beaton, editor of *Women's Own*, toured the factory in order to assure consumers about the quality and advanced characteristics of the product. It was the gleaming factory and its technological modernity that the consumer was encouraged to see as adding value to the product.

The use of on-screen, typically male, presenters was one of the ways in which the authority of the advertising claim was established. Some of these men were scientists or technicians and this format registered the widespread faith in professional experts in the post-war period.[64] The presentation was direct to camera and individualizing in its mode of address.[65] Sometimes this style of authoritative address was combined, as in the case of the OMO ads, with another important source of authority: the 'ordinary housewife'. Here the technique involved the use of testimonials delivered via the presenter to the viewer. It was the apparently spontaneous and authentic response of these women to the virtues of the product that gave the product claims authority.

If testimonials formed one important sub-genre of live-action commercials, then animated commercials formed the other major approach to TV advertising and were used heavily in the early years of ITV, either mixed with live action or as the exclusive form of the advert. Animations made particularly frequent use of jingles in which the story of the advert was carried through song, with the slogan often repeated throughout the advert. The imperative here was the repetition of a simple selling point. A Gallup survey of the first year of commercials on ITV revealed the popularity among viewers of animations and jingles, with the London Press Exchange's advert for Murray Mints emerging as the most popular TV advert. Viewers were apparently enchanted by the amusing animation and its catchy jingle ('Murray Mints, Murray Mints, too Good to Hurry Mints'). *Advertiser's Weekly* captured the popular mood in its praise for the advert. As it suggested, 'the simple, music hall standard [attracts] both ends of the viewing scale. Where Murraymints have the edge on their competitors is in the jingle itself which is now firmly established in the minds of children and adults alike.'[66]

Many of the techniques that were associated with both live action and animated commercials were derived from American advertising and, in this regard, the US industry again constituted a powerful resource for British advertising people. These techniques and styles of advertising were partly carried across the Atlantic by the American practitioners who were hired by agencies in Britain in the early years of ITV. As we have seen, some of these practitioners also disseminated their ideas through the advertising trade press. Their tutorials made evident the American lineage of many of these techniques.

These included testimonial advertising, which had its roots in US press and radio advertising, together with the genres of the documentary commercial, live-action product demonstrations and animations with jingles, all of which were techniques first developed in US TV advertising in the early-to-mid-1950s. Young & Rubicam, for example, produced a celebrated animated commercial for Jell-O, the processed food manufacturer, in 1953 which was subsequently elevated to the industry's 'Clio Hall of Fame'. The commercial used animation to show how Jell-O's instant pudding could help the harassed housewife provide her family with a dessert that needed no cooking.[67] The agency also won industry recognition for its 1954 documentary commercial for Remington's de luxe electric shaver. This used a live-action documentary to demonstrate both the power and the sensitivity of Remington's shaver. In the commercial, the razor is shown to be powerful enough to shave a hair brush, but gentle enough to shave a peach.[68]

'Slice of life' dramas was another genre used in British TV advertising which had its roots in US commercial culture. Derived from serialized fiction in the women's pages of US newspapers in the 1920s, domestic serial dramas were developed and popularized further on US commercial radio. Typically sponsored by the big detergent and washing powder companies, these 'soap operas' were a vehicle for the promotion of their products. One of the longest-running domestic serials, *The Guiding Light*, transferred from US commercial radio to TV in 1952.[69] Not all the techniques developed in US advertising in the early-to-mid-1950s, however, crossed the Atlantic so strongly. Musical extravaganzas, a dominant form used for commercial presentation in the US which drew upon the Broadway musical, were not widely used in Britain. Part of the reason for this stemmed from the different system of commercial subsidy favoured in the two television services. The musical extravaganza was typically used during the commercial segments of the sponsored television programmes which American advertisers paid for and which their advertising agencies produced. This included shows like *Lucky Strike Theater*, the one-hour drama sponsored by the cigarette makers American Tobacco. The sponsored drama included six minutes of air time devoted to promoting the sponsor's brand – and drew heavily upon the Broadway production number.[70]

The closest that TV advertising in Britain came to direct programme sponsorship was in the 'advertising magazines' or 'advertising documentaries' that were a feature of the early years of ITV. Significantly, however, these magazine shows were made not by advertising agencies but by the ITV contractors. They used on-screen presenters to introduce products or services, often from local retailers or businesses. Early examples included *Cooking with the Craddocks*, *Girl with a Date* and *Home with Joy Shelton*.[71] The most celebrated, however, was *Jim's Inn*, first broadcast in 1957 and running for nearly 300 episodes. It was set in the fictitious village of Wemblenham and centred upon Jim and Maggie Hanley, the publicans of the eponymous pub. As familiar in its time as *Coronation Street*'s Rover's Return, *Jim's Inn* wove product presentations into its fictional narrative.[72] The format was popular with small regional advertisers as it cost far less to promote goods on 'ad mags' than it did to buy air time in the form of a spot advert. Under the terms of the Television Act, 'ad mags' did not count as advertising and so were excluded from the amount of advertising per hour that the ITV companies were legally entitled to broadcast. They were eventually banned in 1963 following the recommendations of the Pilkington Report, largely because they were seen to blur the line between consumer advice and product promotion in ways that were felt to be misleading to the public. The cultural critic Richard Hoggart was instrumental in this banning and his comments to other members of the Pilkington Committee revealed the strength of his feelings. As he argued,

> the total suggestiveness of these warm little productions [are] designed to capitalise on viewer's loyalty. Worse, they still often retain a meretricious trace of the idea that they should be shopper's guides. These friendly comperes or meres do their best to suggest that they've thought deeply about possible purchases … and have settled on this particular one. The whole tone of the script and acting suggest someone wise and nice helping you to make a choice … As someone concerned with education, [this is] a very dubious operation; a muddy operation beside which the straight commercials are comparatively clean.[73]

American sponsored television was untroubled by these anxieties and the familiar section of sponsored shows where the performer wove in a message from the sponsor became part of the art of US television advertising.[74] Although this kind of explicit promotion was outlawed on British commercial television, US advertising did, as we have seen, exert a strong influence on British television advertising in the late 1950s. Tellingly, however, American commentators looking at the fledgling system of commercial TV in Britain were less drawn to the 'family resemblances' and more towards the differences between the two advertising systems. Echoing the views of the IPA and *The Times*, which had both praised the 'restraint' of the first commercials aired in Britain, *Time* magazine suggested that British television advertising sounded about as American as 'tea and crumpets'. Harry Wayne McMahan, the leading expert on US TV advertising, was more circumspect but noted the differences between US and UK advertising. As he put it, 'in all the (British) commercials I've seen there is a wonderful simplicity, no gimmicks, and an earnest desire to give information'.[75]

Part of the reason for these perceived differences between the two worlds of advertising was that America was not the only source of ideas and techniques of communication.[76] In the late 1950s and 1960s British TV advertising often drew upon characters and styles from the wider television culture in Britain, especially from situation comedies. Thus, in the late 1960s Findus frozen foods were sold using the character of Alf Garnett, well known from the BBC situation comedy *'Til Death Us Do Part*. The advert followed the format of a sitcom scene. Similarly, Tony Hancock appeared in a series of ads for the Egg Marketing Board. These used his on-screen persona and the style of *Hancock's Half-hour*. In them the comic talked conversationally and directly to the viewer. One of the adverts even playfully acknowledged the paid-for nature of Hancock's testimonial by showing him struggling to remember the slogan. It transpired at one point as he turned around that this was stitched to his back. These sitcom-style ads revealed the way in which the form of the advertising testimonial could be reworked and laced with the important element of humour to lighten the selling process. Humour, not only that of professional comedians but also of ordinary people and everyday situations, became a stock-in-trade of British television advertising.

There were other influences at work too. JWT London's first commercials drew strongly on the tone and mode of address of sponsored documentary film.[77] As I noted in the introduction to this chapter, the agency's early TV commercials for Persil used the documentary format with Ruth Dunning as an on-screen presenter. JWT also ran animated commercials for Persil in the opening weeks of ITV. Like the animated section of the first Ruth Dunning advert, these drew upon the traditions of press and poster advertising and were animations of press adverts.[78] The legacy of poster advertising was also evident in other early television work for Persil. For example, in October 1955 the agency ran a live-action advert featuring the quiz master Robert MacDonald. Directly to camera, MacDonald asked the viewers to take part in the 'Advertising Game' in which they had to guess the name of the brand being advertised on a poster that was being pasted up, square by square, on the screen. When complete, the poster depicted Persil's outdoor advertising campaign.

JWT London's parent company was not always impressed by these early, derivative commercials. Confirming the view of agency insiders that JWT

London struggled in the first five years of ITV to adapt to the new medium, the New York office kept a close eye on London's TV advertising. Ken Shaw, a senior figure in New York, visited JWT London's television department in both 1957 and 1959 to review its progress.[79] In 1959 he made a point of praising the 'enormous progress' that had been made in the quality of the agency's commercials since 1955: 'The lighting is [now] especially good. Hard sell, as we know it in the US, is lacking, but bearing in mind the differences in the respective audiences, this makes sense.'[80] Shaw also praised the good casting undertaken by JWT for their adverts, though he offered a critical note about the performers in the adverts:

> My only criticism of British talent would be the conviction-less voices – women being worse than men – which in general lack production and direction. [Since] the majority of British commercials tend to be of the documentary variety, with the announcer voice-over, and never appearing on camera, the vocal shortcoming of the non-commercial sounding English voice is additionally apparent.[81]

Shaw's views were revealing of the enduring cultural differences between US and British advertising, even within the same US-owned company. This was despite the influence of American advertising on British practitioners. His praise for the improved qualities of JWT London's adverts did reflect, as we will see in the next chapter, their growing confidence in the medium.

Conclusion

If advertising agencies in Britain had begun to get to grips with the new medium of television by the late 1950s, this chapter has argued that this process was dependent upon a set of representational practices which had their origins in US advertising and commercial culture. US advertising was also important as a source of personnel in the early period of commercial TV in Britain, helping to smooth the transition to the new medium. Both in terms of people and representational practices, then, US television, advertising and film making were important resources to advertising agencies in Britain. These trans-Atlantic borrowings were, however, combined with more local influences. This included both BBC-trained staff and, centrally, the British tradition of sponsored documentary film. This latter influence was particularly important. It stemmed from the fact that the commercials production industry, which had been rapidly constituted in the mid-1950s, was staffed by people trained in sponsored documentary film.[82] It was this tradition of home-grown film making, above all, that was important in softening US influences in the early years of British TV advertising, in part through the performance styles which it bequeathed. Along with the verbal cadences of British actors and the restrained style of British producers and directors, these performance styles contributed much to shaping a distinctive tradition of British television advertising in the first decade and a half of ITV's existence.

It is also clear that the legacy of press and poster advertising continued to hang over television advertising in its formative years in Britain. Like the broader television culture as a whole, TV advertising walked backwards into the future not only because agencies were reluctant to embrace the new medium, but also because they drew on forms and techniques from the older technologies of print and posters.[83] If adapting to the new medium of television was a complicated process for agencies, television's growing importance as an advertising medium also served to generate other problems, stemming from the way the new visibility of TV advertising stirred advertising's critics into life. I turn to this debate and the broader reception of TV advertising later in this book.

Notes

1 *The Grove Family* ran from 1954 to 1957. See S. Holmes, *Entertaining Television: The BBC and Popular Television Culture in the 1950s*, Manchester: Manchester University Press, 2008, pp. 38–74.
2 *The Times*, 23 September 1955, p. 5.
3 *Advertiser's Weekly*, 30 September 1955, p. 7.
4 See also S. Schwarzkopf, 'A moment of triumph in the history of the free market', in M. Bailey (ed.), *Narrating Media History*, London: Routledge, 2008, pp. 83–94.
5 C. Jenkins, *Power Behind the Screen*, London: Macgibbon & Kee, 1961, p. 17.
6 C. Mayhew, *Dear Viewer*, n.p., 1953.
7 H.H. Wilson, *Pressure Group: The Campaign for Commercial Television*, New Brunswick: Rutgers University Press, 1961, p. 140.
8 Ibid., p. 138.
9 *Advertiser's Weekly*, 21 October 1954, pp. 180–1.
10 Wilson, *Pressure Group*, p. 138.
11 On American sponsored television in the late 1940s and early 1950s, see L. Samuel, *Brought to You By: Post-war Advertising and the American Dream*, Austin: University of Texas Press, 2002.
12 On the introduction of commercial television, see, inter alia, Wilson, *Pressure Group*; B. Sendall, *Independent Television in Britain, Volume I: Origin and Foundation 1946–62*, London: Macmillan, 1982; J. Corner (ed.), *Popular Television in Britain*, London: British Film Institute, 1991; L. Black, *The Political Culture of the Left in Affluent Britain, 1951–64*, Basingstoke: Palgrave Macmillan, 2003.
13 *Journal of the Advertising Association*, September 1952, p. 2.

14 Quoted in Wilson, *Pressure Group*, p. 125.
15 Ibid., p. 56.
16 *Institute Information*, August 1953, p. 4; see also *Advertiser's Weekly*, 6 August 1954, p. 238.
17 *Institute Information*, September 1953, p. 5.
18 Ibid., p. 4.
19 IPA and ISBA, 1953, *Television, the viewer and the advertiser*, text of a memo to HM Postmaster General, G (8), Pam 627, UCL Special Collections. This was not the first time the IPA had taken a view on commercial television. As early as 1946 the Institute had submitted a pamphlet to the parliamentary Select Committee looking at the workings of the BBC in which it argued in favour of 'controlled commercial broadcasting'. The organization elaborated further on its preferred model of commercial broadcasting in its written submission to the Beveridge Committee on Broadcasting a few years later, proposing that there should be a lifting of the ban on the broadcasting of advertisements on the BBC. Such a move would, it claimed, 'provide industry with a powerful weapon in selling goods … and greatly increase the resources available to the broadcaster for public entertainment'; *Report of the Broadcasting Committee 1949*, 1950–1 Cmd. 8116, Para. 364.
20 IPA and ISBA, 1953, *Television, the viewer and the advertiser*, text of a memo to HM Postmaster General, G (8), Pam 627, UCL Special Collections, p. 4.
21 Ibid., p 10.
22 Ibid.
23 Memo from Ken Shaw to Howard Kohl, 18 August 1959, Edward G. Wilson papers, JWT/Duke, Box 10.
24 Wilson, *Pressure Group*, p. 139.
25 On the Popular Television Association, see Wilson, *Pressure Group*.
26 *The Times*, 2 May 1953, p. 3; 31 August 1953, p. 6; see also letters to *The Times*, 3 August 1953, p. 7; Wilson, *Pressure Group*, p. 188.
27 Orr-Ewing, cited in Wilson, *Pressure Group*, p. 70.
28 Wilson, *Pressure Group*; Corner, *Popular Television in Britain*. The Labour party was strongly opposed to a second commercial channel and threatened to repeal the Act once it returned to power.
29 The idea of 'natural breaks' was deliberately elusive and could mean different things to different commentators. In this sense, it was masterful fudge. For a critical view on 'natural breaks', see the *The Times* editorial on the 'abuse' of natural breaks by the contractors: 'Doing what comes naturally', 12 March 1959, p. 13; see also 3 March 1959, p. 11; 4 June 1966, p. ix.
30 B. Henry, 'The history', in B. Henry (ed.), *Television Advertising in Britain: The First Thirty Years*, London: Ebury Press, 1986, pp. 34–6.
31 All TV advertising had to be cleared prior to transmission by the Advertising Advisory Committee (AAC), a body established by the Television Act. The AAC was concerned with standards of conduct in the new medium and judged commercials in accordance with the 'Principles for Television Advertising' which the committee produced. This established a much higher level of regulation than was the case for press, cinema or poster advertising. The code famously stipulated that

all television advertising had to be 'legal, clean, honest and truthful'; Independent Television Authority, 1955, p. 26.
32. IPA television, cinema and radio sub-committee (TCR), 19 February 1958, IPA/HAT.
33. IPA TCR, 6 March 1957, p. 3; IPA TCR, 9 August 1957, p. 2, IPA/HAT.
34. The IPA's television, cinema and radio sub-committee raised this concern as early as July 1955 and in September of that year decided to ask its own trade relations committee to contact one of the contractors, Granada Television, which had apparently agreed to recognize a production company; IPA TCR, 14 July 1955; 15 September 1955, IPA/HAT. With the drafting of a formal recognition agreement by the Television Programme Companies Association still ongoing in December 1957, the IPA's television, cinema and radio sub-committee again became concerned by reports that nine companies that were not service agencies had been granted recognition; IPA TCR, 4 December 1957, p. 2; IPA TCR, 1 May 1958, IPA/HAT.
35. IPA trade relations committee, 19 February 1963.
36. This was for the *Daily Telegraph* and *Sunday Telegraph*; IPA trade relations committee, 27 August 1963.
37. Advertising Association, *Advertising Expenditure 1960*, London: Advertising Association, 1962, p. 43.
38. *Advertiser's Weekly*, 29 January 1953, p. 190.
39. *Advertiser's Weekly*, 28 October 1954, p. 275.
40. *Advertiser's Weekly*, 23 September 1955, p. 13.
41. McMahan was vice-president of McCann-Erickson, New York in the 1950s. *Advertiser's Weekly*, 10 February 1955, pp. 4–8.
42. Memo from J. Bullmore to directors, 12 May 1965, JWT/HAT, Box 238.
43. *Advertiser's Weekly*, 23 September 1955, p. 13.
44. *Advertiser's Weekly*, 26 August 1954, p. 381.
45. Peter Marsh, interview with the author, 2008.
46. E. Hennessy, *Dorland – History*, n.d., HAT.
47. T. Rayfield, *Fifty in Forty: The Unofficial History of JWT London, 1945–95*, privately published, 1996, p. 74.
48. JWT Television Workshop, 1956, Edward G. Wilson Collection, JWT/Duke, Box 9.
49. Rayfield, *Fifty in Forty*, p. 76.
50. Jeremy Bullmore, interview with the author, 2008.
51. The London Press Exchange initially housed TV in Immedia, its TV, cinema and radio division. In 1958 this was renamed LPE Television Ltd because of the growing importance of TV; *Audio-Visual Selling*, 4 July 1958, p. 1.
52. Stanley Maxted had been an acclaimed war-time correspondent working for BBC Radio Newsreel.
53. Rayfield, *Fifty in Forty*, p. 195.
54. Ibid., p. 12.
55. *The Times*, 21 May 1964, p. vii.
56. *D&AD Annuals*, London: D&AD, 1964–9.

57 Memo from J. Bullmore to directors, 12 May 1965, p. 3, JWT/HAT, Box 238.
58 Office Reconstruction 1962, JWT/HAT, Box 577.
59 J. Caughie, 'Before the Golden Age: early television drama', in J. Corner (ed.), *Popular Television in Britain*, London: British Film Institute, 1991, pp. 22–41.
60 Henry, 'The history', p. 63.
61 *Advertiser's Weekly*, 10 February 1955, p. 6.
62 This account draws on a selection of approximately 600 commercials from the Bradford Film and TV Library transferred to videotape by the BBC for its documentary series, *Washes Whiter* and held at the History of Advertising Trust. They consist of the pre-production copies of the commercials from which the documentary was made. This section also draws on a JWT London compilation tape, *Sixty Years of JWT*, together with agency documentation from the JWT archive (JWT/HAT).
63 *Audio-visual Selling*, 5 September 1958, p. 10.
64 See B. Conekin, F. Mort and C. Waters (eds), *Moments of Modernity: Reconstructing Britain 1945–64*, London: Rivers Oram, 1999.
65 JWT London used the actor Robert Raglan in some of its Persil adverts to underscore the authority of its product claims. See Robert Raglan 62, transmitted October 1961; Raglan A, November 1963; Good News, November 1963; Raglan in Dover, September 1964, Persil Advertising Review (TV) 1955–65, JWT/HAT, Box 160.
66 *Advertiser's Weekly*, 21 September 1956, p. 4. The advert was also praised in a letter sent to *Commercial Television News*, 29 June 1956, p. 10.
67 Samuel, *Brought To You By*, p. 65.
68 Ibid.
69 Holmes, *Entertaining Television*, p. 40.
70 Samuel, *Brought To You By*, p. 19.
71 For a list of Associated-Rediffusion's 'ad mags', see *Commercial Television News*, 30 November 1956, pp. 6–7. The trade press was critical of these early 'ad mags'. See *Audio-visual Selling*, 3 January 1956, p. 6; 9 May 1958, p. 5.
72 See Henry, 'The history'; R. Turnock, *Television and Consumer Culture*, London: IB Tauris, 2007, pp. 145–6.
73 Notes from Mr Hoggart to draft chapter VII of the Report, PRO HO 244/269, 2.
74 See Samuel's comments on the Jack Benny Show; Samuel, *Brought To You By*, p. 71.
75 Ibid.
76 See, inter alia, *Advertiser's Weekly*, 10 February 1955, p. 5; 20 January 1955, p. 144; 20 September 1957, pp. 35–8; 30 September 1960, pp. 24–6.
77 See also 'Ruth Dunning Interviews', 'Grocer', 1955; 'Washing Machine', 1956; and 'Clinic', 1956, JWT/HAT, Box 160.
78 JWT/HAT, Box 160, 1965; see also Persil 'Sailors', 1955 and 'Schoolboy', 1956.
79 The company also sent staff such as Jeremy Bullmore and Colin Clarke over to the USA in 1958 to study US TV advertising for five weeks; Rayfield, *Fifty in Forty*, p. 75.
80 'Impression of JWT London television department and British television generally', memo from Ken Shaw to Howard Kohl, 18 August 1959, Edward G. Wilson papers, JWT/Duke, Box 10.

81 Ibid.
82 See Garrett, in Henry, 'The history'. My thanks go to David Clampin for his thoughts on inter-war British documentary film.
83 On the influence of radio broadcasting and print culture on television formats, see J. Thumin, *Inventing Television Culture: Men, Women and the Box*, Oxford: Oxford University Press, 2004.

5

'All mod cons': television advertising, the housewife and domestic life

Act one of these films is to capture the interest and belief of the housewife. We talk about the 'shock of recognition', but I see it more as a sort of self-congratulatory glow. The viewer agrees that she is the kind of admirable woman she is, and we persuade her that by choosing Persil she will also win recognition from her family and neighbours.[1]

Josephine Mackay's 1965 memo to her senior colleagues about the TV advertising campaign developed for Persil washing powder by JWT London is candid in its assessment of the kinds of feelings and associations that the agency was hoping to stir in its target audiences of housewives. As she suggested, the commercial aimed to invite an identification between the viewer in her role as a housewife with the image portrayed in the advert. It encouraged her to feel good about the social importance of this domestic role and the recognition which she would receive from her family and neighbours in successfully discharging it. Purchasing the product would facilitate this and ensure that she became – or continued to be – the 'kind of admirable woman' depicted in the advert. In seeking to affirm the social importance to women of their role as wives and mothers, JWT's advertising for Persil formed part of a sustained interrogation and elaboration of women's domestic role not only within the agency, but across the world of advertising, commercial culture and public policy in the 1950s and 1960s. As I noted in chapter three, state policy makers, the editors of women's magazines and the manufacturers of domestic technologies and commodities were all linked by a common preoccupation with defining women's primary social role as wife and mother. Drawing on developments in the inter-war years, these protagonists, particularly within commercial culture, saw the role of the 'modern housewife' as socially progressive in character since it allowed women to escape, they argued, from the domestic drudgery of old. This ideal of the 'modern housewife', however, did not stand alone but was intimately connected to the creation of the idea of a 'new household'. With its origins in the early years of the twentieth century this was a home, as Victoria de Grazia has argued, marked by new standards of elementary comfort, like indoor toilets, running water, heat, electricity and piped gas.[2] It was also a home, she further argues, that was first and foremost an American invention and central to the regime of mass consumption developed in the USA in the early twentieth century which came also to dominate Western Europe, especially in the years after 1945. At the centre of the new household, and the lynchpin of the regime of mass consumption, was the modern housewife or 'Mrs Consumer', in her American manifestation.

Advertising, especially television advertising, played an important role in the dissemination of both the ideal of the housewife and that of the new household. In this chapter, I want to reflect on the way TV advertising in Britain represented these conjoined aspects of post-war social change and how it became part of the broader social project to remake domestic life and the ordering of gender relations within it. In doing so, I focus on the way one central aspect of the new home was depicted – the kitchen. Among advocates of the new household, the kitchen occupied a privileged position, being seen as central to healthier, more hygienic and less labour-intensive forms of living. I explore the ways in which TV advertising represented this key aspect of modern domesticity by focusing on commercials which promoted washing powders, washing machines and convenience foods. Two long-running campaigns figure centrally in this account – the advertising for Persil and Oxo cubes. Both campaigns achieved an unusual degree of recognition from the public over their long runs on television. They also reveal how the forms of TV advertising developed by agencies in Britain had an important impact on how post-war consumption and growing material affluence were depicted on television.

Making sense of these commercials requires some further reflection on the broader social forces reshaping the post-war home. In the first part of the chapter, I explore the role played by designers, policy makers and the utility companies in shaping these ideas of domesticity, especially the ideal of the modern kitchen. This ideal, and the moves taken to implement it, need to be seen in a social context in which the ambitions of 'domestic reformers' had to reckon with the actually existing condition of most people's homes and the relatively slow and uneven pace of domestic change for the majority of the population. In part two of the chapter, I consider evidence not only about the dissemination of domestic technologies and the transformations of kitchens, but also about the domestic situations in which many people lived.

This evidence points to a striking gap between images of the ideal home and the circumstances in which much of the population found themselves living. The final section looks in some detail at the way TV advertising depicted modern domesticity and its ordering of gender relations, especially through the way the housewife consumer was represented.

Ideal homes and kitchens

In 1961 the Ministry of Housing and Local Government published a report on the standards of design and equipment within both public and private housing. Titled *Homes for Today and Tomorrow* and subsequently known as the Parker Morris report after the chairman of the committee that had produced it, the publication offered an ambitious vision of how family homes might be improved.[3] It focused on the need for better-planned space in house design and for improved standards of domestic heating so that the available space could be used for everyday activities throughout the year.[4] The report drew upon visits made by the committee to over 600 homes during the summer of 1959 and the autumn of 1960 in which they had studied people's homes and talked to the occupants. Distilling the evidence garnered from these visits, the report noted the transformations that had occurred in most people's lives since the end of the war. It identified this 'new pattern of living' as having been shaped by 'a social and economic revolution' fuelled by rising material standards. This had not only given the majority access to a greater range of domestic goods – like washing machines, televisions, vacuum cleaners and refrigerators – but had shaped a 'revolution in expectations' which public- and private-sector builders needed to take account of.[5] In short, these changes made it timely, in the view of the committee, to 're-examine the kinds of home that we ought to be building'.[6] One of the most notable sections of the report concerned its commentary upon kitchens. Noting that 'the kitchen is the most intensively used room in the house', it felt that in many homes, including those built since the end of the war, the kitchen 'retains some of the character of the nineteenth century scullery'.[7] Drawing on a range of international studies, including those from the USA, Denmark and Holland, the report delineated a precise vision of the way kitchens ought to be planned. This incorporated assumptions about the necessity of fitting into kitchen design space for a range of powered goods and technologies. It also sought to prescribe how the housewife should move around the kitchen. The latter ideas were derived from the advocates of the scientific management of the home and its 'rational' planning. The report thus proposed a didactic model of kitchen design. This was the sequence 'work surface/cooker/work surface/sink/work surface' unbroken by a door or other traffic way.[8] The report suggested that this sequence could be realized in three forms: as a straight line, in the form of an L-shape or a U-shape.[9]

Parker Morris's vision of kitchen design registered over sixty years of thinking and proselytizing about kitchens, much of it pioneered in the USA. This had sought to transform the kitchen from, as Burnett suggests, 'the cheerless scullery populated by servants, to a room that was at the centre of household activity, skilfully planned, equipped with labour saving devices and as a room where family meals were typically eaten'.[10] Two American publications, Mary Patterson's *Principles of Domestic Engineering* and Christine Fredericks' *Scientific Management in the Home*, were especially influential in these developments.[11] Both books initiated a new conception of the kitchen that was elaborated upon by designers in the 1920s, including early enthusiasts in Europe like the Bauhaus school in Germany.[12] Following the lead of writers on 'domestic engineering', US manufacturers of domestic technologies, such as Hotpoint Electrical Appliances Ltd and International Refrigerator, pioneered the development of electrical appliances designed for the new kitchen.[13] These companies were assisted in their promotion of new ideas about kitchen design and domestic living by the electricity supply industry and, to a lesser extent, the private gas supply companies.

In Britain, as Adrian Forty has suggested, it was the search for alternative uses of electricity beyond that of illumination in the street, office and home that encouraged the electricity companies to promote the wider domestic use of electricity. To this end they were heavily involved in the development of domestic electrical appliances and the promotion of their value.[14] These domestic consumer durables were important to the 'new consumerism' of the inter-war years in Britain and included 'domestic aids' like electric cookers, fridges, water heaters, irons, wash boilers and vacuum cleaners.[15] Expenditure on these kinds of goods formed one of the three major areas of household spending in the 1930s – the other two being fuel and light and transport and communications – and were linked to the growing availability of mains power. By 1939 nearly two-thirds of all homes had electricity, the remaining third being largely confined to rural areas.[16] Unlike in the USA, however, the diffusion of domestic consumer durables was a slow process and in the inter-war years, as Sue Bowden has shown, the 'new consumerism' was largely a middle-class phenomenon.[17] Because of this the diffusion of domestic electrical appliances in Britain lagged a generation behind America.[18] In the inter-war years, it was as a source of lighting and power for radios that electricity was consumed.[19]

Three principal factors conspired to inhibit the generalizing of the 'new household' into inter-war Britain. Firstly, as Offer has shown, 'time-using' technologies like radio diffused more quickly than 'time-saving' technologies like fridges, vacuum cleaners and washing aids.[20] Secondly, large consumer durables like fridges remained expensive.[21] Thirdly, until a nationalized electricity industry was created in 1947, the cost of electricity remained high. In fact, it was the reduction in the cost of electricity which did most to stimulate the take-up of powered household technologies in the post-war period.[22] Through the late 1950s and early 1960s, this transformation was evident in relation to two of the most iconic post-war domestic technologies: washing machines and refrigerators. The former rose from being owned by 25% of households in the UK in 1958 to 50% in 1964. Ownership of fridges had a similar steep pattern of post-war growth, reaching 25% of households by 1962 and 50% by 1968.[23]

Building on the innovations of the inter-war years, post-war designers invested heavily in the layout and design of kitchens in order to accommodate the new powered domestic technologies. *Design* magazine, the publication of the Council for Industrial Design, was an important showcase for this work. Between 1955 and 1966 it regularly featured developments in kitchen design and associated domestic technologies. In November 1955, for example, in a survey of kitchen furniture, the magazine depicted new kitchens designed by the upmarket store Heals and the more middle-market manufacturers Hygena and Ezee Kitchens. These included flat-fronted and straight-edged cabinets and cupboards.[24] A few issues earlier, the same 'functionalist' design for kitchen furniture had appeared in the magazine in an article on a small home designed for the Ideal Home Exhibition. Alongside flat-fronted cupboards, the kitchen included a clean-lined gas cooker, a picture window and abstract patterned curtains (Fig. 14).[25] This modernist design idiom also featured in an article from 1958. This showed two kitchen designs put together for the exhibition 'Design in Your Kitchen'. The first of these was a 'luxury kitchen' and included work surfaces and fitted cupboards, fridge, washing machine, ironer, tumble dryer, deep freezer and dish washer. The 'middle income' kitchen was more modest, but included work surfaces and a cooker.[26]

In showcasing these modern kitchens, *Design* recurrently acknowledged that American designers and builders led the way in the re-composition of the post-war interior. As the magazine acknowledged in 1958, 'any discussion of ideal kitchens will inevitably invite comparison with American experiments in

Modern Kitchen, *Design*, 1955, issue 75

kitchen design'. The US company General Electrics also figured prominently in an article on the kitchens of tomorrow.²⁷ The focus on the kitchen as being at the centre of family life, a room in which some of the most advanced domestic technologies and design thinking was located and as a space where women orchestrated the care of their families was strongly evident in the US designs for kitchens. These were preoccupations taken up in British post-war designs. This was the case even as British kitchen designers acknowledged that British kitchens, and kitchen design, lagged behind American developments. Seeking to make a virtue of this deficiency, *Design* magazine suggested that 'our domestic scale' necessitates 'greater refinement and detail'. By this it meant the smaller size of British homes and kitchens compared to the standard of American house design. It saw this more modest form of kitchen design exemplified in the distinct look of cookers sold in the UK. These were the 'hearth-high oven and eye level grill' which indicated a desire 'to achieve comfortable working conditions'.²⁸ Nonetheless, British kitchen designs broadly followed the same principles of design that had produced the kitchen at the heart of the new post-war home in the USA. This deployed a distinctive and highly modern 'functionalist' design idiom in which long and uninterrupted work surfaces and fitted cupboards, together with the set of fridge, washing machine and gas or electric cooker, defined the ideal kitchen.²⁹

Housing, class and the diffusion of the ideal home

As the Parker Morris report had conceded, despite a broad consensus about what the modern home, and especially the kitchen, should look like, many new homes built in the years after 1945 failed to live up to the new design standards. This was particularly notable given the scale of post-war house building. The home-building programme initiated by the 1945 Labour government greatly increased the volume of new housing stock and by 1957 2.5m flats and houses had been built, mostly by local authorities.³⁰ This building programme occurred at the same time as the acceleration of the historical shift towards private-sector home ownership which had begun in the 1930s. In 1945 26% of all houses in England and Wales were owner-occupied, but this had increased to 47% by 1966.³¹ The builders of these private-sector homes were often committed to a vision of modernity in house design, especially in the application of open-plan living to room layout and also in confirming the new centrality of the kitchen. For example, the builder Taylor Woodrow's new 1956 home, selling for £2,155, was sold in terms of its 'dream of a kitchen' complete with stainless steel double sink, fitted cupboards and Formica worktops.[32] Growing owner-occupation and the public investment in housing helped to improve the living conditions of many people. As Selina Todd has shown, while in 1951 only 49% of Liverpool's households had piped water, their own stove, kitchen sink and fixed bath, by 1971 71% benefited from these facilities with the greatest improvement coming in council housing.[33] By 1963 most of the residents surveyed by the University of Liverpool in the central districts of the city had TV sets and some had refrigerators.[34] The growing numbers of married women who worked in paid employment contributed to the rising standards of living of many households. Their number grew strongly between 1951 and 1961, rising from 21.7% to 45.4% of married women, and it was 'luxury' expenditure on goods like TV sets and other domestic technologies that these women's wages helped to fuel.[35]

However, the condition of many homes, especially in the private rented sector, remained at some remove from the ideal of the post-war home. This was largely because many of these properties had been built before the war and had been badly maintained. Edward Perkins, a 67-year-old pensioner interviewed in Liverpool in 1963, rented a small rundown house. He had no cooker and couldn't afford to pay for his electricity on a regular basis.[36] In Manchester, the returns for the 1951 Census revealed that 41% of households did not have exclusive access to a fixed bath and only 56% had exclusive use of piped water, a cooking stove, kitchen sink, toilet and fixed bath. By 1961 over half of families in Manchester were still without a hot water tap.[37] Evidence such as this was to inform the rediscovery of poverty amid apparent affluence by sociologists like Peter Townsend in the early 1960s.[38]

The relatively modest level of material comfort experienced by many working-class households, even if they were not officially poor, was also striking. When another sociologist, Brian Jackson, interviewed young couples for his study of working-class life in Huddersfield in the autumn and winter of 1962 he found them living in relatively poor housing with limited amenities.[39] Mr and Mrs Thackray, for example, were both in their early twenties and rented a small terraced house with a shared outside toilet and no fixed bath, though they rented a TV and had a car – the latter relatively unusual at the time.[40] Another, unnamed couple, also in their early twenties, lived in a small through terraced house with an inside toilet, but no bath, TV or car. The house was relatively well furnished 'with red moquette furniture' and contemporary patterned wallpaper.[41] A similar combination of modest, un-modernized house with a strong investment in decoration and furniture was evident in the small back-to-back house rented by Mr and Mrs Johnson (aged 23 and 21). They shared a toilet, had no bath and rented a TV. Jackson, however, was taken by the way their house was finished. He noted that it was 'decorated beautifully. The wallpaper is modern, not simply contemporary. There is a long olive green settee, a couple of stools, and a dining room suite.'[42] Mr and Mrs Davis were one of the more obviously prosperous couples and materially better off than most of Jackson's young couples. They lived in a new semi-detached house and had a mortgage on the property. It had its own toilet and bathroom. They rented a TV, but had no car. The house was, like many of the other houses Jackson visited, well furnished, but unlike the other couples, the Davises had a modern kitchen. Jackson noted that it was 'crammed with modern equipment, stove, washer, and refrigerator. The wife was pleased to show me around the house, which was spotless.'[43]

The variation in home comforts in Brian Jackson's small sample of Huddersfield households is indicative of the uneven pace of social change in post-war Britain. People living in close proximity could experience very different versions of domestic comfort and convenience. It is this unevenness of social change, as well as the normative pull of the ideal of the 'new household', that is evident in TV advertising in the 1950s and 1960s. It also formed the setting in which the elaboration of the role of the post-war housewife took shape within advertising.

Advertising and modern living

The depiction of the post-war home and the ideal of the new household within television advertising was closely associated with the marketing of a range of domestic commodities, including products like washing powders, detergents, soaps and cleaners, together with processed and convenience foods. These commodities, as I noted earlier, dominated advertising expenditure through the 1950s and 1960s. Almost all the advertising for these goods was aimed at the 'mass-market housewife' and it was this consumer who both figured in the advertising and formed its principal audience. JWT London was especially strongly associated with selling to this group of consumers and Persil washing powder, produced by the giant detergent manufacturer Unilever, was one of the agency's most important accounts associated with these consumers. We can see in its advertising for Persil how the agency elaborated both the idea of the post-war housewife and the domestic world over which she presided. From the end of 1958 JWT London put together a new 'mood'-themed series of commercials for Persil that marked a departure from its earlier television work for the brand. The new series was centred on the depiction of a figure the agency called 'Mum' and ran from 1958 until the late 1960s.[44] Each of the commercials was relatively long, running for either 45 or 60 seconds. They aimed to demonstrate, as the agency put it, 'a mother's love, care and pride in using Persil'. Based around the depiction of one- or two-child families, the idea, as the agency saw it, was to deploy the idea of 'modern non-sentimental family affection'.[45] In the adverts emotion and family bonds centred on the mother and were integral to the presentation of Persil in the commercials. As the account team at JWT noted in 1965, its aim had always been to emphasize the emotional authenticity of the advertising. It suggested

> we have always been at great lengths to make Persil commercials as sincere and convincing as possible … Every mother among our viewers should be able to see herself (perhaps a little as she would like to see herself) in the same situation as the mother on the screen.[46]

The advertising trade press was quick to praise the new commercials, with *Advertiser's Weekly* noting in its regular 'commercial spotlight' feature that the campaign 'broke new ground' in its style and was 'highly commendable'.[47] JWT London itself even featured the Persil advertising in a company advert from the mid-1960s. Using the commercial to show how different the agency was from its competitors, the company advert claimed that 'Persil advertising spoke simply, straightforwardly, and sincerely – a quiet voice that carried above the hysteria of claim and counter-claim'.[48]

The series of 'Mum' commercials certainly portrayed understated emotional dramas based upon the experience of motherly pride and care for the family.[49] The pace and style of the adverts was gentle, with the mothers reflecting with quiet satisfaction, typically shot in medium close up, on their ability to successfully look after their family. At the heart of their satisfaction was the visible proof of the care that they took evident in the whiteness of their wash. The commercials used a recurring device of what the agency called the w/ow (white/off-white) comparison. This showed the shirts of her children or her husband strategically placed next to the less gleaming white shirt of either a schoolfriend, playmate or work colleague. The visual difference in the whiteness of the Persil Mum's items evidenced not just their cleanliness but also the positive social benefits she gained from achieving a white wash,[50] namely, that she was a better wife and mother. As JWT put it, the adverts revealed that 'the Persil user enjoys fulfilment in knowing she is doing the best for her family, with the further reward of earning their increased affection and the respect and approval of her neighbours'. The 'neighbours' were the other women who often appeared in the adverts, seen at the garden gate or at the school gate, and who figured as sources of approval (or sometimes disapprobation), testifying to the whiteness of Mum's wash.

These commercials drew strongly upon the conventions of the 'slice of life' drama and were set to lilting, romantic music. 'Piccadilly', the first in the 'Mum' series broadcast in November 1958, begin with an opening shot of Piccadilly Circus in central London, before moving to a domestic setting. The female voice-over intoned, 'They say the world revolves around Eros. Actually it revolves around Mum. She has to cope with many things – such as getting clothes clean in hard water.'[51] 'Women Alone', transmitted March 1959, was even more reflective. Using a medium shot of Mum at home thinking about her absent family, the advert mixed in shots of her child and husband, emphasizing the comparative whiteness of their clothing next to another child and a neighbour. A male voice-over stated: 'Even Though her family may be apart from her … they are still a part of her … being judged by the care she takes of them … As a wife she uses Persil … As a mother she uses Persil … Persil washes whiter.'[52] This emphasis on personal satisfaction and status that came from being a 'good mother' was also evident in 'Laura Davis', transmitted in March 1961. The commercial was one of a series that focused on the domestic lives of a number of named, individual women. In the commercial we see Mum, Laura Davis, wistfully flicking through women's fashion magazines and wondering if her life had become just a little humdrum. The male voice-over underlines this sense of disappointment, before reassuring Laura Davis – and the viewer – that ultimately it is the love of her family and her ability to look after them that offers the greatest satisfaction. We see her looking lovingly at her husband and baby, before the commercial cuts to a scene of her in her kitchen doing the washing using Persil.[53]

The choice of actresses cast in the 'Mum' series and the way they were styled gave the depiction of the housewife in the adverts a distinctive look and character. Almost all of the women shown were young married mothers, of above-average attractiveness without being too glamorous. Typically they were accessorized with the emblem of the housewifely role: an apron. The aprons were always pristine and the presentation of the housewife usually saw her looking neat and well-groomed, often wearing court shoes, occasionally high heels, and sometimes a string of pearls. This gave the commercials a certain formality and decorousness. It was as if viewers were being invited into homes that were putting on their best public face. Absent were depictions of the slovenly housewife with tousled hair and unfashionable housecoat. As Angela Ince, writing in the upmarket magazine *London Life* in May 1966, sharply noted, 'you never catch Commercial Woman coming down to start the day in an old woollen dressing gown and a grim glare, like any other woman'.[54] In this regard, the image of the housewife in these adverts echoed the ideal presented in women's magazines. This was a married women who took care of her appearance but, in so doing, avoided the twin pitfalls of being either too dressy and narcissistic (the 'overdressed woman') or not concerned enough about how she looked for her husband. In women's magazines and some press advertising, this latter figure was represented by the 'girl with the dressing gown mind'.[55]

The modern housewife of these 'slice of life' commercials was always pictured at the centre of the home and domestic life. Children regularly appeared in these adverts, though they tended to come and go in the narrative, leaving Mum on her own to reflect, positively, on her role in the family. Men, usually husbands, were much more marginal to the adverts and formed the connection to the wider world where they were depicted at the office or shown returning to the home. Conspicuously absent was the domesticated husband of contemporary social commentary who loomed large in the writings of researchers like Mark Abrams and Young and Willmott.[56] The strongly gendered picture of domestic life represented in the commercials reproduced many of the explicit assumptions about women's roles that emerged in public debates during the 1950s and early 1960s, from the work of experts on family life like John Bowlby to the pronouncements in women's magazines. In this regard, television advertising formed part of a wider regime of representation that worked to elaborate an acceptable version of femininity for married wives and mothers. Not everyone, however, found the Persil housewife appealing. Locating it within a broader set of depictions of women in TV adverts for soap, food and household items, an anonymous woman advertising executive writing in *Advertiser's Weekly* in September 1959 chastised her male colleagues for these images of Mum. Contradicting Angela Ince's later assessment, the woman advertising executive complained,

> What woman-loving man could ordain her to be that all-too-often quite frumpish creature who speaks to us from her kitchen sink, from the washing machine, the shopping tour, the housework? Can any man who thinks of the British housewife in these saggy, middle-aged, un-groomed, un-coiffured, too solid and too 'sensible' terms really like women?[57]

What was needed, she urged, was more glamour in the depictions of ordinary women. Interestingly, she thought she had found it in a new campaign for Oxo cubes. This was JWT's 'Cooking with Oxo' series. The anonymous reviewer waxed lyrical: 'Katy [sic] was just the sort of cute and streamlined young housewife most of us would like to think we are … Her hair was attractive and up to date; her dresses … were contemporary, neat and full of sophisticated personality.'[58]

'Katie' did, indeed, mark something of a break from the representation of the modern housewife depicted in the 'Mum' series. JWT had come up with the idea of Katie as part of its attempt to reverse the declining sales of Oxo and the product's association with wartime austerity. The agency decided to move the advertising into a domestic setting and emphasize the product's domestic associations. This represented a shift from the previous advertising strategy which had relied heavily on outdoor advertising and transport sites (such as the sides of buses). To this end, JWT devised a campaign centred upon a young, modern housewife, Katie, and her husband, Philip. Katie and Philip were subtly but clearly middle class, modern and 'nice'. Crucially, they were young and more prosperous than Oxo's established, declining market of consumers. The agency decided to produce the commercials as part of a recurring series. This was initially titled 'Cooking with Oxo', but later became 'Life with Katie'. In the latter commercials on-screen titles were used, confirming the serial nature of the advertising and emphasizing their 'slice of life' character. As the commentary from *Advertiser's Weekly* made clear, however, it was the casting of the character of Katie which was central to much of the distinctiveness of the ads. Played by actress Mary Holland, Katie was young, bright-eyed and trim.[59] While Philip joked in the commercials that he had married her not for her looks but for her cooking, this observation underplayed Katie's physical attractiveness.[60] Her dark, relatively short hair gave her a contemporary look and in the early commercials she has a passing resemblance to Audrey Hepburn's gamine public image. Katie's eye make-up was clearly visible in the ads and this contributed to her relatively styled appearance. Though she dressed conventionally, there was a sense of fashionability about her attire and in an early commercial she appeared wearing a fitted blouse with a raised collar and stylish jacket. Tellingly, Katie rarely appeared in the commercials wearing an apron and when she does it is usually a butcher's-style striped apron and not the highly feminine and flowery style typical of the 'Mum' series.

Mary Holland's performance of the character of Katie was naturalistic and warm compared to the rather stilted and formal demeanour of the Persil mum. Holland brought to the part a more expressive and open personality, imbuing Katie with a quick wit and obvious intelligence. Every inch the loyal and dutiful wife, Katie uses her warmth and charm to manipulate Philip for her own ends.[61] What is striking is the way sexuality surfaces in the adverts. It is carried through the way Katie sparkles in the ads, but more obviously through the displays of physical affection between Katie and Philip. These include a passionate embrace in one of the 'Life with Katie' adverts. In another, which begins with a high-angle shot, Katie and Philip are shown lounging in their sitting room. While Philip reclines on a settee, Katie stretches out on the rug, leaning against him, her hair ruffled and her shoes kicked off in a moment of intimacy.

If the couple are shown enjoying the benefits of a warm and intimate relationship, the commercials also allowed Katie to register some of the frustrations of being a housewife and chief meal provider. On a number of separate occasions through the series, Philip tells Katie at short notice that he is bringing home work colleagues for dinner. While the narrative allows Katie to protest at his thoughtlessness and speak of her downtrodden position, she always rises to the challenge and with grace and good humour delivers a tasty meal. This aspect of Katie's character gained much in contrast to Philip. In the early commercials between 1958 and 1960 Philip was portrayed as an authoritative husband with matinee idol looks. When he was recast, he retained his thoughtlessness, but became bluffer and more childlike. In 'Foggy Night', transmitted in 1967, we see the interplay between Philip's childlike thoughtlessness and Katie's resigned acceptance of his foibles. Having endured a difficult car journey home in thick fog, Philip's first reaction on reaching the house is to tell Katie, 'I thought I'd never see food, or you, again.' While this is a humorous reference to Philip's appetite, the line also allows Katie to offer a knowing, resigned smile at her relative ranking in his affections.

Alongside its elaboration of Katie's version of the modern housewife, one which was both sexier and more open to the demands of the housewife role, the 'Life with Katie' series also displayed the couple's modernity and hinted at a world of social mobility. This was evident, for example, when the couple attend a decidedly middle-class fancy dress party, take a trip to the ballet and eventually move to the country to a house with a rustic cooking range.[62] The depiction of domestic interiors and especially the kitchen was also central to the ads. Katie's kitchen was large, with plenty of work surfaces organized into an L-shape, just as Parker Morris recommended. The kitchen flooring was black-and-white checked vinyl tiles and the kitchen's picture window was adorned with venetian blinds. There was usually a small dining table in the kitchen where Katie and Philip would eat. Their house also had a separate dining room furnished with a low sideboard and modern painting. The rather upmarket standard of their home was underscored by some of the props used in the adverts. These included a contemporary set of coffee pots, the long pile rug in the couple's lounge and tableware from Heals, the upmarket West End furniture store.[63]

Katie's home, and especially her kitchen, were notably more middle class and closer to the post-war ideal than those that appeared in other commercials aimed at the mass-market housewife. At the same time, it remained at some remove from the post-war reworking of the kitchen within progressive middle-class culture. The obvious contrast here was with the vision of 'civilized living' both promoted by and exemplified in the kitchen of Elizabeth David, the cookery writer and doyen of the metropolitan middle class.[64] David was a key cultural entrepreneur and part of a broader movement within progressive middle-class culture in the 1950s and 1960s which looked towards selected elements of 'continental taste' in order to break with the Puritanism and restrictions of British culture. David's cookery books, especially her first, *A Book of Mediterranean Food*, became culinary Bibles for a post-war generation of upper middle-class readers.[65] They are notable for explicitly addressing the domestic situation of this new 'servantless class', a group of upper middle-class Englishwomen required to 'take a far greater interest in food than was formerly considered polite'.[66] In her second book, *French Country Cooking*, David celebrates the centrality of the kitchen to the home and encourages her readers to devote all the resources they could to building up this room. 'It will be', she reassured them, 'the most comforting and comfortable in the house.'[67] David's own kitchen, in the basement of her four-storey Georgian townhouse in Chelsea, exemplified these principles. Mixing selected elements of English and Mediterranean country living it had a floor of oak woodblock, an English farmhouse dresser, a large old pine table set in the middle of the room, an old china sink salvaged from a pre-war scullery, a French armoire and a 'New World' cooker – the only concession to post-war modernity.[68] The pine table was the centrepiece of the room and friends of David recalled how it was the social hub, with 'good food' and 'good talk' enjoyed around it.[69] 'Artistic clutter' was provided by bowls of fruit, plates of salted almonds and olives and jars of preserves.[70] All this represented a radically different shaping of the kitchen not only from pre-war middle-class homes, but from that promoted to the lower middling classes through TV advertising. Elizabeth David herself also cut a different figure from the post-war image of the housewife – including Katie's more sophisticated image. Most tellingly, David was pictured in her kitchen wearing a white cotton full cook's apron and not the highly feminine half-aprons which predominated among TV housewives.

Against the metropolitan setting of Elizabeth David's kitchen and home, TV advertising, including the Persil and Oxo adverts, was set in a defiantly suburban world. In the Persil advert 'Mother Cares', transmitted in April 1959, the housewife-mother was shown in a 1930s semi-detached house, and the 'Mum' series recurrently located the emotional dramas of domestic life in these safe and reassuring spaces; spaces where the streets were tidy and quiet and as orderly as the domestic interiors. As a memo from Josephine Mackay to her colleagues in July 1965 concerning the new Persil commercial 'Garden' made clear, the kind of garden they were seeking to portray was 'of the type one sees from a suburban train'.[71] Notably absent were high-rise flats or more threatening urban settings. The social realism of the commercials, however, did mean that they aimed at verisimilitude by mixing 'modern' domestic technologies with less contemporary styles of decoration and furniture, particularly within the kitchen. In 'Piccadilly', the inter-war semi boasted a kitchen with a plain dresser, country-style chairs and an iron range in the fireplace, alongside a contemporary top-loading washing machine. Similarly, in 'Mother Cares' the 1930s semi featured a modern kitchen complete with black-and-white check vinyl flooring and spindly legged table. In 'Woman Alone', 1959, the setting is a Victorian-style kitchen with a mantelpiece over a fireplace and a large modern dresser. In 'Jill Davis', 1959, we see a house with a large picture window, floral wallpaper on the lounge walls and a stainless steel sink in the kitchen with a top-loading washing machine. 'Cards', 1960, used another inter-war home as its setting, complete with a 1930s-style fireplace. In 'Laura Davis', 1961, the kitchen featured a white gas cooker, fitted cupboards and a picture window with venetian blinds.

The Persil adverts were not unique in this regard. In other commercials for washing powders, washing machines and convenience foods we find a presentation of domestic life which registered the fact that many working-class families still lived in cramped Victorian or inter-war housing. The Findus fish fingers commercial featuring the Alf Garnett character exemplified this and used a version of the Garnett front room from the TV series as the setting. This reproduced the dark, cluttered interior, with its shabby sofa and small dining table. A gleaming white gas cooker is just visible in the background of the scene, hinting at a degree of modernity. The Egg Marketing Board's advertising also depicted an unglamorous image of working-class housing. A commercial from 1963 was set in an inter-war council house and the drama of a young girl getting ready for school depicts a snug but unmodernized home, including a cluttered kitchen. By contrast Tony Hancock's series of adverts for the Board, which were broadcast in 1965, were more clearly located in a modern, if modest, kitchen. Hancock's kitchen featured a picture window, modern floral curtains and slimline fitted cupboards with Formica surfaces, as well as a bright white gas cooker. In a 1961 Hoover Keymatic washing machine advert, the washing machine glides across a spotless, shining vinyl floor, with fitted cupboards, blinds and a picture window creating a bright airy space; and in a 1960 commercial for Tudor luncheon meat we see a bright kitchen replete with Venetian blinds, white-tiled walls and Formica cupboards and gleaming work surface and sink. It was this kind of depiction of 'modern' kitchens that critics of the social realist commercials approved of, since they offered the hope that better standards of kitchen design might become the social norm. As the anonymous female advertising executive whom I cited earlier argued, the problem with many 'slice of life' commercials was that 'kitchen equipment is never the most modern available and usually at best they seem to be examples of that obnoxious "imitation contemporary" that are the bane of so much "modern" British furniture and furnishing'. These images of domestic life were a block to the diffusion of the ideal of the 'new household'.

Conclusion

What is evident from the television advertising aimed at the mass-market housewife for convenience foods, washing powders and washing machines is that it was intimately bound up with the representation of the post-war home and especially the modern kitchen. While these depictions of domestic life were differentiated between the more idealized representations of the 'new household' and those, shaped by the conventions of social realism, that registered the unevenness of social change and the fact that many women still lived in only partially modernized pre-war homes, nonetheless within this range of adverts there is a clear sense of the new horizon of expectations that defined 'modern living' and modern domesticity. This centred upon the importance of domestic technologies like washing machines and modern cookers, together with a recognition that the kitchen was at the heart of family life. This was a representation of modern domesticity in which there was a powerful iteration of the central role played by women within the home.

This representation of women's domestic role offered a very particular depiction of post-war femininity realized through the figure of the modern housewife. As we have seen, while this was a cross-class identity that stretched from working-class to lower middling women, it was also tightly defined as a young, married woman typically with one or two small children. It was notable that the modern housewife was not generally a woman over forty or a single woman. Rather, this identity centred upon the cult of young motherhood. Such was the pull of this ideal that Katie tellingly acquired a small son, David, during the run of the 'Life with Katie' series. The 'slice of life' commercials associated with selling to the mass-market housewife, then, were bound up with strong ideas about the proper ordering of domestic gender relations and familial emotions. These ideas persisted even as the commercials were subject to criticism.[72]

In the USA, this critique of advertising and its selling of the ideal of the post-war housewife was vigorously developed in Betty Friedan's book *The Feminine Mystique*. Published in 1963, Friedan's argument was partly based upon a content analysis of US adverts and offered a withering attack on the way advertising presented the housewife role as the only legitimate one for women to pursue. For Friedan, Madison Avenue defined women solely in terms of their roles 'as man's wife, mother, lover object, dishwasher and general server of physical needs'.[73] Friedan's critique belonged within a broader body of American social criticism of the late 1950s and 1960s, including writers like Vance Packard and David Riesman, that sought to challenge the triumph of post-war consumerism and to reveal its hollowness and social dangers.[74] As we will see in chapter seven, much of this social criticism travelled eastwards across the Atlantic and formed part of the intellectual context in which the advocates of post-war consumerism in Britain, like the advertising agencies, had to operate.

It was not only the criticisms of the way advertising represented growing material affluence, including centrally the post-war home and the housewife, which crossed the Atlantic. As we have seen, the very idea of the 'new household' had its roots in US culture and while there were important European influences upon the shaping of the modern kitchen in particular, the ideals of 'modern living' represented in television advertising in Britain owed much to American ideas. In this regard, TV advertising's depiction of the new household fits into the larger argument that frames this book concerning the need to locate post-war commercial and cultural change in Britain in a wider trans-Atlantic picture. Certainly the example of the new household and the image of the modern housewife support Victoria de Grazia's claim that this was first and foremost an American model central to the new regime of mass consumption that was exported to Europe from the 1920s. The commercials that I have discussed in this chapter also show how US ideals were tailored to the British market. This is clear in both the way that depictions of kitchens embedded them in recognizable social settings and also downplayed any explicit American association. In a similar vein, the images of the housewife within television advertising rendered her as a distinctly British social type. As I noted in the last chapter, it was through casting and the verbal cadences of British actors that the indigenous character of the advertising was established. It is to this reception of television advertising that I want to turn in the next chapter.

Notes

1 Memo from Josephine Mackay to Keith Buckroyd and Denis Lanigan, Persil 'My Mum' campaign, 9 July 1965, JWT/HAT, Box 158.
2 V. de Grazia, *Irresistible Empire: America's Advance Through Twentieth Century Europe*, Cambridge, MA, and London: The Belknap Press of Harvard University Press, 2005, pp. 417–54.
3 Ministry of Housing and Local Government, *Homes for today and Tomorrow*, HMSO, 1961, chairman Sir Parker Morris.
4 Ibid., pp. 2–3.
5 Ibid., pp. 1–2; J. Burnett, *A Social History of Housing 1815–1985*, London: Methuen, 1986, p. 306.
6 *Homes for today and Tomorrow*, p. 2.
7 Ibid., p. 19.
8 Ibid., p. 20.
9 Ibid., p. 21.
10 Burnett, *A Social History of Housing*, p. 280.
11 N. Bullock, 'First the kitchen – then the facade', *Journal of Design History*, 1(3–4), 1988, p. 179.
12 Ibid.
13 T.A.B. Corley, *Domestic Electrical Appliances*, London: Jonathan Cape, 1966, pp. 32–4.
14 A. Forty, *Objects of Desire: Design and Society since 1750*, London: Thames & Hudson, 1986, pp. 182–7.
15 S. Bowden, 'The new consumerism', in P. Johnson (ed.), *Twentieth Century British History: Economic, Social and Cultural Change*, London: Longman, 1994, p. 244.
16 Ibid.
17 Ibid.; S. Bowden and A. Offer, 'The technological revolution that never was: gender, class and the diffusion of household appliances in interwar England', in V. de Grazia and E. Furlough (eds), *The Sex of Things: Gender and Consumption in Historical Perspective*, Berkeley and Los Angeles: University of California Press, 1996, pp. 244–74.
18 Bowden and Offer, 'Technological revolution', p. 245.

19 Ibid.
20 A. Offer, *The Challenge of Affluence: Self-Control and Well-being in the United States and Britain since 1950*, Oxford: Oxford University Press, 1997, chapter 8.
21 Corley, *Domestic Electrical Appliances*, p. 4.
22 Bowden, 'The new consumerism'; D. Sandbrook, *Never Had It So Good: A History of Britain from Suez to the Beatles*, London: Little, Brown, 2005.
23 Bowden, 'The new consumerism', p. 247.
24 *Design*, 1955, 83, pp. 42–3.
25 *Design*, 1955, 75, p. 40.
26 *Design*, 1958, 109, pp. 43–7.
27 Ibid.
28 *Design*, 1958, 109, p. 46; 1957, 97, pp. 43–51.
29 *Design*, 1 July 1966, pp. 48–50; de Grazia, *Irresistible Empire*, p. 278; *Modern Living*, North Thames Gas Board magazine, especially spring 1950, pp. 15–17; spring 1958, pp. 4–5.
30 C. Langhamer, 'The meaning of the home in post-war Britain', *Journal of Contemporary History*, 40(2), 2005, p. 347.
31 Burnett, *A Social History of Housing*, p. 282.
32 D. Kynaston, *Family Britain, 1951–1957*, London: Bloomsbury, 2009, p. 666.
33 Ibid.
34 Ibid., p. 506.
35 D.S. Wilson, 'A new look at the affluent worker: the good working mother in post-war Britain', *Twentieth Century British History*, 17(2), 2006, p. 209; S. Todd, 'Affluence, class and Crown Street: reinvestigating the post-war working class', *Contemporary British History*, 22(4), 2008, p. 506.
36 Todd, 'Affluence, class and Crown Street', p. 506.
37 Langhamer, 'Meaning of the home', p. 350.
38 P. Townsend, 'The meaning of poverty', *British Journal of Sociology*, 13(3), 1962, pp. 210–27.
39 This research was subsequently published as *Working Class Community: Some General Notions Raised by a Series of Studies in Northern England*, London: RKP, 1968.
40 Brian Jackson Archive, Qualidata, University of Essex, SN 4870, File C4.
41 Brian Jackson Archive, Qualidata, University of Essex, SN 4870, File C2.
42 Brian Jackson Archive, Qualidata, University of Essex, SN 4870, File C1.
43 Ibid.
44 Persil Advertising Review, TV, 1955–65, JWT/HAT, Box 160; Persil Care Presentation 2004/295 Box, Unilever Archives.
45 Persil Care Presentation 2004/295 Box, Unilever Archives.
46 Emphasis in original. Persil Creative Strategy, Second Draft, 1965, JWT/HAT, Box 160.
47 'A soap powder advertisement that is completely new', *Advertiser's Weekly*, 4 September 1959, p. 24.
48 *Sunday Times* business section, 2 August 1965, JWT/HAT, Box 160.
49 The titles of the Persil commercials were those used by the agency and did not appear on screen when they were broadcast.

50 The Independent Television Commission banned direct comparison from 1963 though the agency managed to smuggle it in through showing the w/ow comparison on the packet of Persil that featured in the adverts.
51 Persil Care Presentation, Unilever 2004/295 Box 3, n.d.
52 Ibid.
53 Other examples from the 'Mum' series were 'Woman Alone', March 1959; 'Shirley Wilson', April 1959; 'Margaret Sawyer', June 1959; 'Love Starts at Home', July 1959; 'Pyjamas', May 1960; 'Puppy', April 1960; 'Cards', April 1960; 'Hopscotch', May 1960; 'Caravan', March 1961. From November 1962 the adverts explicitly asked 'What is a Mum?' and answered it with 'A Mum is someone who chooses Persil.' JWT/HAT Lever/Persil, 1965, Box 12.
54 A. Ince, *London Life*, 7 May 1966, p. 26.
55 Horlicks' advertising explicitly depicted this social type. See also J. Winship, *Inside Women's Magazines*, London: Pandora, 1987.
56 M. Abrams, 'The home-centred society', *The Listener*, 26 November 1959, pp. 914–15; M. Young and P. Willmott, *Family and Class in a London Suburb*, London: RKP, 1960. Men did feature in bathrooms in commercials for toothpaste and shaving materials. CPV produced an innovative spot advert based on motivation research in 1958. It emphasized a young man, played by the actor Guy de Rochet, sensually stroking his face and narcissistically gazing in the mirror; *Commercial Television News*, 17 January 1958, p. 5.
57 *Advertiser's Weekly*, 18 Sptember 1959, pp. 54–6.
58 Ibid.; *Audio-visual Selling* gave the first Katie commercial a three-star review, suggesting it was a 'very pleasant, happy little spot'; *Audio-visual Selling*, 21 November 1958, p. 8.
59 Mary Holland became so strongly associated with the role that she eventually changed her name to Katie Holland.
60 'Why I Married You/Gravy', 1960; 'Why I Married Her', 1965, JWT/HAT, Tapes H10868, H119868, H106477.
61 See 'New Dish/Grocery Bill Savings', 1960, JWT/HAT, Tapes H10868, H119868, H106477.
62 'Ballet', 1963; 'Fancy Dress', 1966; 'Fog', 1967; 'Workmates', 1968, JWT/HAT, Tapes H10868, H119868, H106477.
63 A 'Gondola' line gravy boat made by Severin Design of Italy and available from Heals was used in one commercial; reply to letter from Mrs A.M. Advent, 26 May 1965, JWT/HAT, Box 203.
64 I am grateful to Frank Mort for alerting me to the significance of David.
65 L. Chaney, *Elizabeth David: A Biography*, London: Macmillan, 1998, p. 245.
66 E. David, *French Country Cooking*, London: John Lehmann, 1951.
67 Ibid., p. 23.
68 Chaney, *Elizabeth David*, pp. 227–9.
69 Ibid., p. 230.
70 Ibid., p. 271.
71 Persil – My Mum, memo from Josephine Mackay/Joe Houley to Mr Buckroyd, 29 July 1965, JWT/HAT, Box 158.

72 *Advertiser's Weekly*, 18 September 1959, pp. 54–6.
73 Friedan, cited in D. Horowitz, *Betty Friedan and the Making of the Feminine Mystique: The American Left, the Cold War and Modern Femininism*, Amherst: University of Massachusetts Press, 1998.
74 See Horowitz, *Betty Friedan and the Making of the Feminine Mystique*.

6

Welcome intrusion? Television advertising and the viewing public

I am a widow with three strapping sons. They each start the day with 'tingling freshness', their hair the envy of their pals. They have a 'square meal' breakfast plus a 'pinta' with it. They drive on petrol 'with a tiger in it', take packed lunches made of bread 'full of sunshine'. I am, meanwhile, 'whistling through the washing up' and at lunchtime I get cracking with my little mate the Lion … I do though [worry] how to make the housekeeping money stretch. It's a pity there isn't a commercial that can tell me![1]

This letter from Mrs B. featured in the *Daily Mirror*'s regular 'Live Letters' page, nestled amid its typical array of quirky daily trivia and ribald observation. Her letter was notable for the way it dramatized the presence in her life of television commercials, and their irritatingly catchy slogans. Although her comments revealed a certain enjoyment of the form of the television commercial and a desire to show off her knowledge of their communicative idioms to her fellow readers, they also betrayed an anxiety about the financial consequences of being drawn into the consumption of these advertised goods. Mrs B.'s contradictory response to TV commercials – at once drawn to them and anxious about their effects – signalled a more widely shared ambivalence among the viewing public. As such it offers us a way into considering how viewers responded to television advertising in the first decade and a half of its existence, the period from the inception of ITV in 1955 through to the first major reorganization of the service in 1968 and the introduction of colour transmissions in 1969. These developments ushered in a changed ITV network and new representational possibilities for advertisers, effectively bringing to a close ITV's and TV advertising's formative years.[2]

Exploring the reception of TV advertising in this period is important because the viewers of advertising have remained a nebulous and shadowy presence within critical accounts of post-war consumer society. Like other attempts to understand historical audiences and readers, the fact that viewers of TV commercials in the 1950s and 1960s have left few traces in the archives of their relationship to the new form of persuasion clearly presents a significant obstacle to any attempt to understand how they viewed commercials at the time. However, as Jonathan Rose has argued in relation to working-class readers through the nineteenth and twentieth centuries, it is possible to begin to piece together the intellectual and subjective responses of these historical actors. Against those pessimistic critics who have suggested that no evidence could exist of how ordinary people read or experienced their leisure, Rose draws on the example of scholars in 'book history' to tap the existing archival resources which open up the 'mystery' of the common reader. He finds them and their experiences in memoirs and diaries, school records, social surveys, oral history, library registers and letters written to newspapers.[3] Like earlier cultural studies of consumption, Rose is concerned to attend to working-class readers as engaged actors who 'absorb, interpret and respond' to cultural forms rather than as a mass audience who have things done to them by texts. For Rose, they were involved in a reading of their culture, at once intellectual and emotional, and were transformed by the experience (especially, for Rose, in their encounter with classic literature and fiction).[4]

This chapter, in seeking to draw out evidence of viewers' responses, focuses on two key sources. The first is surveys and qualitative studies undertaken by the advertising industry which recorded attitudes towards advertising, and TV advertising in particular. The second is letters written by viewers about the advertising that they watched. The letters are a particularly precious historical resource. Through them we can see how television and TV advertising communicated a sense of immediacy and eventfulness in the lives of those who watched it. It was this which stimulated them to write to advertisers about the commercials they had seen on television. Their written responses speak to a broader, but distinctive, historical experience of the new medium of television. For this first generation of post-war TV watchers – or 'TV lookers' as one of the women I cite later described the still new habit of watching television – TV's novelty and power to communicate directly and instantly was conjoined with an older culture of letter writing. Their epistles show how television became central to everyday life in the late 1950s and 1960s and how viewers were prompted by its vivid presence in their lives. It was this property of television in general, and TV advertising in particular, that engaged viewers and helped to embed television's commercial messages in the lives of the mass audience. The chapter explores this reception of commercials with particular reference to the adverts which have figured centrally in this book so far: those aimed at the mass-market housewife for products like washing powder and convenience foods. As we will see, viewers of these commercials were strongly engaged by the fantasies of modern life and femininity that they circulated. Their reactions allow us to explore the pull of these depictions of contemporary consumption.

Viewers' reactions to TV advertising did not occur in a vacuum but were shaped by other cultural forms. One of the most important was the popular press. Fleet Street's mass circulation dailies played an important role in mediating the reception of commercial television and TV advertising for their readers. With the habit of daily newspaper reading well established in the 1950s and 1960s and with the popular press commanding genuinely mass readerships, the reaction of the best-selling national dailies to ITV and TV commercials mattered. In this chapter, I focus on how the two biggest-selling popular papers, the *Daily Mirror* and the *Daily Express,* covered ITV and TV advertising. Both papers had a complex relationship to the new commercial TV service and to television advertising in particular. The growing popularity of television from the mid-1950s as a source of news, information and entertainment represented a substantial challenge to the popular appeal of newspapers. At the same time, the arrival of ITV and with it a new form of advertising threatened to take revenue away from the mass circulation daily press. The Beaverbrook Group, publishers of the *Daily Express*, were particularly hostile to ITV and denigrating of television advertising. The company issued a statement in *The Times* in November 1958 where it made this antipathy clear, suggesting that the '*Daily Express* and television are in different fields' and 'that commercial television is not a medium suited to the presentation of many important products'.[5] The *Daily Mirror* and the Mirror Group were much more positive about ITV and reacted to the competition that it posed by buying a financial stake in one of the ITV contractors.[6] However, both papers also, over time, helped to gently weave TV commercials into the fabric of national life. This was a process that they handled in different ways and in this chapter I consider the differences, as well as the similarities, in how the *Mirror* and the *Express* covered ITV and TV advertising. In doing so, I ask at what point and in what way did the commercials themselves become newsworthy? What did this newsworthiness tell us about the reception of television advertising?

Popular newspapers, television and TV advertising

The breaking of the BBC's broadcasting monopoly and the creation of ITV in 1954 was undoubtedly a watershed moment in post-war British life. The arrival of ITV gave new impetus to the establishment of television as a mass medium in Britain, helping to expand the take-up of the joint TV and radio licence and the acquisition, either through rental or hire-purchase, of a television set.[7] Held down by the austerity of the immediate post-war years and by the limited nature of the BBC's television service, ITV's arrival encouraged the 'roof top revolution' that saw aerials sprouting from homes in working-class neighbourhoods in increasing numbers from 1953 onwards.[8] By the early 1960s over 85% of the population had access to domestic sets. This compared to a figure of less than 1% in March 1948.[9] Television underwent a subtle process of domestication during these years as the mass of the population found a place for TV in their homes and their domestic routines. The cultures of viewing that developed revealed how television's entry into the home was often shaped by its position as a status symbol and marker of 'being modern'.[10] At the same time, viewers, especially middle-class families, were often initially concerned to control the uses of the new medium for fear of family life unravelling. As a 35-year-old laboratory technician worried,

> I believe that television makes family home life almost impossible. For 2–3 hours every evening the family must sit in darkness looking at the screen – mother cannot knit, father cannot read, the children skimp their homework and stay up late. No one can have a conversation, no letters get written, and friends calling are not welcomed since they break the sequence.[11]

Television, however, very quickly became embedded in the domestic routines of most households. In the process private life was itself subtly reorganized around the new rhythms of television viewing, with meal times and domestic chores fitted around the growing importance of 'watching the box'. At the same time, television became a topic of conversation at work and between family members. If it contributed to what the market researcher Mark Abrams saw as an increasingly 'home-centred society', television also extended the sense of belonging to a national community which radio had already helped to establish in the 1930s and 1940s, and the national daily popular press before that.[12]

As television viewing grew, ITV took an increasingly large share of the audience.[13] By the end of 1959 it could claim 70% of the viewers able to receive both BBC and ITV services. Registering this split in the audience share for the two channels, Richard Hoggart suggested that ITV felt, to many viewers, more like their channel, the people's channel: 'For Us and not Them', in Hoggart's characteristic formulation.[14] Not everyone, however, was enthusiastic about the new service. Not watching ITV became something of a point of principle for middle-class viewers and this antipathy could cut across political affiliations. The Labour party was home to many of ITV's sharpest critics.[15] Harold Wilson's self-confessed love of *Coronation Street* notwithstanding, it was the growing recognition of the fact that Labour voters constituted most of the ITV audience that begin to soften the party's views towards ITV through the 1960s, though many senior figures and rank and file members continued to resist the attractions of ITV.[16] In doing so they were joined by dissenting paternalistic Tories like Lord Hailsham in their concern about the moral dangers of ITV.[17]

This scrutiny of ITV was also evident in the popular press. The national morning popular press was at the zenith of its popularity in the 1950s and although circulations begin their long post-war decline from the mid-1950s, the habit of reading a popular daily paper was firmly established for the mass of the population. It contributed to the almost universal participation in the reading of newspapers, with over 85% of the population reading a newspaper every day.[18] The newspaper market was dominated by the mass circulation national dailies, with the *Daily Mirror* and the *Daily Express* leading the way and commanding 38% and 33% respectively of the readership of national daily papers. Their nearest rival for the popular newspaper reader was the *Daily Mail* with 18% of the market, while the upmarket *Times* and *Guardian*, in comparison, reached 2% and 1% respectively of newspaper buyers.[19] In terms of political affiliation, the *Mirror* and the *Express* staked out the mainstream political divide of the period, with the *Express* committed to the Conservative party and the *Mirror* a Labour-supporting paper.[20] Since the 1930s the *Express* had combined its allegiance to the Conservative party with a positive and optimistic view of the social changes associated with growing consumerism.[21] Through the 1950s and 1960s the *Express* celebrated the signs of popular affluence and the new opportunities for ordinary people to improve their lives that flowed from this.[22] A 'home-centred', consumer-orientated society fitted with the paper's individualistic view of social life and its conception of the social order as made up less of social classes so much as individuals and their families striving to better themselves.[23] The paper itself attracted large amounts of consumer advertising and its half-page display ads were an important shop window on the world of post-war consumption.

The *Mirror* was slower to respond to growing post-war affluence and struggled through the late 1950s to accommodate its model of class divisions and solidarities inherited from the war with the social changes being wrought by popular prosperity.[24] This did not stop its advertising manager promoting the paper in the advertising trade press as the best newspaper to reach the newly affluent working class. When the *Mirror*'s editorial pages did attempt to connect with affluence they did so, in the first instance, through young people. As A.C.H. Smith notes, after the 1955 election the paper ran a weekly 'Teen Page' and elsewhere articles on fashion, exotic food, new cars and other goods, leisure and investments 'witnessed the paper's acceptance of an unprecedentedly affluent society'.[25] By the mid-1960s the paper had fully embraced the positive benefits of growing prosperity.[26]

Television was an important symbol of post-war affluence and the ownership or rental of a television set was one of the consumerist markers of the time. The arrival of ITV coincided with the expansion of consumer spending from the mid-1950s. The responses and reactions of the *Mirror* and *Express* to television and especially ITV interestingly complicated the way both papers addressed the social changes associated with affluence. For a paper supportive since the 1930s of the social benefits of popular consumerism, the *Express* was strikingly hostile to ITV. On the opening night of the service, the paper's 'Opinion' column drew attention to the small number of TV sets that were able to receive ITV. Introducing a theme that it would return to regularly for the next decade and a half, the column also compared the costs of television advertising unfavourably with those of the press. Looking forward, it prophesied a bleak future for ITV, asserting that it was unlikely that 'advertisers will find commercial television an economic proposition … The standards [of ITV programmes] are bound to deteriorate rapidly by comparison with the BBC … The whole set up is futile in its present form.'[27] The paper also took great delight in the early financial difficulties of the ITV companies. This 'morning flop' was how it described ITV's 'staggering losses' three months into the new service and the paper repeatedly compared the 'downward slide' of ITV's programmes with those of the BBC.[28] When the ITV companies began to prosper and turn financial losses into profits, it was these profits and the monopoly advantages of ITV that the *Express* railed against. The paper referred to ITV as a 'tycoons' paradise' and called upon the government to recoup money from the ITV contractors in order to cut the television licence fee.[29]

The publication of the Pilkington Report on broadcasting in June 1962, which was critical of ITV, gave the *Express* further opportunities to attack commercial TV.[30] Under the headline 'The Guilt of Commercial TV', the *Express*'s 'Opinion' column underlined the paper's support for the findings of the report and, in particular, the concerns it had expressed about the excessive profits of the contractors and the triviality of much of ITV's output.[31] A longer feature article in the paper encouraged the Conservative government to use the Pilkington Report to make good the mistake it had made in introducing commercial television. As the paper put it, ITV was one of the 'seamier sides of what is known as the "affluent society". The swollen profits of commercial television [are] blatant examples of this.' The Tory party, it went on, should use the recommendations of the report to 'end this unhappy chapter in its history' by tackling the problem of ITV (and especially the monopoly) that it was seen to have created.[32] The article was accompanied by a cartoon by Cummings depicting Sir Harry Pilkington offering Prime Minister Harold Macmillan a chance to put the 'naughty genie' of ITV back in its bottle.[33]

Unlike the *Express*, the *Mirror* was an enthusiastic supporter of ITV. Whereas its rival had downplayed the launch of the new service, the *Mirror* heralded its arrival. Six days before the first ITV broadcasts, the paper alerted its readers to the 'show business bombshell' that was about to 'burst on the world of British entertainment'. Waxing lyrical, it claimed that

> In approach, speed and methods, the new programmes will make those of the BBC … look like a visual version of the Third Programme … the new material will burst on Britain's home screens with all the pent up excitement of a travelling funfair.[34]

On the day of ITV's launch in the London area, the *Mirror* offered warm salutations to the new service. 'Good luck ITV!' the *Mirror* proclaimed, adding, 'Good viewing to all our readers'.[35] The *Mirror*'s leading article continued the support for ITV at the end of its first week of broadcasting. Toasting ITV as a 'quickfire success', the leader claimed that 'its programmes have been entertaining and balanced. In general, the advertising has been expertly handled. The outlook for the viewer is bright.'[36] This enthusiastic support for ITV was turned into a commercial investment in the new service six months later. In April 1956 the *Mirror* told its readers that it was joining ITV. It did so by buying a stake in Associated Television, the contractor which held the London weekday franchise.[37] A little later the paper sought to promote ITV by sponsoring its own television awards show, broadcast on ITV. The show was based on a nationwide poll of *Mirror* readers and celebrated the best performers and shows on commercial television.[38]

This support for ITV found favour among the *Mirror*'s readers. In March 1957 one such reader, Mrs Mason from Nuneaton, set out at length her enthusiasm for commercial television. Against those critics who saw television – and especially ITV – as disrupting family life, Mrs Mason praised its capacity to draw the family together. As she suggested,

> you cannot overestimate ITV's role in home-making here in the Midlands. It has bought a sparkle to the fireside … Husbands stay at home with their wives now. And can you blame them when they have got 'Gun Law' on instead of a Hobson's Choice of sixty minutes of ballet … We see ITV as the gayer younger sister to BBC's more staid Aunt.[39]

Mrs Mason's praise for ITV ventriloquized the *Mirror*'s own desire to defend ITV against its detractors. When the Pilkington Report was published, the *Mirror* sought to protect ITV from the criticisms of the committee, in part by seeking to play down the significance of the report.[40] The *Mirror* also sought to embarrass the committee's chairman, Sir Harry Pilkington, on the day the House of Commons debated the report by publishing a large photo of his step-daughter, April Wilding, on its front page. April was about to make a 30-second television commercial, a fact the *Mirror* thought represented a certain contradiction in the Pilkington family's attitudes towards ITV.[41]

The *Mirror*'s depiction of April Wilding was notable not only as an effort to embarrass Sir Harry, but also for the way it fitted into the *Mirror*'s wider coverage of TV advertising through the coverage of the actresses and models that appeared in commercials. Prior to the launch of ITV, the *Mirror* had alerted its readers to 21-year-old Jean Clark, a London fashion model, whom they could expect to see in the months ahead in commercials on ITV. This approach continued in August 1956 when the paper ran a feature on 'Glamorous model Gina Egan', who acted in TV commercials.[42] The newsworthiness of the models in commercials was a persistent, recurring feature of the *Mirror*'s coverage of television advertising, especially through the 1960s. It included the paper's series on 'TV Lovelies' and culminated, in 1968, with the launch of the *Mirror*'s 'Telebird' feature. Many of the 'telebirds' were actresses/models whose faces were familiar from commercials.[43] This kind of coverage of commercials fitted into the *Mirror*'s well-established use of 'pin-ups' in the pages of the paper in the 1950s and 1960s. As Adrian Bingham has shown, the pin-up flourished in Fleet Street in these years, with the *Daily Mirror* leading the way. Pin-ups of pretty girls – be they film stars, bathing beauties, models or actresses in commercials – offered sexualized depictions of attractive young women that pushed at the boundaries of what was publicly acceptable in terms of depicting erotic imagery. The pin-ups offered a carefully coded representation of female sexuality which centred upon the display of cleavage and exposed legs. More explicit portrayals of full-frontal nudity or pubic hair were circumscribed.[44]

The depictions of the models and actresses who featured in TV commercials precisely followed these conventions of representation and were part of the visual, erotic titillation offered by the *Mirror* to its male readers.[45] There were, however, occasional exceptions to these depictions of the actresses in commercials. One notable instance of this occurred when the *Mirror* featured Mary Holland, the actress who played Katie in the Oxo commercials. Katie's modern but homely on-screen persona did not fit with the ideal of the glamorous model or actress and so, acknowledging this, the *Mirror* depicted her rather differently as a young mum at home. It was also undoubtedly the case that Katie's unique status as the most well-known and popular character in TV advertising affected her presentation in the paper. As the *Mirror* itself acknowledged, Mary was the most 'extraordinary "personality" that television has ever produced. The only actress who ever climbed to nationwide fame through a commercial.'[46]

As well as covering the young actresses who appeared in the commercials the *Mirror* was also enthusiastic about 'famous' TV animals who appeared in adverts. It reported on celebrity animals from commercials like Dash the Old English sheepdog, 'Big Louis' the great Dane, Jeremy the bear, Arthur the cat, the P.G. Tips chimps, Pedro the bloodhound and Sparkie Williams, the 'world's richest, most famous and most talkative budgie', who had become a star of commercials.[47] This recognition awarded to animals in adverts was sufficient to register in the *Mirror*'s regular comic strip, *The Perishers*, and even crossed over into its political cartoons.[48] For example, in October 1968, the Conservative party was depicted by Franklin as a cat forced to choose between two unpalatable varieties of cat food, Powellism and Heathism, in a play on the television advertising of branded cat food.[49] For the *Mirror*, then, whether in political cartoons, comic strips or its coverage of the actresses and animals who appeared in ads, TV commercials formed an increasingly taken for granted element in the entertaining and newsworthy material that it offered its readers. In this regard, it fully embraced television commercials and the broader culture of commercial television.

The *Express* was very slow to cover television at all as a subject of critical discussion, let alone TV advertising. When the paper did periodically review television programmes, it was generally highly critical, especially of ITV.[50] A review of Granada TV's three-hour broadcast of Tolstoy's *War and Peace* was preoccupied by the distracting nature of the commercial breaks in the programme. As the paper's reviewer put it,

> I had deluded myself into believing that on this occasion there would be no commercials. More fool me. They flowed as fast as ever, their distracting jingles interrupting the flow and completely nullifying what could have been Granada's finest hour. Tolstoy and toilet tissues, Napoleon and nappies, Alexander, Emperor of all Rome and cake mix are impossible table companions.[51]

Despite this hostility to ITV and television commercials, the *Express* did begin to briefly cover television ads, particularly from 1962 onwards when the ITV network had effectively achieved national coverage. Like the *Mirror*, one form this took was light-hearted interest in the animals that featured in commercials.[52] The human stars of adverts also began to appear more regularly in the *Express* in the mid-1960s. The paper ran a photo-news spread on the boxer Billy Walker, notable for bringing 'glamour' to the world of boxing by appearing in TV adverts for hair cream and beer.[53] The female models in commercials were also considered newsworthy by the paper. Like the *Mirror*, attention to the 'pretty girls' who appeared in commercials was one of the recurring ways in which the *Express* covered television advertisements.[54] Thus, a story on Jutta Peusch, a roulette croupier, pictured her in a bikini and made much of the fact that she would be more familiar to readers from her appearances in commercials.[55] The *Express*'s coverage of these models was often linked to the paper's gossip and society page edited by William Hickey.[56] Hickey was an *Express* institution and brought titillating coverage of high society to the paper's largely suburban readers. In his regular column he introduced his readers to, among others, society debutantes and the daughters of the aristocracy. There was sometimes a connection between high society and the world of advertising as these young women were either involved in modelling in TV commercials or were considering working in advertising. Thus, Hickey's page introduced Gina Warwick, a former debutante, who had been advertising crisps on television.[57] She was picture in a low-cut black dress that revealed her cleavage and her neatly folded bare legs. Hickey also ran a feature on the 'pretty daughters' of the Ambassador to Paris. One of the daughters, Jane, confessed that she was 'looking for something in advertising'.[58]

This interest in the links between the world of commercials and 'society girls' was counterbalanced on Hickey's page by his concern to remind *Express* readers of the enduring power and style of press advertising. Toeing the paper's party line, a large part of the William Hickey page on 24 September 1965 was devoted to a gushing review of a press advert for an airline featuring Marlene Dietrich. For Hickey, Dietrich was a 'symbol of every gorgeous, haughty, feminine extravagance imaginable'.[59] In February 1967 Hickey sang the praises of the whole-page adverts for H.J. Heinz that had appeared in the *Express* that week. As Hickey told his readers,

> the lesson the advertising hammers home is that no other form of advertising whatever matches the power of the newspaper advertisement when the customer's attention is needed for more than a fleeting glance; when a challenging story has to be told; cogent facts presented in a manner most likely to linger in the mind.[60]

If the *Express*'s coverage of TV commercials was muted by its general hostility to ITV and its concern to promote the greater power of press advertising, from the early 1960s it had begin to register the newsworthiness of TV ads. The paper's framing of their newsworthiness in terms of attractive young women and funny animals echoed the coverage of television advertising given in the *Mirror*, though it made much less aggressive use of pin-ups. How, though, did the readers of these papers and the wider viewing public react to TV advertising? What was the reception of commercials among the public at large?

Viewers' attitudes to television advertising

Between 1961 and 1969 the advertising industry, under the auspices of the IPA, conducted a number of extensive surveys of public attitudes towards advertising. The British Market Research Bureau was responsible for many of these and combined social surveys with small group discussions of television commercials. Together with studies done by individual agencies, this body of research offered some suggestive insights into popular attitudes towards TV advertising through the 1960s. BMRB's first survey was conducted between September and October 1961 and began with the simple question: 'Do you approve or disapprove of advertising? A little or a lot?'[61] Eighty-four per cent of respondents stated that they approved of advertising and the approval rating for advertising remained between 70% and 80% in the subsequent BMRB surveys through the 1960s. In passing this judgement on advertising it was clear that, by 1961, the public associated advertising almost exclusively with TV commercials. Thus, over two-thirds of respondents said that they saw most advertising on TV. When asked to give an example of an advert that they could remember, nearly half gave an example of a TV commercial, with only a quarter citing a poster advert and just over 10% a press or magazine advert.[62]

BMRB's research in both 1961 and 1966 pressed further on the different attitudes held by the public towards press and TV advertising. This revealed a downside to the greater visibility of TV advertising. Here the public, by a significant margin, claimed to prefer press advertising to TV advertising, with nearly two-thirds of the 1961 sample finding press advertising more 'useful', compared to just under half for TV.[63] Tellingly, however, the same survey revealed that the majority found TV advertising more entertaining.[64] The entertainment value of TV adverts was significant. Viewers revealed their preference for them even as they often simultaneously felt that advertising should be informative rather than entertaining.[65] This contradiction was confirmed by a later study. It revealed that while viewers felt that newspaper adverts were 'educational' and 'informative', they saw TV adverts as the most entertaining.[66] If television adverts were more entertaining, however, their intrusive nature could also provoke a critical reaction. Many viewers felt that the adverts 'interrupt programmes and spoil programme continuity'.[67] This theme was persistent across the surveys. As a commentary by the BMRB authors on the 1966 survey noted, for some viewers of TV advertising 'there is too much of it, it is repetitive and spoils TV'.[68]

The surveys also revealed that there were class differences in viewers' attitudes and feelings towards commercials. The 1966 survey showed that dislike of TV advertising rose as one went up the social scale, with AB (upper middle-class) viewers less enthusiastic about commercials than DE (working-class) viewers.[69] Corroboration of some of these views surfaced in the small-scale qualitative studies produced by BMRB and JWT. BMRB's study from June 1966 was based upon group discussions with 13 married couples living in London. In the discussions the middle-class couples expressed strong dislike of TV advertising and instinctively felt critical of all advertising. The working-class couples, on the other hand, accepted advertising's place on television. They did, however, dislike advertising featuring presenters whom they felt talked down to them or with whom they could not identify. This was a significant reaction given the central role played by on-screen presenters in some forms of TV advertising. Conversely, the middle-class couples liked presenters, especially if they were either honest or outspoken or regarded as experts in their fields.[70] These same middle-class viewers expressed a strong dislike of advertising jingles – they thought them 'loud' and 'trivial' – while the working-class couples saw them as an acceptable part of advertising.[71]

Not all the opinions expressed in the study diverged along class lines. The interruptive nature of TV adverts caused general disapproval and the interruption was felt to be worse the better the programme being watched.[72] The repetition of advertising and the recurrence of advertising for similar products in the same evening stirred the displeasure of all the couples, especially if the adverts were for washing powder.[73] There was also a recurring claim, expressed most strongly by the middle-class couples, of a preference for informative and straightforward adverts that used techniques like product demonstration. Conversely, commercials that relied on 'mood' or 'fantasy' were most strongly criticized.[74] As the BMRB authors suggestively argued, such claims needed to be treated with caution. The group discussion setting and wider social pressures meant respondents were keen to find rational reasons for liking certain kinds of adverts, as its earlier survey had also suggested. At the same time, even middle-class viewers were as likely as working-class viewers to talk about humorous or entertaining elements in adverts when asked to describe specific commercials that they liked.[75]

If humour and entertainment represented important ways in which viewers were drawn into an engagement with TV commercials, then identification with the social types portrayed in them and with their depictions of everyday life was also important. A piece of qualitative research undertaken by JWT for Persil washing powder in 1966 focused upon the reactions of a small group of nine respectable working-class housewives (C class, aged 20–50). The women were asked to reflect on their feelings towards the children and mothers depicted in commercials. The discussion revealed the strong identification these women had with the maternal role depicted in the adverts and with the attributes of motherly sentiment and sentimentality. The women expressed these feelings through what they said about enjoying the portrayals of children which showed them as high-spirited, spontaneous and natural – as getting into all kinds of mischief, without being really troublesome or delinquent. Portrayals of this kind seemed to chime with these women's ideas of normal child development and expressiveness and to place them – the maternal figure – as a reassuring presence in the adverts; there to bring solace and comfort to a child that needed love and protection. Depictions of children with frailties or imperfections seemed to particularly invite these sentiments. 'I like a child with a gap in its teeth – it's appealing.' 'The Milky Bar kid with glasses – I love the Milky Bar kid.' 'Or a boy with a great big gash over his face [who] has just fallen down.' 'A boy with blood running down his leg or with a plaster on it … far more natural than a boy with his socks pulled up.'[76]

The depiction of mother–child relationships in commercials that drew out these responses from the working-class women represented a powerful affirmation of the ideal of maternal femininity that washing powder adverts repeatedly asserted through the 1950s and 1960s. As we saw earlier, however, these depictions of housewife-mothers were challenged by the adverts that JWT produced for Oxo. The popularity of the character of Katie in the series was evident in correspondence that Oxo received from viewers concerning the commercials. The company passed these letters on to its advertising agency to respond to. Thus, in the files of the agency, there is an intriguing collection of 35 letters that have survived. They date from April–December 1965, with the vast majority being written between October and December. The letters are from ordinary viewers (with one exception) and represent their reactions to the Oxo commercials. Of the 35 letters, four were from men, one was from two single women and the remaining 30 were from married women. The gender composition tells us much about who the adverts were targeted at, as well as perhaps something about the gendering of letter writing in most households. The writers lived in all corners of mainland Britain: from Perthshire, Liverpool, Rochdale, Co. Durham, Oldham through the Midlands (Birmingham and Walsall) to the Home Counties and eastern England (Southampton, Guilford, Bournemouth, Woodingdean).

The writing style, expression and vocabulary of the correspondents, together with the material form of the communication, gave insights into their educational and class backgrounds. A couple of the letters were typed, though the majority were handwritten. A few used headed notepaper. The most formal came from a male Health Officer, writing in a quasi-professional capacity, and offered an elegantly composed and concisely expressed set of observations about the adverts. A significant minority of the other notes and letters could also have come from the 'letter-writing classes'. Thus, Mrs B. Jeavers, of Erith in Kent, not only used headed notepaper, but deployed both a formal mode of address and a confident writing style: 'Dear Sir, I am a regular user of Oxo cubes and have also watched with interest the TV ads "Life with Katie".' Another writer, Mrs G. Neal of Warwickshire, was equally formal and proficient in her writing, beginning 'I am aware that this is small matter, but one I find really irksome.' She also revealed her (respectable) class position when she referred in her letter to 'Katie's daily' – that is, her 'daily domestic helper' – making the gravy in the ad.[77]

The majority of the letters, however, were more hastily thrown together and paid little attention to formal punctuation or syntax. They were urgent, impromptu responses to watching the adverts, and often deployed the vivid present tense in their descriptions. They might also sign off the letter with a blunt, direct expression of their feelings about Oxo or the advert. Sometimes they ended with an injunction to Oxo to improve the ads. As such, these letters revealed much about the subaltern class position of their authors. Thus, an anonymous female 'TV looker' from Birmingham opened with a paragraph-long sentence, using commas instead of full stops to signal a change in the direction of the narrative in a breathless and vivid recapitulation of the advert. Mrs K. McCulloch of Glasgow also wrote a short note that consisted of a single paragraph without punctuation. Mrs McDonald offered a direct and unstructured opinion that showed that little thought had gone into the composition of the letter, though its substantive content was evidently heartfelt. Some of these women also sent their thoughts on scrappy postcards or tiny cheap sheets of paper. The material form of the letter shed further light on their senders' households – these were homes without the letter-writing paraphernalia of more socially secure families.

Cutting across the different correspondents were some common concerns. Of the 35 letters, 17 concerned the issue of hygiene. In fact, one particular advert stirred a strong response from these viewers. In the advert, as the majority of writers took trouble to reconstruct, Katie returned from shopping and, having put down her shopping bag, crumbled an Oxo cube into a jug of water without first washing her hands. This act of poor domestic hygiene prompted indignant responses. Mrs Jeavers complained: 'What good housewife would come in after a morning's shopping and crumble an Oxo cube to make gravy without washing her hands first? Urgh! Need I say more!'[78] Mrs Hannen signed off her letter of complaint, 'yours hygienically', while Mrs King was affronted by the way the poor hygiene of Katie undercut her other positive attributes: 'Katie is a very well groomed girl and she has a lovely home, but her cooking hygiene is not good.'[79]

This attention to domestic hygiene revealed something not only about the contemporary public discourse on hygiene, but also the highly respectable impulses of these viewers. It fitted with the general appeal of Katie's 'niceness', her well-groomed appearance and the aspirational dimensions of her lifestyle. Mrs King made the connection explicitly between Katie's well-groomed looks and her 'lovely home' and standards of domestic living. Mrs Hollis worried that another commercial showed Katie frying onions while dressed to go out. 'She will smell pretty dreadful', she suggested. Katie's status as the exemplar of a well-groomed, attractive young wife sometimes meant that viewers directly sought to emulate her lifestyle. Thus, three letters enquired about the gravy boat used by Katie in the ads and other viewers asked for copies of the recipe for the meal she was cooking.[80] Another viewer worried that Katie's standard of spoken English was slipping and wrote to suggest that the makers of the adverts correct her use of the phrase 'more subtler flavour' – though, in fact, as the agency pointed out, Katie had in fact used the phrase 'more succulent'.[81]

The status of Katie was also capable of attracting more obsessive and perverse interest. Thus, E. Lester from Oldham made the following request:

> Dear Katie, you are a very beautiful girl, would you please send me a photograph of yourself and if possible a pair of your cast off false eyelashes, I quote eyelashes because they can be easily posted. Your husband? makes his food look so very good, and I have become an Oxo <u>addict</u> myself, by you and Philip's persuasion. And would you please tell me whether you are an actress or whether you are just on the adverts. P.S. Good luck to you, Philip and the baby, although it may not be yours.[82]

The letter, unusual though it was, did reveal the investment viewers could have in the emotional life of the adverts. This was an investment that partly stemmed from the long-running nature of the campaign. Mrs Jeavers confessed to being someone who had 'watched with interest the TV ads "Life with Katie"', while Mrs Rafferty revealed that she 'liked to watch Katy and Philip'.[83] Some viewers complained when Katie and Philip did not appear in the adverts. Thus, Mrs Collison lamented their absence from a commercial in December 1965:

> What has happened to Katie and Philip? My family and I have decided that your present advert on TV does not do your product justice. Previous advertisements with Katie and Philip were in our opinion the best on TV. Even my 6 year old son stopped his play to watch, Philip seemed to be thriving on Katie's cooking with Oxo, and Katie well, she's a love … We miss Katie and Philip, so please can we have more of their adventures?[84]

Mrs Grady was also irritated by Katie and Philip's absence and threatened to boycott Oxo if they were not reinstated: 'If you do not put her and her hubby's voices on the screen again I'll discontinue my order and go for synthetic flavoured soup powder which are also quite tasty … Katie makes home look so alluring people who don't care for Oxo are very tempted to give it a try.'[85]

Evidently, for many of these correspondents, Katie and Philip were real presences in their lives, knowable in the same way that real people were knowable.[86] Staff at JWT who replied to these viewers' letters were complicit in this sense of Katie as a real, knowable person. Their replies identified Katie as a character with an ongoing existence beyond the adverts.[87] The pull of Katie and the serial nature of these long-running Oxo adverts invites a comparison with the form of television soap opera and its intense paralleling of the rhythms of real life.[88] Viewers, however, could also distance themselves from the drama, even as they continued to invest in the narratives. In doing so, they revealed a familiarity with the codes and conventions of TV commercials. Thus, two young nannies wrote to Oxo with an idea for a new commercial. Discussing their lack of success at securing boyfriends, the pair revealed that they eventually decided to follow Katie's lead and use Oxo in their cooking. 'And by golly it worked! Oxo does give a meal man-appeal ... Maybe you could use the idea for a new advert for Oxo.'[89] They went on to describe an advertising scenario: 'Two girls always sitting and waiting for the telephone to ring after giving two dinner parties, both thinking of Oxo at the same time! A third dinner party with Oxo (of course) brings results – wedding bells!'

Their letter revealed the extent to which by the mid-1960s viewers were familiar with the conventions of TV adverts and could play the role of advertising copywriter. Even as they did so, these correspondents shared with other viewers who took the trouble to write to Oxo an enormous investment in the sagas of Katie and Philip.

Conclusion

The character of Katie, as the *Mirror* acknowledged in its profile of the actress who played her, was uniquely well known and was able to draw out particularly strong subjective responses from the viewers – particularly the married women – who watched the commercials. Given this it would be wrong to see the reactions that she generated as necessarily typical of how viewers responded to and felt about the majority of commercials. Nonetheless, the pull of the character and the 'slice of life' drama in which she appeared was echoed in the investment which viewers made in the entertaining quality of other TV adverts. Certainly, the surveys and studies produced by the advertising industry showed how television advertising had become effectively synonymous with advertising *tout court* by the early 1960s, partly through its power to engage viewers in the stories that it told and the compelling diversion that it offered. The pull of TV advertising, however, could also work against the advertiser. As a form of persuasion, spot adverts were much more intrusive and interruptive than press and magazine advertising. They literally came into the living room and intruded upon not only the programmes broadcast on ITV, but also the private domestic space of viewers. The use of sound and moving images in TV advertising made this intrusion into the home more direct and immediate than was the case with print-based advertising – though these also, but with less immediacy, brought the outside world into the home. The way that commercials interrupted programmes could thus stir a more negative reaction from viewers. When they were felt to do this – especially when the programme they interrupted was enjoyable and engrossing – viewers switched from being well disposed towards adverts and became hostile to them. In this regard, viewers could vacillate between being drawn towards advertising and enjoying it as entertainment and disliking the way it spoiled their television viewing. Certain genres of advertising, like the use of on-screen presenters and loud jingles, could provoke the dislike of different sections of the viewing public, though middle-class viewers were often the most publicly critical of all commercials.

The coverage of television advertising in the popular press might not have helped to soften these antagonisms, but it did work to legitimate the cultural presence of TV adverts through the way they were woven into the fabric of the papers as newsworthy objects. There were importance differences, as I noted, in how the two biggest-selling papers covered TV commercials. The *Daily Express* was much less enthusiastic than the *Mirror* about all of the output of commercial television and its hostility may have confirmed the views of its more respectable readers about the horrors of ITV, including its advertising. By the early 1960s, however, even the *Express* was forced to register the newsworthiness of TV ads. It did so, as we saw, through the coverage of the 'pretty girls' who appeared in the commercials. The *Mirror* took this style of coverage further and largely absorbed the reporting of commercials into its extensive use of the 'pin-up'. They became part of the titillation that it offered its male readers.

If the pin-up was one form of public fantasy within which commercials were inscribed, more important was the way the commercials themselves circulated a powerful fantasy of 'ordinary femininity'.[90] The working-class women interviewed by JWT about the Persil commercials revealed a clear desire to identify with the maternal role depicted in the advertisements. It was the detailed letters about Katie and the Oxo sagas, however, which were most revealing of how married women (mainly) felt about the depiction of femininity and modern living in the adverts. The letters showed the appeal of the fictional lives of Katie and her family. For many of the women who wrote to Oxo, these figures were a real and tangible presence in their lives. The adverts – and Katie in particular – also allowed them to disclose their desires for the life which Katie had and their identification with her. Much of the pull of the commercials came from Mary Holland's compelling performance, especially her ability to combine vulnerability and assertiveness. But it was also her well-groomed appearance, her 'niceness' and the way she handled the role of being housewife in a way that was both highly contemporary and yet not disruptive of gender divisions or norms of femininity which clearly spoke to the aspirations of the viewers and their views of the gendered dynamics of domestic life. We might also see in their reactions to Katie a confirmation of her English-Britishness. None of the women who wrote to Oxo refer to Katie's ethnicity, but they assume that she is (a bit) like them in the way they talk about her and her life. Certainly, the descriptions of her as 'well-groomed', as a 'love' and as having a 'lovely home' deploy the idioms of English-British civility and ideas of the English in particular as essentially a 'nice', 'decent', 'orderly' and 'essentially private' people.[91] In the same way, the women who were interviewed about the Persil commercials were drawn to their idealized, but recognizable, depictions of suburban British family life. These were suburbs where the front gardens and pavements were orderly, tidy and where private life was securely sequestered behind the garden gate and the front door.

Notes

1 Letter from Mrs B., *Daily Mirror*, 14 June 1962, p. 25.
2 New ITV franchises were awarded in 1968. Some of the contractors who had made up the early ITV network lost out in this reorganization. The most notable casualty was Associated-Rediffussion, the holder of the London weekday franchise and the contractor which had launched the ITV service in London in 1955. Colour broadcasting began on ITV in 1969, following the early lead taken by BBC2 where colour had been pioneered in 1967. BBC1 begin colour transmissions from 1970.
3 J. Rose, *The Intellectual Life of the British Working Class*, New Haven and London: Yale University Press, 2002, p. 1.
4 Rose, *Intellectual Life of the British Working Class*, p. 3. See also M. Houlbrook, 'A pin to see the peepshow: culture, fiction and self-hood in Edith Thompson's letters 1921–2', *Past and Present*, 207(1), 2010, pp. 215–49.
5 'The press and television', *The Times*, 25 November 1958, p. 7.
6 The Mirror Group bought shares in ATV in 1956.
7 Sandbrook suggests that by 1956 half of all televisions were bought on hire-purchase. Of course, many viewers would have rented rather than bought their televisions. D. Sandbrook, *Never Had It So Good: A History of Britain from Suez to the Beatles*, London: Little, Brown, 2005, p. 384.
8 Between 1946 and 1964 there were two TV channels – channel 1 (BBC) and channel 9 (ITV). They were joined by BBC2 in 1964. John Hartley's claim that without the spread of domestic fridges television would not have been possible is not borne out by the facts in Britain. The spread of television was earlier and quicker than that of the fridge. J. Hartley, *The Uses of Television*, London: Routledge and Kegan Paul, 1999, chapter 8.
9 T. O'Sullivan, 'Researching the viewing culture: television in the home, 1946–60', in H. Wheatley (ed.), *Re-viewing Television History: Critical Issues in Television Historiography*, London: IB Tauris, 2007, p. 162.
10 See T. O'Sullivan, 'Television memories and cultures of viewing, 1950–65', in J. Corner (ed.), *Popular Television in Britain*, London: British Film Institute, 1991,

pp. 158–81; O'Sullivan, 'Researching the viewing culture', especially p. 162; Mass Observation Panel on Television, Report no. 3106, April 1949, p. 11, Mass Observation Archives, University of Sussex.
11 Mass Observation Panel on Television, Report no. 3106, April 1949, pp. 27–8.
12 M. Abrams, 'The home-centred society', *The Listener*, 26 November 1959, pp. 914–15; O'Sullivan, 'Television memories and cultures of viewing'; O'Sullivan, 'Researching the viewing culture'; P. Scannell, *Radio, Television and Modern Life*, Oxford: Blackwell, 1996; R. Turnock, *Television and Consumer Culture*, London: IB Tauris, 2007; C. Johnson and R. Turnock (eds), *ITV Cultures: Independent Television over Fifty Years*, Maidenhead: Open University Press, 2005; J. Thumin, *Inventing Television Culture: Men, Women and the Box*, Oxford: Oxford University Press, 2004.
13 For a more sceptical view of ITV's contribution to the rise in television viewing, see Turnock, *Television and Consumer Culture*, pp. 26–9.
14 R. Hoggart, 'BBC and ITV after three years', *New Left Review*, 1958, 5, pp. 32–6.
15 L. Black, *The Political Culture of the Left in Affluent Britain, 1951–64*, Basingstoke: Palgrave Macmillan, 2003.
16 Wilson relaxed by reading thrillers and watching television. His favourite programme was *Coronation Street*: 'The people in it seem to be real', he told the *Daily Express* in November 1962, cited in B. Pimlott, *Harold Wilson*, London: Harper Collins, 1992, p. 267.
17 L. Black, *Redefining British Politics: Culture, Consumerism and Participation, 1954–70*, Basingstoke, Palgrave Macmillan, 2010; Black, *Political Culture of the Left in Affluent Britain*; M. Jarvis, *Conservative Governments, Morality and Social Change in Affluent Britain, 1957–64*, Manchester: Manchester University Press, 2005.
18 A. Bingham, *Family Newspapers? Sex, Private Life and the British Popular Press, 1918–78*, Oxford: Oxford University Press, 2009, p. 16.
19 M. Abrams, *The Newspaper Reading Public of Tomorrow*, London: Odhams, 1964, p. 63. The *Daily Mirror* had overtaken the *Daily Express* as the most popular daily paper in 1949 and for younger readers the *Mirror* was easily the most widely read paper, reaching almost half of those aged between 16 and 44 and with a strong representation among young married couples. The *Express*, on the other hand, was significantly more popular among older readers, though it did also successfully attract readers from all social classes. The *Mirror* scored highly amongst the mass working-class market. A.C.H. Smith, *Paper Voices: The Popular Press and Social Change, 1935–65*, London: Chatto & Windus, 1975, p. 12.
20 The *Mirror*'s conversion to the Labour cause only dated back to the mid-1930s. It had started as a Conservative-inclined women's paper under the proprietorship of Alfred Harmsworth, owner of the *Daily Mail*. The *Mirror* was relaunched in 1935, going downmarket and becoming left-leaning. The style of the paper was dramatically changed. Two popular American papers, the *New York Daily Mirror* and the *New York Daily News*, were an important influence on the new-look *Mirror* and it was from these papers that the new *Mirror* took one if its new features, strip cartoons. The London office of JWT was instrumental in this transformation of the *Daily Mirror*, acting as a consultant on the redesign. See Bingham, *Family*

Newspapers?, p. 21; R. McKibbin, *Classes and Culture: England 1918–51*, Oxford: Oxford University Press, 1998, p. 506.
21 Quoted in Smith, *Paper Voices*, p. 158.
22 Ibid., p. 163.
23 Ibid., p. 167.
24 Ibid., p. 150.
25 Ibid.
26 Ibid., pp. 150, 180.
27 *Daily Express*, 22 September 1955, p. 4; see also *Daily Express*, 25 September 1955, p. 2.
28 *Daily Express*, 2 December 1955, p. 1; 3 December 1955, p. 4.
29 *Daily Express*, 8 December 1959, p. 8; 4 May 1962, p. 10.
30 *Daily Express*, 28 June 1962, p. 5.
31 *Daily Express*, 28 June 1962, p. 6.
32 *Daily Express*, 29 June 1962, p. 6.
33 *Daily Express*, 28 June 1962, p. 6; 8 September 1962, p. 6. The paper also published extracts from H.H. Wilson's critical study of the launching of ITV, *Pressure Group*. See 17 May, 1962, pp. 11–12.
34 *Daily Mirror*, 16 September 1955, p. 9.
35 *Daily Mirror*, 22 September 1955, p. 4.
36 *Daily Mirror*, 29 September 1955, p. 2.
37 *Daily Mirror*, 21 April, 1956, p. 2.
38 *Daily Mirror*, 28 July, 1962, p. 7.
39 'This housewife says – I really do love Lucy & Co.', *Daily Mirror*, 1 March 1957, p. 9.
40 *Daily Mirror*, 23 June 1962, p. 9; 28 June 1962, pp. 14–15.
41 *Daily Mirror*, 18 July 1962, p. 1.
42 *Daily Mirror*, 23 August, 1956, p. 7.
43 See, inter alia, *Daily Mirror*, 13 October 1965, p. 4; 30 October 1965, p. 11; 7 January 1965, p. 21; 16 April 1968, p. 4; 12 December 1968, p. 7; 5 January 1969, p. 9.
44 Bingham, *Family Newspapers?*, p. 203.
45 See also F. Mort, 'The Ben Pimlott Memorial Lecture 2010: the permissive society revisited', *Twentieth Century British History*, 22(2), 2011, pp. 277–8.
46 *Daily Mirror*, 13 February 1962, p. 11. She later featured in the *Sunday Times* magazine: 'Beautiful Katie – is it the girl or the gravy that gives a meal man appeal', *Sunday Times*, 15 January 1968, p. 12.
47 *Daily Mirror*, 5 December 1962, p. 3; 6 February 1965, p. 19; 31 August 1966, p. 5; 18 February 1967, p. 11; 15 February 1968, p. 9; 14 November 1968, p. 17.
48 *Daily Mirror*, 5 August 1964, p. 10.
49 *Daily Mirror*, 11 October 1968, p. 19.
50 *Daily Express*, 19 August 1959, p. 6.
51 *Daily Express*, 27 March 1963, p. 4.
52 *Daily Express*, 5 December 1962, p. 15; 6 December 1962, p. 12; 26 February, 1968, p. 7; 24 February 1967, p. 9.

53 *Daily Express*, 30 March 1965, p. 5.
54 *Daily Express*, 24 August, 1962, p. 1.
55 *Daily Express,* 27 August, 1962, p. 2.
56 On Hickey, see Smith, *Paper Voices*, p. 155.
57 *Daily Express*, 1 May 1956, p. 3.
58 *Daily Express*, 28 April, 1965, p. 3.
59 *Daily Express*, 24 September 1965, p. 3.
60 *Daily Express*, 2 February 1967, p. 3; see also 30 March 1968, p. 3.
61 IPA, *As Others See Us – a study of attitudes to advertising and to television advertising*, IPA Occasional Paper, 17, 1966, p. 1.
62 Ibid., p. 9.
63 This view of press advertising as helpful and informative was expressed in the late 1930s in a study on 'Reactions to Advertising' undertaken by Mass Observation, 1938, pp. 28–9, Box 1/A, Mass Observation Archives, University of Sussex.
64 IPA, *As Others See Us*, p. 10.
65 J. Treasure, 'Advertising and the public', IPA Conference, November 1969, p. 5, HAT/JWT, Box 25.
66 The Mass Observation study 'Reactions to Advertising' presented views that also saw press advertising as educating people, especially the working classes, on manners, cleanliness, neatness and 'keeping the bowels open', pp. 20–1.
67 IPA, *As Others See Us*, p. 10.
68 Ibid.
69 Ibid., p. 14.
70 Ibid., pp. 4–5.
71 In group discussions on television conducted by the journalist and anthropologist Geoffrey Gorer in 1957, two of the working-class mothers commented that their children liked the commercials, with the wife of a sheet metal worker revealing that 'My little son likes to sing "Omo means brightness"'. G. Gorer, group discussion, television, 21 August 1957, Geoffrey Gorer papers, Box 3/B, Ms52/1/7/3/5/2, University of Sussex.
72 'Attitudes to Advertising – Pilot, Report on Group discussions, June 1966', p. 3, BMRB/BGL/28103, JWT/HAT.
73 Ibid.
74 This echoed concern expressed by a number of the members of the Pilkington committee.
75 'Attitudes to Advertising – Pilot, Report on Group discussions, June 1966', p. 5, BMRB/BGL/28103, JWT/HAT.
76 Ibid., p. 7.
77 Letters from William T. Murphy, 28 October 1965; Mrs G. Neal, 5 December 1965; Mrs B. Jeavers, 5 December 1965, JWT/HAT, Box 203.
78 Letter from Mrs B. Jeavers, 5 December 1965. See also letter from Mrs G. Neal, 5 December 1965, JWT/HAT, Box 203.
79 Letter from Mrs L. King, 6 November 1965.
80 Letters from Mrs C. Harrison, 26 April 1965; Mrs A. Advent, 26 May 1965; Mrs V. Leighton-Young, 22 March 1965.

81 Reply to letter from Mrs D. Lucas, 25 March 1965.
82 On the erotics of advertising, see a letter from Mrs J. Moore to Persil asking for information on the male voice-over artist on their commercials. She felt 'his voice is so soft and gentle … I just sit enthralled when I hear that voice'. Letter from Mrs J. Moore, 17 February 1966, JWT/HAT, Persil 1966, Box 319.
83 Letters from Mrs G. Neal, 5 December 1965; Mrs Rafferty, 25 November 1965.
84 Letter from Mrs I. Collison, 1 December 1965.
85 Letter from Mrs M. McGrady, 16 December 1965.
86 The phrase is adapted from Paddy Scannell on soap operas. See Scannell, *Radio, Television and Modern Life*, p. 158.
87 See reply to E. Lester from M. Batchelor, 3 June 1965: 'Katie has asked me to send you a photograph of herself. P.S. Katie – being a woman – is not prepared to divulge whether she wears false eyelashes or not.'
88 Scannell, *Radio, Television and Modern Life*, p. 103.
89 Letter from Misses G. Sill and S. Burdenuik, 14 February 1966.
90 Charlotte Brunsdon, *The Feminist, the Housewife and the Soap Opera*, Oxford: Clarendon Press, 2000, introduction.
91 A. Light, *Forever England: Femininity, Conservatism and Literature between the Wars*, London: Routledge, 1991, p. 11.

7

'Trading on human weakness': advertising, morality and consumer desire

At the Advertising Association's conference held at Eastbourne in May 1953, delegates were treated to a speech on 'The Place of Consumer Choice in a Socialist Economy' by Aneurin Bevan, the former minister for Health and Housing and darling of the Labour left. It was a speech which left the majority of the delegates feeling angry and frustrated.[1] With characteristic melodrama, Bevan attacked advertising as 'one of the most evil consequences of a society which is, itself, intrinsically evil' and 'sponsored television', then being actively discussed, as its most insidious form.[2] Challenging the views of his audience that consumer choice was assisted by advertising, Bevan argued, conversely, that 'you use your arts to push a product down our throats which we would not think of taking if you left us alone'. Under a socialist economy, he suggested, the consumer would actually have more choice than at present 'for in competitive society the consumer is passive, besieged, assaulted, battered and robbed'. 'I know that you are decent people', he conceded, 'but you are harnessed to an evil machine which is doing great harm to modern society. I hope you will be kept in check.'[3]

George Pope, honorary secretary of the AA, who was chairing Bevan's session, stumbled in his response to this strident attack and suggested that if commercial television came then 'something really English and not American' would be introduced. Others present in the hall took the opportunity offered by Bevan's speech to propose a more robust defence of their industry.[4] They included Philip Stobo, a copywriter at the agency S.H. Benson. He suggested that advertising was central to rising living standards in an affluent society and from this flowed 'nicer clothes, wider travel, richer leisure'. 'Forget Bevan', he concluded, seeking to stir the AA audience, 'Forget our other critics too. We are not the custodians of morality … We are salesmen of the will to want.'[5]

Philip Stobo's bold defence of advertising's role in the progressive improvement in the material standards of life signalled a wider intent from within the advertising industry to refine arguments about its value to society at large and introduced themes that were to be repeated through the late 1950s and 1960s.[6] This defence of advertising was stirred not just by Bevan's attack, but by a sustained public debate about advertising's social role. Labour ministers, MPs and party members were joined not only by a section of the Conservative party, but also by journalists, churchmen and even the BBC in their antipathy towards the industry.[7] The emergent consumer movement, especially in the form of the Consumers' Association (formed in 1957), was another source of anti-advertising feeling. Its members, drawn from middle-class and educated backgrounds and with a faith in science and technology, were critical of advertising because they felt that it misled the consumer and misrepresented products.[8] The almost obsessive fascination with and scrutiny of advertising was further encouraged by a body of social criticism, some of it emanating from the United States, which focused on the negative social consequences of advertising as part of a broader critique of post-war affluence. The most widely read of these US critics in Britain was Vance Packard. Packard's American criticism was complemented by home-grown attacks on advertising from writers and academics. In these critiques of advertising, left-leaning writers like Richard Hoggart shared much in common with right-wing Leavisite critics like Frank Whitehead in their view that advertising trivialized genuine human emotions and offered an impoverished conception of the 'good life'.[9] Sensitivity to the influence of advertising was also sharpened by the growing role of marketing people over the presentation of politics. If the 1959 General Election was the first television election, then it was the expansion of the use of paid-for advertising undertaken by advertising agencies both within government and for the main political parties that also raised the stakes in the public debate on advertising's influence.[10] The idea that politics could be sold like soap powder troubled critics like Dennis Potter, for example, just down from Oxford and with his illustrious career as a television playwright ahead of him. In a scathing commentary on the 1959 General Election, Potter railed against the way the Labour party had accommodated itself to consumerism-fuelled apathy. The 1959 election, for Potter, had seen the debate between the parties recast so that it felt like 'a bitter trade struggle between Nescafe and Maxwell House or Pink Camay and Palmolive'.[11]

In this chapter I explore the critique of advertising and the responses that it stimulated from within the advertising industry. In doing so, I look at the period marked by the controversies around the introduction and subsequent growth of commercial television and the reactions to the first decade of television advertising. For its critics, the establishment of commercial television in 1955 had led, as many had feared, to a lowering of cultural and moral standards. Television advertising figured prominently in these concerns and the adverts that appeared between programmes, as much as the programmes themselves, were seen as a symptom of the negative drift of social change. Such concerns were important in fuelling the renewed attack on advertising. There was a long-standing critique of the practice going back to the nineteenth century and many of the luminaries of British intellectual life in the 1930s and 1940s had developed critical readings of advertising and commercial persuasion. The arrival of ITV served to rekindle these concerns and precipitate a new assault on advertising and the industry that produced it.[12] This debate pointed to sustained disagreements between advertising's critics and the industry over the meaning and significance of post-war affluence and advertising's role in these social changes. At the heart of this was the airing of competing understandings of consumer choice and consumer freedom, of differing conceptions of the role that the state should play in regulating market processes and divergent opinions about what the limits of commercial influence and interference ought to be in the mass media, especially broadcasting. But more tellingly there were also at work in the public exchanges different ideas of human motivations and desires as puritan notions of self-restraint and self-control advocated by critics rubbed up against more self-expressive views of human beings and their relationship to the world of goods proposed by advertising people. These were intellectual divisions that cut to the heart of the post-war affluent society and its expanded ethic of consumption.

This chapter focuses on three key set-piece moments in the debate on advertising that were filtered through the machinery of Parliament and the party system, as well reflecting on the more familiar terrain of social and cultural criticism. There is a good reason for this emphasis. In the committee rooms where witnesses were cross-examined and oral testimonies and written statements scrutinized and pored over, we see not just the critics of advertising having their say, but also the representatives of British advertising seeking to refute the charges being made against their industry and developing an intellectual defence of their commercial practices.[13] I explore these exchanges by beginning with the *Report of the Committee on Broadcasting* published in 1962. Chaired by Sir Harry Pilkington, of the glass manufacturing family, and notably featuring Richard Hoggart among its members, the Pilkington Committee represented the first response from within government to commercial television and television advertising since the passing of the 1954 Television Act. Its considerations and ultimately its conclusions had a significant bearing on how British broadcasting developed in the 1960s and the constraining of commercialism within this sector.[14] Importantly, the report also had powerful things to say about television advertising. From Pilkington, I turn to another parliamentary report produced in the same session of Parliament. This was the *Report of the Committee on Consumer Protection*, better known as the Molony Committee after its chair, the QC J.T. Molony. The Molony Report addressed the existing state of statutory consumer protection and consumer rights and the growing demand, particularly from the consumers' movement, for greater consumer protection. Advertising and sales practices figured centrally in its deliberations and the Molony Committee served, like the Pilkington Committee, to air more widely held criticisms of advertising. Finally, I turn to the Labour party's advertising commission and consider its central arguments about advertising's economic and cultural influence. Before exploring the deliberations of these committees and the commission, I reflect on the arguments made by influential social critics which permeated the committee rooms of these proceedings and which contributed to the intellectual atmosphere in which they operated. I focus on the two most high-profile critics of advertising of the late 1950s and 1960s, Vance Packard and Richard Hoggart.

The critics of advertising

Just as it was the origin of many of the advertising ideas and practices that I have already discussed in this book, so America was one of the quarters from which the critics of advertising came in the 1950s. The best-known was the American social commentator Vance Packard. Packard's social criticism was developed in a trilogy of books published between 1957 and 1960 that each tackled different aspects of the problems of post-war affluence.[15] Of the three books, *The Hidden Persuaders*, published in the US in 1957, had the biggest impact. It centred on the rise of motivational research and the use of depth interviews in American market research and advertising. Packard detailed the way practitioners like the celebrated market researcher and pioneer of motivational research, Ernest Dichter, sought to influence and manipulate the mind of the consumer by using a range of insidious techniques drawn from the psychological sciences. In one of the most famous examples from the book Packard described how Dichter helped the US car maker Chrysler to develop a new line of cars based on his understanding of the 'deeper sexual yearnings' of male consumers. Chrysler dealers had found that they sold more cars if they put convertibles, soft-topped sports cars, in the showroom window, despite the fact that most customers bought sedans, the standard family car. Dichter concluded that the men purchasing the cars saw the convertible as a symbolic mistress and this is what drew them to the showroom. However, once there they bought the sedan 'just as [they] once married a plain girl who [they] knew would make a fine wife and mother. Symbolically he marries the sedan.'[16] Dichter suggested that Chrysler could capitalize on these symbolic associations of types of car by creating a new model, the hardtop, which was a 'union between the wife and the mistress'.[17] As Packard notes, the hardtop soon became the most successful new car style introduced into the American market.[18]

Packard set himself against these clever but insidious techniques of commercial manipulation, arguing that they were illegitimate because they invaded the 'privacy of our minds' and undermined the freedom and autonomy of the individual. Against them he championed the virtues of 'plain speaking' and the moral worth of 'producer values', ideas that owed much to the provincial Methodism of Packard's Bradford County upbringing.[19] He was not alone in taking such a stand. His critique of commercial manipulation shared much with other liberal critiques of affluence that appeared in America through the 1950s and early 1960s. In this regard Packard belonged in the company of writers like David Reisman, William Whyte and C. Wright Mills, all of whom emphasized the social costs of affluence. Moreover, as Horowitz suggests, Packard's books appealed to the same liberal-minded audience addressed by his contemporaries: individuals who worried about the downsides of affluence, while enjoying its material benefits.[20]

The Hidden Persuaders was first published in Britain by Longmans in 1957, and then reprinted as a Penguin Special in 1960 and as a Pelican Book in 1962. A publishing success among the wider reading public, it did not go unnoticed by the advertising industry. Industry insiders partly read it as an instructive guide to US research techniques, especially motivation research.[21] A reviewer in the *Journal of the Advertising Association* coolly acknowledged the force of Packard's argument. *The Hidden Persuaders* had, he suggested, 'set the commercial world talking' because of the way it offered a seductive sense of the way advertising might play on consumers' fears and motivations.[22] Other industry commentators, however, were sceptical about the claims he made, particularly about motivation research. The market researcher and Labour party supporter Mark Abrams, writing in the *Journal of the Advertising Association* in February 1958, sounded such a note of caution. He argued, 'My own view is that it is highly unlikely that advertising men and market research workers are becoming effective "hidden persuaders" or successful "mass manipulators" on the basis of such work [motivational research].'[23] Others were more directly critical of Packard's melodramatic comments on motivational research, with its Cold War overtones of brainwashing and propaganda. As another review of *The Hidden Persuaders* in the *Journal of the Advertising Association* complained, 'such a misleading presentation of the subject makes the book dangerous – in that to lay readers it can cause unnecessary misgivings about the entire advertising profession … to present this subject in a lurid and sinister light, with premonitions of 1984 and worse, is quite farcical.'[24]

Packard's image of the 'hidden persuaders' certainly had the power to shape how advertising's critics described the industry. At the 1963 Labour party conference a delegate claimed that the creation of the new position of director of publicity had been a terrible event for the party and that Labour had 'no need to resort to "hidden persuaders" of their own to win elections'.[25] A few years later IPA Forum quoted the comments of one of the Church's commentators on advertising, the Revd Rogers, a senior Methodist minister. Reflecting on the morality of advertising, he claimed 'consumers suspect that they are being obliquely got at by clever exploiters – the persuaders, hidden or half-hidden'.[26]

Another sceptical reviewer of Packard from outside the advertising industry was to have a greater impact on the critical debates about advertising – Richard Hoggart. Hoggart reviewed Packard's *The Wastemakers* in the *Observer* in 1961. He was notably testy and critical in his response to the book, harshly suggesting that it was 'a symptom of the ills it describes. It is a concocted, a gimmick book – to be consumed while its theme is fashionable and then discarded like last week's Kleenex.'[27] Hoggart's own arguments about advertising and post-war affluence were to be influential in a different way from Packard's. At the heart of this, of course, stands *The Uses of Literacy*, one of the most revered and widely read accounts of the effects of emergent prosperity upon working-class life.[28] The book was notable for the way it read contemporary social change – the world of milk bars, juke box boys and the 'shiny barbarism' of post-war commercial culture – through the lens of cultural decline. If much of the emotional punch of the book stemmed from its evocation of the robust and honest virtues of working-class life in the era before post-war affluence, then the power of this account was heightened by the sense of panic about the social changes of the early 1950s that threatened the world described. As Francis Mulhern has argued, the book tells a story of 'decline already far gone, perhaps irretrievable'.[29] It is also a book shaped by a set of solid moral convictions that owe much, as Stefan Collini has shown, to the residues of a secularized Protestantism.[30] For Hoggart, hardship is held to encourage 'effort, self-control and social purpose', while prosperity brings only 'passivity, indulgence and selfishness'.[31] This moral compass shapes *The Uses of Literacy* and Hoggart is damning in his analysis of the new forms of 'mass art' – pulp fiction, magazines and popular songs – for 'overexciting' and eventually 'killing' taste. It is these forms of 'shiny barbarism' which 'unbend the springs of action' among working people.[32] *The Uses of Literacy*, however, is remarkable for depicting a culture which is fundamentally pre-television. Television merits only a brief reference halfway through the book when Hoggart refers to its capacity to give viewers a sense of 'communion'.[33] Advertising in general is only briefly mentioned and TV advertising not at all.[34] This omission from Hoggart's writing, however, was not to last long. In 1958 he reviewed the first three years of ITV for *New Left Review*.[35] In the essay, he recognized the popularity of commercial television among working people and the way that it picked up on traditions of popular entertainment. Nonetheless, in his comments on television advertising Hoggart conceded nothing to its potential appeal to 'ordinary viewers' and launched a scathing attack on it. There was in the flow of TV adverts, he claimed, 'the fever of alternation between crude "spots", "hard" and "soft" sells, jingles, insistent echo chamber repetitions, halting infants' voices (a particularly nasty form)'. The adverts, overall, were, he concluded, 'feeble if unpleasant things'.[36]

This punchy, dismissive attack on television advertising was given a more thoughtful rendering in a lecture which Hoggart gave the following year. Published as 'The Uses of Television' in the January 1960 edition of *Encounter*, Hoggart proposed a more precise critique of TV commercials. His first objection was that they encouraged 'self-indulgence' among working-class and lower middle-class viewers. The adverts offered, he claimed, a picture of life in which these viewers were 'asked to find acceptable' the idea that they 'deserve this chocolate' or 'owe it to themselves to have this refrigerator'.[37] Such invitations to 'self-indulgence' from commercials led on to his second objection, which was that they encouraged consumers to make 'irrational choices'. Contrasting TV advertising with the ambitions of the Consumers' Association to foster rational consumer choice, Hoggart argued that the adverts were 'forms of bastard art based largely on emotional appeals often irrelevant to the rational case for using the product'.[38] Bound up with these emotional appeals was the third problem with TV adverts for Hoggart. This concerned the 'picture of life' which 'young working class and lower middle class wives and husbands' were being offered. It was, for Hoggart, a bright, unreal world,

> a congenitally innocent world, a world prior to the knowledge of good and evil, in which all the young girls have that wonderful Jamesean exclamation mark between their eyebrows … and even middle-aged fathers look no more than nicely weathered by sinless winds. But it is a bodiless world and Sir Robert Fraser, like the Father Christmas in a big store, is the public relations host to it.[39]

Such a 'picture of life' – essentially 'childish, inadequate and euphoric' – and finding its fullest expression in washing powder and soap adverts 'grossly distorted' the nature of married love and family life and other human relationships. [40]

The Pilkington Report

Hoggart's uncompromising arguments about television advertising and ITV in general drew him to the attention of civil servants looking for members of the proposed broadcasting committee established by Prime Minister Harold Macmillan in 1960. Or at least that was the view of a suspicious mind like Sir Robert Fraser, chairman of the ITA.[41] Whatever the precise reasons for his appointment, Hoggart proved to be an influential member of the committee. His membership gave him the opportunity to directly address those advertising people who had been the targets of his opprobrium. The *Report of the Committee on Broadcasting* was an important piece of public policy centred on the future of broadcasting in Britain.[42] The committee was established by the government in 1960 principally because the 1954 Television Act was due to expire in 1964 and the BBC's Charter was also up for renewal in June 1962. In addition, the availability of new broadcasting frequencies and with them the option of new television channels meant the government needed to act to consider the future of broadcasting.[43] The report produced by the committee was notable for its powerful vision of broadcasting. In chapter three it argued that television ought properly to be 'in a constant and sensitive relationship with the moral conditions of society'.[44] Television producers, it argued, had an obligation to lead and not simply follow public tastes; there was an imperative to innovate and experiment and producers needed to move beyond common experience and preferences in order to expand the horizons of viewers. In the process, the report suggested, television needed to think of addressing overlapping minority audiences rather than only or predominantly mass audiences. This vision of the social responsibility of British broadcasting provided the benchmark against which the report evaluated the television services offered by both the BBC and the ITA. While conceding that there had been some 'fine achievements' within television since the mid-1950s (including in the areas of television drama, current affairs, in some comedy and in the development of news bulletins), the report noted the preponderance of 'disquiet' and 'dissatisfaction' with television in many of the submissions to it. It was this sense of disquiet and dissatisfaction that set the tone for the report. It identified the ITV companies as the principal source of these concerns. It was they, it argued, which were largely responsible for the fact that there were too many superficial and 'cheaply sensational programmes' on television. Arguing that 'the BBC knows good broadcasting [and] by and large they are producing it', the report claimed that the ITV companies, on the other hand, were principally responsible for the erosion of moral standards depicted on television.[45]

It was out of this assessment – and the critique of ITV – that the report set out to review television advertising. While it noted the concern of organizations like the Advertising Inquiry Committee (AIC), a lobby group founded by Labour MP and long-term critic of advertising Francis Noel-Baker, that some adverts were misleading, the report felt 'the greatest concern by far was about the general social consequences of television advertising, and more particularly, about the nature of the appeal made by some adverts'.[46] The report went on: 'too many adverts played on impulses which were discreditable; for example, upon acquisitiveness, snobbery, fear, uncritical conformity, and "keep up with the Jones"'. Advertising also undermined 'fine impulses like love, manliness and maternal pride'.[47] Challenging the views of Sir Robert Fraser, the ITA chairman, who had claimed under cross-examination that the image of life portrayed in television adverts was 'a pleasing one', the Pilkington Report suggested the authority that he chaired should amplify the Principles of Television Advertising so as to make it more difficult for advertisers to make false or misleading claims.[48] Warming to its theme, the report chided Sir Robert and the ITA:

> The charge is not that it is wrong to add to the gaiety or pleasure of life by using this or that product. The criticism is rather that advertising too often implies that, unless one buys … the product, one will have cause for shame, or loss of self-respect, or cannot hope for happiness. [Such appeals] trade on human weakness.[49]

These concerns with the values promoted in TV adverts and their broader corrosive effects on the public were evident in the committee proceedings of the report, notably so when the members of the committee cross-examined the representatives of the advertising industry. The exchanges between these protagonists were illuminating because they revealed much about not only the committee's concerns about television advertising, but also how advertising people sought to counter the criticisms of their industry. In the questioning of a group of advertising men representing the IPA, the committee focused upon the new force of television as a medium of communication and the influence advertising was having upon commercial television as a whole. Richard Hoggart, in particular, forcefully suggested that television advertising surely had a 'more immediate emotional impact' than press advertising.[50] Pressing home his point, he offered an example of the differences between press and TV advertising. He chose a recent advert for a patent medicine. In the press advert, the copy had declared, 'Take so and so's pills, they're hospital tested.' He went on,

> There is a difference between the impact of that appearing in a newspaper and the impact of a 'commercial' in which a man ... a pretty dignified old character – looked out of the screen and said ... 'Take so and so's pills' and then in a deep voice full of every foreboding said 'They are hospital tested'. The statement was thus of an almost entirely different kind in its impact on a great number of people who are not particularly sophisticated.[51]

Dan Ingman, a member of the IPA's television and radio committee, was defensive in reply, seeking to underplay the differences between the two campaigns. As he put it, 'It seems to me not to matter in the slightest whether people get more worked up about this because it is spoken rather than printed. The important point is, are they hospital tested, not whether this is said or printed it seems to me.'[52] To which Hoggart dismissively replied that that 'hospital-tested' was a 'meaningless phrase'.

The discussion then switched to the broader question of the balance between the public-service obligations of ITV and its commercial value as a medium to advertisers. Sir Harry Pilkington picked up on a line in the IPA's written submission where it had grandly identified the role of advertising as providing a service to the general public. Clearly irritated by this attempt by the IPA to appropriate the language of public service to a commercial practice, Pilkington challenged the IPA men on what they saw as advertising's public duty. Sinclair Wood, a former IPA president, was the most forthcoming of the IPA representatives and he offered a firm defence of advertising's social role – its service to the public. This social role sprang from advertising's contribution to the rise in living standards through increased consumer spending. Echoing Stobo's response to Bevan in 1953, Wood proceeded to emphasize how mass production had made possible higher standards of living through making many previously luxury goods available to the majority. Mass production, however, required 'mass selling': 'It is in our interests as a nation, both from an exporting point of view and from the raising of the people's standard of living that goods should be sold effectively. If this nation were not allowed to practice ... salesmanship then we would begin to be materially less effective as a nation.'[53] To this end, modern mass communications 'should be at the service of legitimate commerce and business' and more television air time should be available to 'commercial mass communication'.[54]

Sinclair Wood's arguments offered a justification for the IPA's demand for a second commercial channel and the lengthening of the broadcasting day. It was these arguments in favour of greater commercialization of ITV that stuck in the minds of the committee members and Richard Hoggart noted in his own record of the oral evidence that the 'IPA said they want a selling medium'.[55] Hoggart's written comments to the secretary of the Pilkington Committee during the drafting of the final report also revealed how far apart were the views of at least one influential member of the committee and those of the representatives of advertising. Hoggart pressed the committee to recognize the corrupting power of TV adverts and their crass style. As he put it,

> We ought to grasp the nettle about television advertising as little engaging emotional dramas ... [though] compared with real television drama writers ... the guys who write these little advertising dramas are like Soho strip joints to Verdi – they have the techniques and tricks but nothing to say ... all virtuosity and no virtue.[56]

This withering critique, with its overtones of television advertising being sleazy and manipulative, was echoed in other comments Hoggart made during the committee proceedings. When members of the Independent Television Contractors Association appeared before the committee in July 1961, Hoggart, along with other committee members, interrogated them on how the ITCA judged some of the claims made by commercials. Hoggart was less concerned about the use of fantasy in adverts, an issue raised by other committee members in relation to commercials for Camay and Knights Castile soap. Rather he was concerned with the 'ones which try to be nearly real'.[57] In particular Hoggart reflected on commercials made for Fairy Liquid and Persil washing powder. These adverts, he suggested, were socially problematic because they used a range of important human emotions, such as 'mother love' and 'Aunty love', and linked these with the use of the product. In the process, the commercials not only hijacked these values, but reduced the complexity of human relationships. As Hoggart put it, 'Now let us see as many happy homes as we can on TV, [but] always bearing in mind that the happy home has to be worked for very hard by the business of living together with one another in a state of tension and mutual needs and desires.'[58] Hoggart's criticisms fed into the final recommendations of the report and are evident in its concern about the way commercials used 'the excitement of fiction and the compelling reality of the everyday' to persuade viewers.[59] Informed by this thinking, the Pilkington Committee recommended that the ITA should develop further effective restraint of television advertising.[60]

Molony Committee

Published in the same parliamentary session as the Pilkington Report, the Molony Report addressed the issue of consumer protection and concerns placed on the political agenda by the lobbying of groups like the Consumers' Association.[61] Its focus, therefore, was very different from that of the Pilkington Committee. However, as with the deliberations of the committee on broadcasting, the advertising industry found itself forced to defend its commercial practices and to counter a whole set of arguments made against advertising that were meticulously recorded by the Molony Committee. In its initial submission to the committee in November 1959 the IPA had sought to position advertising as a help to the consumer. As it argued, 'the present day use of brand names is a customer's assurance of quality and standard'.[62] Moreover, any concerns about misleading advertising that might arise from the small number of disreputable companies could be addressed by strengthening the professional bodies, like the IPA itself, which currently exercised voluntary control over the industry by promoting higher professional standards. As the IPA noted in a letter to Mr S. Mitchlemore, the secretary to the Molony Committee, 'wherever any dubious technique which has been mooted e.g. the use of hypnosis and subliminal advertising, this Institute has taken quick action against its use'.[63]

The confident tone of the IPA's original submission was punctured by the questions put to it by Mitchelmore prior to its meeting with the Molony Committee. These questions summarized the main concerns that had been expressed to the committee by other witnesses and focused on the nature of contemporary styles of advertising communication. As Mitchlemore put it,

> Broadly, the impression seems to be that a good deal of advertising has abandoned any serious attempt to portray the product; that it aims, rather, at coupling a brand name with a much-lauded (but not necessarily significant) characteristic

or with pleasant or irrelevant associations and at pressing home its message with sustained vigour and technique whilst the bemused consumer buys by dubiously-founded instinctive reaction, instead of by considered choice and with regard to his true needs.[64]

Among the advertising techniques that Mitchlemore went on to detail as being particularly problematic were 'rigged demonstrations of products, irrelevant associations, personal testimonies and claims that cannot be positively disproved'.[65] He went on, 'the speed, persistence and vigour of the techniques leaves little scope for the consumer to spot the sleight of hand'.[66]

The IPA, in its reply to Mitchlemore, bristled at the charges. It sought, again, to differentiate between the small number of disreputable adverts and agents who might make false or misleading claims, and the majority of advertising agencies, especially IPA members, who were committed to maintaining and improving standards of advertising. While this miscreant minority could be dealt with by the use of the existing merchandise marks legislation, the IPA sought to resist further moves to protect the consumer from advertising by recourse to new statutory means. The IPA also offered a strong defence of the importance of persuasion in advertising and the ability of consumers to distinguish between the emotive and factual content of adverts. As they put it,

> [We see no harm in the fact that] much advertising is not purely factual. In our opinion ... the manufacturer and his agency [rightly] use techniques to attract attention and to persuade – sometimes to persuade emotionally. It is all part of legitimate selling ... The man on the Clapham omnibus and the ordinary housewife can distinguish between the 'factual content' and the 'mood of ads'. Surely a reasonable trust in the values and critical judgement of ordinary people is the basic element in any form of democratic society.[67]

Furthermore, it claimed, the problem for British society was not so much advertising threatening the interests of the consumer, but rather that British industry did not 'sufficiently proclaim the merits of its goods in the export markets' through advertising. If there remained concerns about the effects of advertising on consumers, then the IPA felt that a tightening of existing voluntary controls was sufficient to reassure the public. This included, centrally, the creation of a new advertising standards authority 'manned by experienced people from inside the advertising industry' that could consider any complaints against advertising.

These arguments had some impact on the final recommendations of the Molony Committee. The committee proposed no new statutory controls over advertising and the final report also supported the view put forward by the

IPA and the AA that false or misleading advertising could be best addressed by the tightening up of the merchandise marks legislation. These recommendations support Matthew Hilton's contention that the Molony Report was heavily pro-business and cautious about promoting full-blown state consumerism.[68] There was, however, a telling qualification added by the committee to its generally sympathetic recommendations on advertising. It claimed that many 'legitimate' methods of advertising continued to divert consumers from making a 'sound choice'.[69] It detailed these as follows: 1) most advertising had abandoned factual presentation and was persuasive rather than informative; 2) it made meaningless claims about products, particularly based on comparative merit, without indicating against what the product was being compared (i.e. 'washes whiter', 'lasts longer' etc.); 3) testimonials were bought rather than being spontaneous; 4) it played on people's emotions; 5) it made misleading claims about the performance of, particularly, domestic appliances; and 6) the industry was inadequately restrained by the law.[70] The report felt that, taken together, these charges were serious and required that the advertising industry should be made subject to tighter control. As it suggested, 'it has been recognized that the impact of television is so forceful and intimate, especially on the young, that this medium requires a heightened standard of restraint peculiar to itself and it is questioned whether the proper level of restraint has been achieved'.[71] These ideas fed into the Molony Report's final recommendations, which proposed a strengthening of the existing machinery for judging the suitability for broadcast of adverts and the creation of a new regulatory body, the Advertising Standards Authority, to police breaches in the Code of Advertising Practice.[72] This would be made up not only of advertising people, as the IPA and AA had proposed, but also individuals from manufacturing, the press and television, the world of education, the trade union movement and politics, together with an independent chair.[73]

The Reith Commission

The ambition of the Molony Committee to improve the standard of television advertising rested upon a distinction between sound consumer choice and its distortion by certain techniques of advertising and persuasion. This understanding was also evident in the deliberations of the Labour party commission into advertising.[74] Chaired by Lord Reith, the first director-general of the BBC, the commission was made up of senior academics, economists and representatives of the advertising industry. It had been established by the

Labour leader Hugh Gaitskell in 1962.[75] Gaitskell's decision to establish the commission sprang from his concern that the Labour party needed to be attentive to the views of a young, university-educated generation. He had already set up a party youth commission in 1959 to look at the problems of this age group and the same audience was in mind when the advertising commission was created.[76] The advertising report was also motivated by Gaitskell's own critical feelings towards advertising. As he told the *Daily Mail* in January 1961, '[there is] something rather nauseating and humiliating about those [TV] commercials … when people are regarded as sort of objects on which the ad men can get to work'.[77] The report went to some lengths to document the serious social consequences of advertising. Echoing themes present in the Pilkington and Molony reports, the Reith Report expressed concerns about the intrusiveness of advertising and the way it was 'constantly being impressed upon the public eye or ear in peremptory fashion'.[78] Advertisements were also having a corrosive effect on language. As the report noted, 'as advertisers strive to outdo each other … the superlatives … in which they deal become drained of all significance and force'. This had the effect, it continued, of 'debasing language and blunting its communicative power, not only within advertising, but for ordinary users of the language as well'.[79] Worse followed, for the report, in terms of the effect of advertising on consumer behaviour. Like the Molony Report, the Reith Report felt that advertising techniques were bound to distort choice in the 'direction of irrationality'.[80] This meant that even within a world of proliferating consumer goods, consumers were unable to make rational choices between them, with a consequent diminution of their liberty. Advertising, it argued, 'substitutes vague sentiments and fantasies for a genuine assessment and perception of the quality of goods'. More than that, advertising agencies did not regard it as part of their responsibility to encourage a 'cool and practical' assessment among the consuming public.[81]

The force of these comments on advertising prompted the advertising men on the commission – who included Brian MacCabe, a senior figure in both the AA and IPA, and the eminent market researcher and London Press Exchange director, Mark Abrams – to put forward a reservation to paragraphs 377–98. They challenged the claims about advertising promoting irrationality, suggesting that they did not agree with the 'implication that all irrationality of behaviour is necessarily to be deplored, nor do [we] think that choices made at a subconscious and undeliberate level are always necessarily irrational'.

A further challenge to the eventual recommendations of the commission was evident in the lengthy replies given to it by J. Walter Thompson. Like

MacCabe and Abrams' reservations, JWT defended the fact that advertising made emotional and not strictly rational appeals to the consumer. The agency claimed that not only did consumers expect some emotional pleasure from the goods they bought, but emotional appeals added to the subjective value of the goods.[82] As the agency argued, 'the emotions used to express the subjective value are almost invariably positive ones. They include such emotions as pride, love, security, patriotism ... In each case they are designed to add to the consumers' pleasure in buying and using a product.'[83] Choice for the consumer, then, was rightly an amalgam of logical and emotional judgements. Advertising helped the consumer in both regards by being not only a central source of information on goods, but by providing these added subjective values upon which judgement between products could be made. JWT did concede, however, that there were certain emotions that advertising should avoid using or stimulating. Approvingly citing chapter eight of Richard Hoggart's *The Uses of Literacy*, JWT claimed that advertising should avoid appealing to inadequacy and invoking fear, loneliness or hate among consumers.[84]

In its final recommendations, the Reith Report was not persuaded by the case made by advertising witnesses, including those from JWT. While the report conceded that advertising had a necessary part to play in a 'modern mass producing economy', it felt that the consumer needed better protection from the advances of the advertising industry and that the industry's own self-regulation was not good enough to do this. Reiterating a central theme of the report, the recommendations argued that consumers needed more independent information on goods. This would be a corrective not only to misleading advertising, but would act as an 'incentive for advertising to use rational methods of persuasion'.[85] To this end, the Reith Report proposed that the role of the Consumer Council established by the Molony Report should be expanded into a National Consumer Board (NCB) paid for by a levy on advertising.[86] The report also recommended that advertising agencies should be required, where practicable, to place their names on adverts (including on television), in order to encourage 'higher quality in advertising'.[87]

Unsurprisingly, the representatives of advertising were hostile to these proposals and concerned that the Wilson government might act to implement them. The AA rushed out a press release based on advance publicity of the report which reasserted the argument that statutory regulation and oversight was unnecessary given the strong commitment to self-regulation and high standards pursued by organized advertising. The AA was especially hostile to the NCB. Advertising, it felt, was already an instrument of consumer protection and the NCB's involvement in product testing would lead to the diminution of consumer choice. As the AA proclaimed, the NCB would lead to state-sponsored choice and a reduction in product ranges. This would, it claimed, 'deny the public the right to exercise adult judgement in spending their money. Even in Communist countries it is now being found necessary to offer consumer choice.'[88]

Conclusion

The Advertising Association's protestations against the Reith Report were in the end unnecessary. The Wilson government, embroiled in an ongoing sterling crisis and concerned with reducing government spending, quietly shelved the recommendations of the Reith Report. In any case, its proposals concerning the need for greater consumer protection and for tighter regulation of advertising had been more expeditiously met by the establishment of the ASA and the Consumers' Council in the wake of the Molony Report. The government did seek to respond to one of Reith's recommendations, however. This was for more research into the economic and social effects of advertising. The Board of Trade was tasked with establishing a study of the economic effects of advertising. Despite extensive preliminary work, this study too was ultimately scrapped as the Treasury pressed for government departments to take their fair share of cutbacks in public expenditure in 1968.[89] The failure of the Board of Trade to produce its study and the acknowledgement from within government that little was still known about advertising's economic and social effects represents a striking and revealing summation of over a decade of debate and discussion about the industry from within the machinery of government, party politics and beyond. The absence of sustained academic study of advertising had done little to deter the protagonists in the highly charged debate about the industry. Part of the explanation of this gap between contemporary knowledge of and opinion about advertising from both its critics and its supporters lies in the fact that all protagonists felt that something important was at stake in the reflections on advertising; issues to do with the social changes unfolding in British society through these years as it became a more consumer-orientated society. The uneven, protracted and contested nature of this process was evident in a displaced form in the interrogation of advertising and especially television advertising. These commercial forms seemed to signal the emergence of an expanded form of commercial authority and communication that rivalled established sources of social power and recognition.

Viewed retrospectively, one of the most compelling features of the debate about advertising – and specifically its critique – was the moralism that coloured the arguments. With their emphasis on waste, bad taste and the corruption of consumers, this sensibility shared much with what Daniel Horowitz has called, in the US context, 'modern moralism'. The moralistic nature of much of this critique was both its greatest virtue and its greatest shortcoming. While it allowed the critics to pose important ethical questions to advertising, the moralistic tone prevented a sustained engagement with the utility and pleasures of goods promoted by advertisers. Moreover, it enabled advertising people in response to float a positive vision of advertising and its role in legitimating consumers' desires for a better life expressed through the world of goods. Such arguments supported a more self-expressive conception of consumers that counterposed the small pleasures of everyday consumption with the ideal of self-control and restraint defended by advertising's critics. Perhaps most telling were the contrasts between the models of consumer choice and its associated freedoms and liberties that were held by the critics and defenders of advertising. If the critics recurrently asserted the consumer freedoms that could flow from 'sound choice' and 'cool' decision making, then advertising people mobilized an expanded conception of the mixture of logical and emotional dimensions that shaped choosing and the importance, notably, of added 'subjective values' in the acquisition of goods.

In fact, it was the emotional and symbolic dimensions of goods and the way these should properly enter the process of consumer calculation that set the defence of advertising apart from its critics. Through such understandings, advertising people pieced together an optimistic account of advertising's social and economic role. This kind of intellectual defence was important for key sections of the advertising industry. While they may have over-reacted to the charges of their critics and to the minor tinkering of government regarding statutory controls of advertising, the desire to give legitimacy to advertising as a practice served to strengthen the hand of those 'respectable reformers' within advertising who had long sought to raise the public standing of the industry, especially among educated opinion. Respectable reformers within bodies like the IPA and AA and urbane agencies like J. Walter Thompson had most to gain from these arguments and most readily came forward to take on advertising's critics. But it was also clear that advertising people felt, certainly by the mid-1960s, that they had the wind of history in their sails, that their vision of the self-expressive possibilities of consumption and its little freedoms was in the ascendency. Rising advertising expenditure and booming private-sector consumption gave them the belief that for all the irritation of critics like Hoggart and Packard and the machinations of parliamentary committees and the Labour party advertising commission, theirs was the vision that was prevailing.

If advertising could tell a compelling story about the world of goods and its freedoms, however, its critics were successful in exerting certain pressures on the industry and in mining deep cultural reservations within British society towards commercial persuasion. These cultural blocks to unrestrained commercial expression helped to entrench the political compromises that had shaped the very foundations of commercial television and TV advertising in Britain. While critics might have continued to balk at its output, they undoubtedly contributed to the containment of TV advertising in Britain and to the conduct of the advertising industry. These cultural and political pressures formed part of the reason why TV advertising in Britain did not look like that produced in America, despite the influences that this book has traced. And it helped to inform the moves by an agency like JWT London to present itself as a self-consciously British business.

Notes

1 *Journal of the Advertising Association*, July 1953, pp. 10-17; November 1953, p. 22.
2 *The Times*, 2 May 1953, p. 3. One is reminded by this speech of Bevan's inflammatory attack on the Conservative party under Lord Woolton made in 1948, when he described the Conservatives as 'lower than vermin' and Toryism as 'organised spivvery'. On Bevan's oratory, see D. Smith, *Aneurin Bevan and the World of South Wales*, Cardiff: University of Wales Press, 1993, pp. 246–58; M. Foot, *Aneurin Bevan, Volume 2*, St Albans: Paladin, 1975, pp. 234–53.
3 *Advertiser's Weekly*, 7 May 1953, pp. 234–5.
4 Ibid., p. 236.
5 Ibid.
6 Ibid.
7 See, for example, the BBC broadcast by the consumer journalist Marghanita Laski, 'Why I hate advertising', *Listener*, 28 October 1965, pp. 653–4; the BBC TV programme introduced by Kenneth Horne, titled *Let's Imagine a World Without Advertising*, 19 January 1962; and *Choice*, the BBC consumer testing programme of the mid-1960s. The Advertising Association certainly felt that the BBC was hostile. Its 'Public Relations for Advertising' document suggested 'not only is the BBC as a whole likely to be critical of advertising, but many of its key staff are from the sort of intellectual circles where hostility to advertising is almost an article of faith'; AA, 1960, p. 2, HAT AA/8/1/1. See also 'IPA, IPR protest to BBC', *Advertiser's Weekly*, 28 April 1955, p. 159.

8   See M. Hilton, *Consumerism in the Twentieth Century: The Search for an Historical Movement*, Cambridge: Cambridge University Press, 2003, pp. 199–205; L. Black, *Redefining British Politics: Culture, Consumerism and Participation, 1954–70*, Basingstoke: Palgrave Macmillan, 2010.
9   R. Hoggart, *The Uses of Literacy*, Harmondsworth: Penguin Books, 1957; 'The case against advertising', in R. Hoggart, *Speaking to Each Other, Volume 1: About Society*, Harmondsworth: Penguin Books, 1971 [1965], pp. 205–11; D. Thompson, *Discrimination and Popular Culture*, Harmondsworth: Penguin Books, 1964; D. Potter, *The Glittering Coffin*, London: Victor Gollancz, 1960; R. Williams (ed.), *The May Day Manifesto*, Harmondsworth: Penguin Books, 1968, pp. 41–4; National Union of Teachers, *The Teacher Looks at Advertising*, London: National Union of Teachers, 1963.
10 There was an established tradition of state-sponsored advertising stretching back to the First World War, and during the inter-war period bodies like the Empire Marketing Board used advertising to promote Britain's interests. The Conservative party hired the services of an advertising agency in 1929 and from 1948 Lord Woolton, the party's chairman, expanded the role played by advertising in the party's campaigning by hiring the agency Colman Prentis Varley. Senior figures in the Labour party felt that CPV's advertising had helped the Tories to win the 1959 election. Labour ran its first national press advertising campaign in 1963. See D. Wring, *The Politics of Marketing the Labour Party*, Oxford: Palgrave, 2005; J. Pearson and G. Turner, *The Persuasion Industry*, London: Eyre & Spottiswoode, 1965, chapter 19; M. Abrams, 'Opinion polls and party propaganda', *Public Opinion Quarterly*, 28(1), 1964, pp. 13–19; R. Rose, *Influencing Voters: A Study of Campaign Rationality*, London: Faber & Faber, 1967; 'Special report: convert to advertising: Britain's Labour party', *JWT News*, 7 June 1963, pp. 5–6.
11 Potter, *The Glittering Coffin*, p. ii.
12 See F.R. Leavis, *Mass Civilization and Minority Culture*, London: Folcroft, 1930; G. Orwell, *Keep the Aspidistra Flying*, London: Victor Gollancz, 1936. J.B. Priestley's post-war critique of 'ad-mass' had its roots in his earlier, pre-war writings; J.B. Priestley, *English Journey*, London: Heinemann, 1935. Economists of the inter-war period also offered a sustained criticism of advertising. The most important were A. Marshall, *Industry and Trade*, London: Macmillan, 1919; H. Simons, *A Positive Programme for Laissez-faire*, Chicago: University of Chicago Press, 1934. On these economic arguments against advertising, see R. Harris and A. Seldon, *Advertising in Action*, London: Hutchinson, 1962.
13 These parliamentary committees addressing advertising were part of a tightening up of legislation affecting the advertising industry. This included the Merchandise Marks Act 1953, the Television Act 1954, the Hire Purchase Act 1957 and the Trade Descriptions Act 1968. In 1961 the government also introduced a levy on television advertising expenditure. The tax was paid by the contractors. A ban on the television advertising of cigarettes was introduced in July 1965.
14 Perhaps the most notable consequence of the report was the introduction of BBC2 at the expense of a second commercial channel.
15 These were *The Hidden Persuaders*, New York: David MacKay, 1957; *The Status*

Seekers, New York: David MacKay, 1959; and *The WasteMakers*, New York: David MacKay, 1960.
16 Packard, *The Hidden Persuaders*, p. 77.
17 Ibid.
18 Ibid. See also pp. 70–1, 88–9.
19 D. Horowitz, *Vance Packard and American Social Criticism*, Chapel Hill, NC: University of North Carolina Press, 1994, p. 222.
20 Ibid.
21 Something similar happened with Packard's *The Status Seekers* which was read by advertising people as a guide to ideas of class-consciousness and status. See *Journal of the Advertising Association*, April 1958, pp. 28–9; June 1960, pp. 29–30; *Advertiser's Weekly*, 15 January 1960, p. 20.
22 *Journal of the Advertising Association*, June 1960, p. 29.
23 *Journal of the Advertising Association*, February 1958, p. 12.
24 *Journal of the Advertising Association*, April 1958, pp. 28–9.
25 Pearson and Turner, *The Persuasion Industry*, p. 261.
26 IPA Forum, 1967. The influence of Packard's book was evident in a letter to *The Times* from Terence Morris, lecturer in sociology at the LSE. Morris echoed Packard's concern about the way motivational research attacked the 'privacy of the individual'. 'Is it legitimate', he asked, 'to discover hidden anxieties and play on them for commercial gain'; *The Times*, 17 April 1959, p. 15.
27 Cited in Horowitz, *Vance Packard*, p. 202.
28 The critique of post-war commercial popular culture found in *The Uses of Literacy* and Hoggart's other writings reverberated in the work of kindred spirits at the time. See, especially, Potter, *The Glittering Coffin*, p. 25.
29 F. Mulhern, 'A welfare culture?', *Radical Philosophy*, 77, May/June 1996, p. 29.
30 S. Collini, 'Richard Hoggart: literary criticism and cultural decline in twentieth century Britain', in S. Owen (ed.), *Richard Hoggart and Cultural Studies*, Basingstoke: Palgrave Macmillan, 2008, p. 41.
31 Ibid.
32 Hoggart, *The Uses of Literacy*, p. 157.
33 Ibid., p. 154.
34 Ibid., pp. 207–9, 256.
35 R. Hoggart, 'BBC and ITV after three years', *New Left Review*, 1958, 5, pp. 32–6.
36 Ibid., p. 34.
37 R. Hoggart, 'The uses of television', *Encounter*, January 1960, p. 44.
38 Ibid., p. 43.
39 Ibid., p. 44.
40 Ibid., p. 43. The common ground shared by left-leaning writers and Leavisite criticism was underlined when Hoggart offered his most direct attack on advertising in 1965. Writing in the advertising trade paper, *Advertiser's Weekly*, Hoggart set out the case against advertising. At the heart of his critique of this 'shabby business' was a contention that advertising fundamentally exploited human frailty. Hoggart claimed that it was culpable for 'emotionally abusing its audience'. As he suggested, 'recognising that we all have fears, hopes, anxieties, aspirations,

insecurities, advertisers seek not to increase our understanding of these feelings and so perhaps our command of them, but to use their existence to increase sales.'
41 R. Hoggart, *An Imagined life: Life and Times 1959–1991*, Oxford: Oxford University Press, p. 62.
42 Post Office, *Report of the Committee on Broadcasting 1960*, 1961–2 Cmnd 1753.
43 J. Milland, 'Courting Malvolio: the background to the Pilkington committee on broadcasting 1960-2', *Contemporary British History*, 18(2), 2004, p. 78.
44 *Report of the Committee on Broadcasting*, Para. 42, 15.
45 Ibid., Para. 149, 46. The report focused on the depictions of violence in particular. See Para. 166–86. The report was also troubled by the size of cash prizes in quiz programmes and the humiliation of members of the public in 'party game' items, Para. 178–83.
46 Ibid., Para. 244. The Advertising Inquiry Committee was founded in 1959 with the aim of highlighting any advertising that broke the code of practice established under the 1954 Television Act. The AIC claimed that 5–8% of all advertising on television was false or misleading and thus in breach of the Principles of Television Advertising.
47 *Report of the Committee on Broadcasting*, Para. 244–5.
48 Ibid., Para. 252.
49 Ibid., Para. 252–4.
50 Committee on Broadcasting, notes of a meeting held at Cornwall House, Waterloo Road, London, S.E.1, on Tuesday 25 July 1961, PRO HO 244/269, p. 5.
51 Ibid., p. 6.
52 Ibid.
53 Ibid., p. 8.
54 Ibid., p. 9.
55 Notes from Mr Hoggart to Draft Chapter VII of the Pilkington Report, p. 4, PRO HO 244/269.
56 Ibid.
57 ITCA Evidence to the Committee on Broadcasting, 25 July 1961, PRO HO 244/585, pp. 7–9.
58 R. Hoggart, ITCA Evidence to the Committee on Broadcasting, 25 July 1961, PRO HO 244/585, pp. 18–19. Another member of the committee, the actress Joyce Grenfell, was troubled by an advert for Bluinite Tide, p. 9.
59 *Report of the Committee on Broadcasting*, Para. 253, 80.
60 Commenting in the 1990s on the reception of the Pilkington Report, Hoggart argued that it had helped to improve ITV. As he suggested, people tend to remember ITV as 'behaving well from its inception ... but in its first eight or nine years it [ITV] behaved like an Oxford Street barrow boy'; Hoggart, *An Imagined Life*, p. 71.
61 Board of Trade, *Final Report of the Committee on Consumer Protection*, 1961–2 Cmnd 1781.
62 IPA Memorandum to the Committee on Consumer Protection, 18 November 1959, PRO BT 258/900.
63 Reply to letter from the Secretary of the Committee, 31 May 1961, PRO BT 258/900. The IPA established a committee which eventually banned its members

from using subliminal advertising. See *The Times*, 7 October 1957, p. 5.
64 Letter from S. Mitchlemore to J.P. O'Connor, Director of IPA, 31 May 1961, PRO BT 258/900.
65 Ibid.
66 Ibid.
67 Reply to letter from the Secretary of the Committee, 31 May 1961, PRO BT 258/900.
68 Hilton, *Consumerism*, pp. 224–8.
69 *Final Report of the Committee on Consumer Protection*, Para. 230
70 Ibid., Para. 239–41.
71 Ibid., Para. 535.
72 Ibid., Para. 258.
73 Sir Arnold Plant, Professor of Commerce at LSE, was its first chair 1962–65. On the composition of the authority, see, *Advertiser's Weekly*, 27 July 1962, p. 5.
74 *Report of a Commission of Enquiry into Advertising*, 1966, Labour Party Advertising Committee Records, University of Essex, Special Collections.
75 Lord Reith has next to nothing to say about the commission in his diaries, though he recalls that Gaitskell had initially approached him to chair a commission on the funding of political parties; I. McIntyre *The Expense of Glory: A Life of John Reith*, London: Harper Collins, 1994, p. 358.
76 P.M. Williams, *Hugh Gaitskell: A Political Biography*, London: Jonathan Cape, 1979, p. 389.
77 Ibid., p. 391.
78 *Report of a Commission of Enquiry into Advertising*, Para. 374.
79 Ibid., Para. 373.
80 Ibid., Para. 379.
81 Ibid., Para. 379.
82 Advertising Commission Replies to Questionnaire Ref. RD 282/June 1962, p. 57, J. Walter Thompson Company Ltd, JWT/HAT, Box 255. See also the essay by Tom Corlett of J. Walter Thompson in *IPA Forum*, May 1968, p. 11, for a similar argument.
83 Advertising Commission Replies to Questionnaire Ref. RD 282/June 1962, p. 58, J. Walter Thompson Company Ltd, JWT/HAT, Box 255.
84 Ibid.
85 *Report of a Commission of Enquiry into Advertising*, Para. 412.
86 Ibid., Para. 412.
87 Ibid., Para. 480.
88 Advertising Association Statement on the Reith Commission Report, 21 June 1966, released midnight 23 June 1966, Labour Party Advertising Committee Records, 1 July 1966, University of Essex, Special Collections.
89 The study was delegated to the Economic Research Unit. See, inter alia, 'The Selection of the Research Team for Advertising Study', 21 July 1967, ERU, PRO BT 213/492; Research Proposal for a Study of the Economic Effects of Advertising, 4 September 1967, BT 213/497; letter to J.B. Heath, notes by Mitchelmore, 3 January 1968, BT 213/492.

Conclusion

In his memoir of life at JWT London from the late 1940s to the early 1970s, Peter Yeo, who had worked as an account representative for the company, concluded on a melancholic note. His story of JWT in its prime, with its host of colourful characters and its sometimes demanding and quirky clients, came to a close with the acknowledgement of decline and failure. From his retirement home in the Balearic island of Mallorca, Yeo had read that JWT had fallen on 'bad times' and been taken over 'by a company called Wire and Plastic Products'. 'How humiliating', he confessed, 'for the agency that had ruled the roost for so long, to be bought up by a company that had made its millions out of supermarket trolleys – the trolleys in which all those JWT advertised products had been wheeled around.'[1]

Yeo's reference to the aggressive takeover in 1987 of JWT by WPP, the company headed by Saatchi & Saatchi's former financial director Martin Sorrell and built out of his purchase of the Kent-based manufacturer of shopping trolleys, signalled not just a transformation in the fortunes of 40 Berkeley Square, but also of the parent company as a whole. WPP's takeover of JWT, including all of its US offices, formed part of a programme of acquisition and expansion in which it also acquired another giant of US advertising (and the world's fifth largest), Ogilvy & Mather. These aggressive moves by a British-owned advertising and marketing business into the field of American advertising were not unique. Sorrell's former employers Saatchi & Saatchi had led the way through the 1980s, not just toppling JWT London from the top of the agency rankings in Britain in January 1980, but six years later buying the American agency Ted Bates. At the time Bates was the fourth largest agency network in the world.[2] These developments were part of the emergence of new global centres of advertising. They also included the rise of important multinational Japanese and French agencies, alongside the new global power of

British advertising. As such, these developments represented a historic reversal of the international dominance of American advertising in the second half of the twentieth century and brought to an end a distinctive period in the history of Anglo-American advertising relations.

Endings, however, are not always as clear-cut as they look. The global rise of British advertising and the 'British invasion' of the US advertising industry self-evidently represented not the withering of trans-Atlantic advertising relations, but a re-ordering of their power relations and the direction of influence. This kind of shifting of the gears within trans-Atlantic advertising and commerce had happened before at the beginning of the 'American Century'. In the 1930s European émigrés to the US had brought with them ideas that were to inform the development on US soil of new approaches to consumers and commodities. These included the seeds of 'motivation research' within studies of consumer behaviour, as well as design innovations associated with European modernism, including the 'functionalism' of the Bauhaus school. The latter helped to shape US industrial design and architecture, including kitchen design.[3] These continental European influences, developed and extended in the USA, later returned to Europe (including Britain) in the post-war period to transform European advertising and product design under US commercial leadership.

The relative decline of US advertising in the late 1980s and the rise of British advertising needs to be seen as part of this longer history of ongoing exchanges which have helped to create the structural convergences and 'family resemblances' between the consumer-orientated economies and cultures of Western Europe and North America.[4] The convergence of advertising practices and approaches to mass consumption which have grown out of this 'commercial Atlantic' should not lead us, however, to overlook the continuing importance through the twentieth century of national traditions in advertising, commerce and consumption. If this book has sought to tell the story of post-war advertising in Britain and its relationship to growing material affluence as part of an international history of commercial change, I have also argued that trans-Atlantic influences in advertising and the consumer economy were typically reworked and articulated through the grammar of national difference. One of the central contentions of the book, in fact, has been to suggest that US advertising took distinctive directions in Britain. Viewing the process of 'Americanization' from the inside, through the activities of J. Walter Thompson, formed a key focus for my arguments. This generated less a sense of the wholesale transfer of US practices and their overwhelming of indigenous advertising traditions than a picture of the reworking and hybridizing of these practices as they were adapted to local cultural and business conditions. We saw this across a number of key areas of agency practice. US-derived market research techniques, including motivation research, were selectively drawn upon in the UK and combined with established traditions of British economic measurement and research. BMRB, JWT's research subsidiary, made use of official statistics and home-grown sociology in its attempts to map post-war social change, alongside psychological approaches to consumer behaviour. In press advertising, JWT notably developed styles that combined the conventions and traditions of its parent company with cultural resources drawn from British and continental photography and film making. In the late 1960s this included picking up on the dynamic image making associated with 'Swinging London'. And we saw how in the development of television advertising the hybridizing and indigenizing of US practices contributed to the development of a distinctive British tradition. While this tradition had its roots in interwar developments in sponsored documentary film making and the traditions of press advertising in Britain, it was stimulated by the appropriation and reworking of US influences as well. The movement of US practices eastwards across the Atlantic served was a spur and a resource, productively generating approaches to TV advertising which were distinct from US approaches while often drawing on their example.

This was certainly the case in the genre of adverts aimed at the massmarket housewife. These commercials have occupied a privileged position in my account in large part because the housewife was post-war advertising's key consumer target, being associated with some of the most heavily advertised goods, especially on TV. The commercials aimed at the housewife drew strongly on the tradition of the 'slice of life' drama which had its roots in American commercial culture. But as we saw in the case of both Persil's and Oxo's TV advertising, the commercials rendered the depiction of the housewife and her home as distinctly English-British entities. They did this through the casting and styling of the women who represented the 'ordinary housewife' in these commercials and in their choice of domestic and social settings. This indigenizing of the 'slice of life' drama had a second, further consequence. It worked to domesticate the ideal of the 'housewife-consumer' and the model of the 'new household' which had their origins, at least in part, in US culture.

If one key dimension of the cultural significance of these commercials, then, was the way they helped to render the 'new (post-war) household' as something that was compatible with British domesticity, they also gave a normative force to this ideal. As chapter five argued, in the late 1950s and 1960s there was a big gap between the way that TV advertising represented domesticity and the living conditions of many Britons. Viewers could often only dream of owning the kind of Parker Morris-approved kitchen which Katie presided over. The commercials, especially for Oxo, were not only in this regard 'aspirational', but also normative. They established the idea that this was what homes – especially kitchens – should look like. At the same time the adverts offered women viewers powerful fantasies of contemporary femininity in the form of the progressive 'modern housewife'. Their seductiveness certainly caught the eye of the Pilkington Committee, which described these 'slice of life' commercials as using all 'the excitement of fiction and the compelling reality of the everyday'.[5]

As we saw in chapter six, at least some viewers were riveted by the sagas of Katie in particular. The long-running serial nature of the adverts helped to make Katie knowable to them in the same way as real people in their lives. This kind of reaction to the adverts paralleled the response which media scholars have identified in the watchers of soap operas.[6] As I argued, however, there was also a more precise historical experience of viewing TV adverts and TV in general that came through in the reception of the Persil and Oxo commercials. In the late 1950s and 1960s watching television retained something of its novelty for the first generation of post-war TV viewers. This novelty sprang from not only the relative scarcity of television's output, but also from TV's immediacy and directness as a medium of communication. While, as the experts on making commercials put it, 'seeing was believing', TV also had a phenomenological influence upon viewers. As Paddy Scannell has powerfully argued, TV could create the sense among viewers of both being at home watching the programme and yet caught up in the unfolding of the drama on the screen. This 'double consciousness' fostered by TV was – and is – most powerful with live broadcasts and the vivid eventfulness that they create.[7] But we can also see it the responses of women viewers to the Oxo adverts. They revealed this sense of being caught up in the unfolding of Katie's life as they watched at home. Importantly some of these viewers expressed their immersion in Katie's world by writing letters to her and the makers of the commercials. The pull of TV, its immediate presence in viewers' lives, met an older culture of letter writing in the 1950s and 1960s. It was the coming together in these immediate post-war years of both technologies of communication – television and letter writing – which was historically distinctive and which helped to embed the commercial fables in the lives of their viewers. Writing offered a way of reflecting on the commercials and helped to consolidate their significance to those watching.

It was not only 'ordinary viewers' who could be engaged by TV adverts. So could rather differently placed observers – cultural and social critics, policy makers and large sections of the main political parties. Their reactions formed part of the critical and intellectual context in which post-war advertising developed. As we saw, the arrival of TV advertising provoked a largely negative and critical reaction from this body of informed opinion. The debate about advertising led by its critics takes us to the heart of the cultural significance of the developments in post-war advertising which I have charted. For its critics, the new visibility and pervasiveness of TV advertising was part of a wider set of problems associated with growing material affluence. Informed by a body of cultural criticism, some of it American in origin, commentators and policy makers in government and many within the political parties took issue with the styles of persuasion developed by advertising agencies and the model of life which they represented. The cultural critic Richard Hoggart was an especially influential observer. Hoggart took to task what he saw as the unreal nature of the way soap and washing powder commercials, in particular, depicted family life. He suggested that they smoothed over the way that families had to balance the competing needs and desires of their members while building a shared life together. He also chastised the adverts for exploiting family emotions, especially mother love.

Hoggart's observations about advertising fed into the machinery of public policy. As we saw in chapter seven, he was an influential member of the Pilkington Committee and it is possible to see his thinking informing the committee's published criticisms of TV advertising. Certainly the report's dislike of the way that commercials promoted acquisitiveness, crass materialism and status-striving bore the mark of Hoggart's anti-commercialism and moralism. This kind of thinking had direct policy implications, informing the containing of commercialism within British TV until the early 1980s. One consequence of this was the limiting of advertising air time on British TV. Despite the particular force of his critique, however, Hoggart's views were not unique and his general moral antipathy to advertising and consumer culture was shared by large sections of educated opinion and within the cultural and political elites. It also reached down to the grassroots of both the Tory and Labour parties.

Alongside the responses to advertising from these quarters, there was also another distinctive strand to the critique of advertising which first surfaced in the mid-1960s. This concerned the depiction of the housewife-consumer. While, as we saw in chapter five, there was some discussion within the advertising industry about the way commercials depicted the housewife, it was the criticisms developed by second wave feminists in the United States which began to more seriously problematize the apparently secure cultural value of these representations. Betty Friedan's pioneering assault on what she saw as the negative social consequences of advertising for women was derived from an analysis of US press, not TV, advertising. It nonetheless managed to capture some of the, as-then unspoken, feelings of dissatisfaction about the post-war 'cult of domesticity'. This had privileged the near-exclusive emphasis on the housewife role as married women's primary career. Friedan saw advertising as complicit in promoting these values. Her critique of post-war US advertising crossed the Atlantic in the late 1960s and began to influence a home-grown critique of the 'cult of domesticity' found not only in advertising, but in adjacent forms of commercial culture and public policy. By the early 1970s her arguments had begun to influence the thinking of the emerging women's liberation movement in Britain. Challenging depictions of femininity – including the housewife role – within advertising and consumer culture became one of the formative preoccupations of second wave feminism.[8]

Advertising people did not register the early American feminist critique of their practices in the 1960s, but they were certainly aware of critics like Richard Hoggart and Vance Packard. Both writers stimulated them to develop a robust defence of their practices. At its upper echelons, the advertising industry took on its critics and engaged in an ideological defence of advertising's role in a culture of growing material affluence. Motivated by an optimistic vision of consumption, it articulated an understanding of consumer subjectivity rooted in the idioms of self-expression and pleasure-seeking. Releasing consumers' desire for goods from the tradition of British puritanism and assembling them as more hedonistic subjects was central to both the intellectual project and technical strategies of post-war advertising. In fact, legitimizing the 'will to want' and the quotidian freedoms of 'getting and spending' bound together the ideological defence of advertising and the technical process of assembling the consumer and commodities which it performed. In its ideological defence, the industry increasingly felt through the late 1950s and 1960s that it had the wind of history in its sails and that its critics were locked into defending the values of an older social order.

If advertising people had some success in legitimating the stimulation of consumer desires, particularly among those consumer groups whom they targeted, the anxieties expressed by their post-war critics about the negative drift of affluence-driven social change did have the power to limit the more aggressive styles of promotion. This included US-derived techniques of 'hard sell' that agencies could have turned to. Furthermore, the views of advertising's critics in the 1950s and 1960s have continued to cast a shadow over critical thinking and have found favour with more recent commentators on post-war affluence. The economic historian Avner Offer has done most to rekindle this critique of the social consequences of the rising levels of material affluence over the last sixty years in both the US and Britain. Offer's arguments, in fact, owe much to the legacy of anti-commercial and moralist critiques of consumer society that were prevalent within the intellectual and political culture of the 1950s and 1960s. His spirited assault on the dangers of affluence emphasizes the corrosive effects of post-war prosperity on well-being, self-control and other forms of prudence. For Offer, the drive for innovation and novelty at the heart of consumer society undermined well-being, creating a focus on short-term pleasures and in turn generating new feelings of dissatisfaction. For Offer, true well-being is founded not upon the abundance of goods, but upon a balance between present and future needs. This requires people to develop self-control and the capacity for 'prudence'. Long-term rewards follow from the cultivation of these capacities and their associated commitment strategies – capacities and strategies undermined by affluence and its 'hedonic treadmill'.[9] Advertising emerges as one of the particular villains of Offer's critique. He sees the arts of persuasion as playing an important role in the paradox of affluence, offering illusory forms of intimacy that intrude upon authentic interpersonal relations.[10]

It is clear that the expansion of popular prosperity in the post-war period was bound up with a deeper cultural shift within British society, one echoed in the rest of Western Europe. This hinged upon the shift from a culture of restraint and deferred gratification to a culture of self-expression and hedonism. This was a movement which the French sociologist Pierre Bourdieu saw bound up with the rise of an ethic or morality of 'pleasure as duty'. More recent commentators like Todd McGowan have similarly described this as a shift from a 'society of prohibition' towards a society of 'commanded enjoyment'.[11] Offer is right to see the deep-rooted social consequences of this shift and his idea of the 'hedonic treadmill' of affluence echoes Bourdieu's and McGowan's assessments. Against Offer's analysis, however, it is necessary to recall the positive social benefits that growing material affluence in the 1950s and 1960s brought the majority of Britons. As both Richard Hoggart and

Raymond Williams forcefully acknowledged at the time, it was not possible to simply dismiss rising standards of living among working-class and lower middle-class groups as crass materialism or the adoption of bourgeois values. Hoggart, in particular, offered a typically poignant, autobiographical sense of social progress in *The Uses of Literacy* when he invoked memories of his grandmother and mother and how their lives would have been eased if they had brought up their families in the mid-twentieth century. As he put it, 'they wanted these goods … and services not out of greed of possessions, … but because lack of them made it very difficult to live … a "decent life"'.[12]

Possessing a washing machine, having access to effective cleaning products, convenience foods, a well-heated home with enough space to turn around in, an indoor toilet and bathroom, a television and cheap fashionable clothing enhanced the lives of those populations who had historically been materially deprived. Post-war advertising was good at communicating the positive benefits of these everyday goods and in assembling the arts of modern living which flowed from them. The faith shown by advertising people in the virtues of a consumerist vision of the good life articulated a sense of the possible in a period when memories of scarcity and privation for the majority were real and tangible. The problem, of course, as Offer and others suggest, comes from the continual cranking up of standards of living and the elevation of what counts as basic needs within consumer society. These are trends which have accelerated in advertising and consumer culture since the 1960s. The problem of advertising-driven affluence, however, is not just about the relentless escalation of consumption norms. In and of themselves advertising and the associated devices of the consumer economy cannot – and historically did not – create an equalization of the standard of living across British society and the wider 'commercial Atlantic'. In a society like Britain there remained substantial inequalities of income and access to resources which consumer society in the 1950s and 1960s did little to change. Rising levels of consumption associated with the inclusion of the mass of the population in consumer markets in the era of affluence also contained its own logics of symbolic division and hierarchy. As Bourdieu famously showed, these worked to reproduce class-cultural divisions even in a period of narrowing class differentials in levels of consumption. How you dressed, your choice of curtains and sofa, whether you watched ITV, as much as how you spoke, affirmed class differences rather than blurring them.

In recent years a reinvigorated consumer movement has sought to re-engineer how consumer markets might function by seeking to re-imagine consumer choice so that it includes a set of ethical judgements and is not simply based upon the pursuit of private wants and the 'hedonic treadmill'. In the case of an organization like Fairtrade, for example, such an approach does not seek external means to soften the differential access to consumer goods. Rather it seeks to redefine consumption/production relations in specific commodity markets.[13] This has meant trying to bridge the gap between Western consumers of goods like chocolate and coffee and their producers in other parts of the world in order to create better terms of trade. In a similar way, environmental critiques of 'over-consumption' have aimed to redefine consumer choice by drawing attention to the finite nature of resources like water and raw materials associated with 'inconspicuous' forms of consumption like washing, showering and heating. The escalation of social norms in these areas of practice makes greater demands upon energy and water resources.[14] Both interventions in consumer culture aim to create an ethical citizen-consumer whose individual desires are tempered by collective responsibilities.

This attempt to shape citizen-consumers across a range of consumer markets and settings represents an honourable political project. But there is a nagging question which lurks at its heart which comes from the values promoted in the 'affluent' 1950s and 1960s. Namely, how do you set limits on consumption? When is enough, enough? For all their power, models of the citizen-consumer deploy a rationalist model of human action. This is poor at grasping what advertising people and market researchers have known since the 1940s: that the problem of consumer subjectivity, for both advertising and its critics, is that it is shaped by emotional dynamics and investments in goods which are not exclusively rational. Furthermore, advertising has contributed to the linking of private-sector consumption with an ethic of freedom. Setting limits on this freedom is a difficult problem and requires disentangling consumers from the apparatus of advertising and consumption. The advertising practitioners who have figured centrally in this book were part of the problem with their belief in the transformative power of rising material affluence and the modest freedoms of everyday consumption. They were also complicit in the production of dissatisfaction and the need for novelty and innovation in consumption practices. But they were not alone in not having a very good answer to the question of how societies might temper consumers' 'will to want', while protecting the social gains of post-war affluence.

Notes

1. P. Yeo, *Reflections on an Agency*, n.d., unpublished typescript, p. 53, HAT.
2. See S. Nixon, *Hard Looks: Masculinities, Spectatorship and Contemporary Consumption*, London: UCL Press, 1996; A. Mattelart, *Advertising International: The Privatisation of Public Space*, London: Routledge, 1991, pp. 1–48.
3. On European design innovations and their influence on US design, see P. Sparke, *An Introduction to Design and Culture in the Twentieth Century*, London: Allen & Unwin, 1986, pp. 3–52; Sparke, *Electrical Applicances*, London: Unwin Hyman, 1987. American commercial design also developed design styles distinct from European modernism, especially in car design. On 'streamlining', see Sparke, *Introduction to Design and Culture*, p. 52, and D. Hebdige, 'Towards a cartography of taste 1935–62', in *Hiding in the Light*, London: Comedia, 1988, pp. 45–76.
4. There were parallel developments in the field of public policy. On the European influence on American social policy in the 1930s and 1940s, see D. Rogers, *Atlantic Crossings: Social Politics in a Progressive Age*, Cambridge, MA: Harvard University Press, 1998.
5. Post Office, *Report of the Committee on Broadcasting 1960*, 1961–2 Cmnd 1753, Para. 253, 80.
6. See P. Scannell, *Radio, Television and Modern Life*, Oxford: Blackwell, 1996.
7. Ibid.
8. M. Wandor (ed.), *The Body Politic: Writings from the Women's Liberation Movement in Britain, 1969–72*, London: Stage 1, 1973; A. Oakley, *Housewife*, London: Allen Lane, 1974; S. Rowbotham, *The Past is Before Us*, London: Pandora, 1989; J. Mitchell, 'Women: the longest revolution', *New Left Review*, November/December 1966, pp. 11–37; Birmingham Feminist History Group, 'Feminism as femininity in the 1950s?', *Feminist Review*, 5, 1979, pp. 38–65.
9. A. Offer, *The Challenge of Affluence: Self-Control and Well-being in the United States and Britain since 1950*, Oxford: Oxford University Press, 2006, pp. 1–4, 358.
10. Ibid., pp. 103–6.
11. T. McGowan, cited in Y. Stavrakakis, *The Lacanian Left: Psychoanalysis, Theory and Politics*, Edinburgh: Edinburgh University Press, 2007.
12. R. Hoggart, *The Uses of Literacy*, Harmondsworth: Penguin Books, 1957, p. 139.
13. K. Wheeler, *Fairtrade and the Citizen Consumer: Shopping for Justice?*, Basingstoke: Palgrave Macmillan, forthcoming; N. Clarke, C. Barnett, P. Cloke and A. Malpass, 'Globalising the consumer: doing politics in an ethical register', *Political Geography*, 26(3), 2007, pp. 231–49.
14. See, inter alia, E. Shove, *Comfort, Cleanliness and Convenience: The Social Organization of Normality*, London: Berg, 2003; K. Soper, *Troubled Pleasures: Writings on Politics, Gender and Hedonism*, London: Verso, 1990; Soper, 'Rethinking the good life: the citizenship dimension of consumer dissatisfaction with consumerism', *Journal of Consumer Culture*, 7(2), 2007, pp. 205–29; F. Trentmann, 'Citizenship and consumption', *Journal of Consumer Culture*, 7(2), 2007, pp. 147–58; M. Hilton, *Prosperity for All: Consumer Activism in an Era of Globalization*, New York: Cornell University Press, 2009; A. Chatriot, M.-E. Chessel and M. Hilton (eds), *The Expert Consumer: Associations and Professionals in Consumer Society*, London: Ashgate, 2006.

Bibliography

Unpublished primary sources

Geoffrey Gorer Papers, University of Sussex, Box 3/B Ms52.
History of Advertising Trust
    Advertising Association AA 1–13
    George Butler Collection GB/1–5
    The Colman, Prentice and Varley Archive, 21/73
    Hennessy, E., *Dorland – History*, n.d.
    Institute of Practitioners in Advertising IPA 1–17
    J. Walter Thompson Company Archives
    Records of the London Press Exchange
    Yeo, P., *Reflections on an Agency*, n.d.
John W. Hartman Center for Sales, Advertising and Marketing History, Duke University
    J. Walter Thompson Company Archives, Edward G. Wilson papers
    Papers of Samuel William Meek
Mass Observation Archive, University of Sussex
    File Reports: A10 Reactions to Advertising; 14–1949 Mass Observation Panel on Television
    Topic Collection (1937–60): Commercial Advertising 1938–47 TC 22; Commodities, 1941–64, TC 78
National Archives Public Records Office, Kew
    Board of Trade Papers, PRO BT 64, BT 213, BT 244, BT 250, BT 256, BT 258, BT 315
    Home Office Papers, PRO HO 244
    Prime Minister's Office Papers, PRO PREM 13, PREM 11
National Galleries of Scotland, Edinburgh, Ashley Havinden Archive GMA
Unilever Archives, Port Sunlight, Unilever Director's Conference
University College London, Special Collections, Gaitskell Papers, G (8)
University of Essex, Qualidata, Brian Jackson Archive, SN 4870
University of Essex, Special Collections
    The Labour Party Advertising Committee Records
    Report of a Commission of Enquiry into Advertising, the Labour Party, 1966

Official publications and House of Commons Parliamentary Papers

Board of Trade, *Final Report of the Committee on Consumer Protection*, 1961–2 Cmnd 1781.
Ministry of Housing and Local Government, *Homes for today and Tomorrow*, London: HMSO, 1961.
The Public Schools Commission, first report, London: HMSO, 1968.
Post Office, *Report of the Broadcasting Committee 1949*, 1950–1 Cmnd 8116.
Post Office, *Report of the Committee on Broadcasting 1960*, 1961–2 Cmnd 1753.
Report of the Royal Commission on the Press, 1961–2, 1961–2 Cmnd 1811.

Newspapers, periodicals and journals

Adam
Advertiser's Annual
Advertiser's Weekly
Advertising Review
Audio-visual Selling
Commercial Television News
Commentary
D&AD Annual
Daily Express
Daily Mirror
Design
IAOTL (In and Out the Lane)
Institute Information
IPA Forum
IPA News
Journal of the Advertising Association
J. Walter Thompson Company News
Kompass
London Life
Modern Living
Round the Square
Statistical Review of Independent Television
The Times
Unilever House Magazine

Secondary works

Abrams, M., *Education, Social Class and Newspaper Reading*, London: IPA, 1963.
Abrams, M., 'The home-centred society', *The Listener*, 26 November 1959, pp. 914–15.
Abrams, M., 'New roots of working class Conservatism', *Encounter*, May 1960, pp. 57–8.
Abrams, M., *The Newspaper Reading Public of Tomorrow*, London: Odhams, 1964.

Abrams, M., 'Opinion polls and party propaganda', *Public Opinion Quarterly*, 28(1), 1964, pp. 13–19.
Abrams, M., *Social Surveys and Social Action*, London: Heinemann, 1951.
Abrams, M., *The Teenage Consumer*, London: London Press Exchange, 1959.
Abrams, M., and Rose, R., *Must Labour Lose?*, Harmondsworth: Penguin Books, 1960.
Advertising Association, *Advertising Expenditure*, London: Advertising Association, 1953.
Advertising Association, *Advertising Expenditure 1960*, London: Advertising Association, 1962.
Advertising Association, *Advertising Expenditure 1960–73*, London: Advertising Association, 1974.
Anon. (Jill Neville), 'Writing the ads', *New Left Review*, March/April 1966, pp. 15–20.
Arvidsson, A., 'The therapy of consumption, motivation research and the New Italian housewife 1958–62', *Journal of Material Culture*, 5(3), 2000, pp. 251–74.
Black, L., *The Political Culture of the Left in Affluent Britain, 1951–64*, Basingstoke: Palgrave Macmillan, 2003.
Black, L., *Redefining British Politics: Culture, Consumerism and Participation, 1954–70*, Basingstoke: Palgrave Macmillan, 2010.
Blythe, I., *The Making of an Industry: The Market Research Society 1946–86*, London: Market Research Society, 2005.
Bingham, A., *Family Newspapers? Sex, Private Life and the British Popular Press, 1918–78*, Oxford: Oxford University Press, 2009.
Bingham, A., *Gender, Modernity and the Popular Press in Inter-war Britain*, Oxford: Oxford University Press, 2004.
Birmingham Feminist History Group, 'Feminism as femininity in the 1950s?', *Feminist Review*, 5, 1979, pp. 48–65.
Booker, C., *The Neophiliacs: A Study of the Revolution in English Life in the 50s and 60s*, London: Collins, 1969.
Bowden, S., 'The new consumerism', in P. Johnson (ed.), *Twentieth Century British History: Economic, Social and Cultural Change*, London: Longman, 1994, pp. 242–62.
Bowden, S., and Offer, A., 'The technological revolution that never was: gender, class and the diffusion of household appliances in interwar England', in V. de Grazia and E. Furlough (eds), *The Sex of Things: Gender and Consumption in Historical Perspective*, Berkeley and Los Angeles: University of California Press, 1996, pp. 244–74.
Bradbury, M., *Dangerous Pilgrimages: Trans-Atlantic Mythologies and the Novel*, London: Secker & Warburg, 1995.
Breward, C., 'Clothing desire: the problem of the British fashion consumer c. 1955–1975', ESRC *Cultures of Consumption* working paper series, 7, 2004, unpublished.
Breward, C., and Gilbert, D., 'Anticipation of the new urban cultural economy: fashion and the transformation of London's West End', in M. Hebler and C. Zimmermann (eds), *Creative Urban Milieus: Historical Perspectives in Culture, Economy and the City*, Frankfurt and New York: Campus Verlag, 2008, pp. 159–78.
British Market Research Bureau, *The New Housewife*, London: BMRB, 1967.
Brunsdon, C., *The Feminist, the Housewife and the Soap Opera*, Oxford: Clarendon Press, 2000.
Bullock, N., 'First the kitchen – then the facade', *Journal of Design History*, 1(3–4), 1988, pp. 177–92.

Burnett, J., *A Social History of Housing 1815–1985*, London: Methuen, 1986.
Callon, M., Meadel, C., and Rabeharisoa, V., 'The economy of qualities', *Economy & Society*, 31(2), 2002, pp. 194–217.
Callon, M., Milo, Y., and Muniesa, F. (eds), *Market Devices*, Oxford: Blackwell, 2007.
Callon, M., and Muniesa, F., 'Peripheral vision: economic markets as calculative collective devices', *Organization Studies*, 26(8), 2005, pp. 1229–50.
Caughie, J., 'Before the Golden Age: early television drama', in J. Corner (ed.), *Popular Television in Britain*, London: British Film Institute, 1991, pp. 22–41.
Chaney, L., *Elizabeth David: A Biography*, London: Macmillan, 1998.
Chatriot, A., Chessel, M.-E., and Hilton, M. (eds), *The Expert Consumer: Associations and Professionals in Consumer Society*, London: Ashgate, 2006.
Church, R., and Godley, A. (eds), *The Emergence of Modern Marketing*, London: Frank Cass, 2003.
Church Gibson, P., 'From up north to up west? London on screen 1965–67', *The London Journal*, 31(1), June 2006, pp. 85–107.
Clarke, N., Barnett, C., Cloke, P., and Malpass, A., 'Globalising the consumer: doing politics in an ethical register', *Political Geography*, 26(3), 2007, pp. 231–49.
Collini, S., 'Richard Hoggart: literary criticism and cultural decline in twentieth century Britain', in S. Owen (ed.), *Richard Hoggart and Cultural Studies*, Basingstoke: Palgrave Macmillan, 2008, pp. 33–47.
Conekin, B., Mort, F., and Waters, C., 'Introduction', in *Moments of Modernity: Reconstructing Britain 1945–64*, London: Rivers Oram, 1999, pp. 1–21.
Corley, T.A.B., *Domestic Electrical Appliances*, London: Jonathan Cape, 1966.
Corner, J. (ed.), *Popular Television in Britain*, London: British Film Institute, 1991.
Crichton, J., 'A major influence on economic growth', in IPA, *Fifty Years of Growing Responsibility*, London: IPA, 1967, pp. 16–26.
David, E., *French Country Cooking*, London: John Lehmann, 1951.
Davidoff, L., Doolittle, M., Fink, J., and Holden, K., *The Family Story: Blood, Contract and Intimacy, 1830–1960*, London: Longman, 1999.
De Grazia, V., *Irresistible Empire: America's Advance Through Twentieth Century Europe*, Cambridge, MA, and London: The Belnap Press of Harvard University Press, 2005.
Despland, M., *Bastide on Religion, the Invention of Candomble*, London: Equinox Publishing, 2008.
Dichter, E., *The Strategy of Desire*, New York: Doubleday, 1961.
Djelic, M.-L., *Exporting the American Model: The Post-war Transformation of European Business*, New York: Oxford University Press, 1998.
Downham, J.S., *BMRB International: The First Sixty Years*, London: BMRB International, 1993.
Downham, J.S., Shankleman, E. and Treasure, J.A.P., *A Survey of Market Research in Great Britain*, London: BMRB, 1956.
Doyle, P., 'Advertising expenditure and consumer demand', *Oxford Economic Papers*, 20(3), 1968, pp. 394–416.
Fitzgerald, R., *Rowntree and the Marketing Revolution, 1862–1969*, Cambridge: Cambridge University Press, 1995.
Fletcher, W., *Powers of Persuasion: The Inside Story of British Advertising*, Oxford: Oxford University Press, 2008.
Foot, M., *Aneurin Bevan, Volume 2*, St Albans: Paladin, 1975.

Forty, A., *Objects of Desire: Design and Society since 1750*, London: Thames & Hudson, 1986.
Fox, S., *The Mirror Makers: A History of American Advertising and its Creators*, New York: Morrow, 1984.
Gilroy, P., *Ain't No Black in the Union Jack: The Cultural Politics of Race and Nation*, London: Routledge, 1987.
Gilroy, P., *The Black Atlantic: Modernity and Double Consciousness*, London: Verso, 1993.
Glucksmann, M., *Women Assemble: Women Workers and the New Industries in Inter-war Britain*, London: Routledge, 1990.
Goldthorpe, J., and Lockwood, D., 'Affluence and the British class structure', *Sociological Review*, 11(2), 1963, pp. 133–63.
Goldthorpe, J., Lockwood, D. Bechoffer, F., and Platt, J., *The Affluent Worker in the Class Structure*, Cambridge: Cambridge University Press, 1969.
Gurney, P., 'The battle for the consumer in post-war Britain', *Journal of Modern History*, 77, 2005, pp. 970–5.
Hall, S., 'The big swipe', *New Left Review*, 1959, 7, pp. 50–3.
Hall, S., 'A sense of classlessness', *New Left Review*, 1958, 5, pp. 26–32.
Harris, R., and Seldon, A., *Advertising in Action*, London: Hutchinson, 1962.
Hartley, J., *The Uses of Television*, London: Routledge and Kegan Paul, 1999.
Hebdige, D., 'Towards a cartography of taste 1935–62', in D. Hebdige, *Hiding in the Light*, London: Comedia, 1988, pp. 45–76.
Hennessy, P., *Having It So Good: Britain in the Fifties*, Harmondsworth: Penguin Books, 2007.
Henry, B (ed.), *British Television Advertising: The First Thirty Years*, London: Ebury Press, 1986.
Henry, H., *Motivation Research: Its Practice and Uses for Advertising*, London: Crosby Lockwood & Son, 1958.
Henry, H., *Motivation Research and the TV Commercial*, London: ATV Series, 1959.
Higgins, D., *The Art of Writing Advertising*, Lincolnwood, IL: NTC Business Books, 1965.
Hilton, M., *Consumerism in the Twentieth Century: The Search for an Historical Movement*, Cambridge: Cambridge University Press, 2003.
Hilton, M., *Prosperity for All: Consumer Activism in an Era of Globalization*, New York: Cornell University Press, 2009.
Himmelweit, H., Oppenheim, A.N., and Vince, P., *Television and the Child*, Oxford: Oxford University Press, 1958.
Hobsbawn, E., *Age of Extremes: The Short Twentieth Century*, London: Michael Joseph, 1994.
Hoggart, R., 'BBC and ITV after three years', *New Left Review*, 1958, 5, pp. 32–6.
Hoggart, R., 'The case against advertising', in R. Hoggart, *Speaking to Each Other, Volume 1: About Society*, Harmondsworth: Penguin Books, 1971 [1965], pp. 205–11.
Hoggart, R., 'Changes in working class life', in *Speaking to Ourselves: Essays on Society*, Harmondsworth: Penguin Books, 1971, pp. 45–61.
Hoggart, R., *An Imagined Life: Life and Times 1959–1991*, Oxford: Oxford University Press, 1991.
Hoggart, R., *The Uses of Literacy*, Harmondsworth: Penguin Books, 1957.
Hoggart, R., 'The uses of television', *Encounter*, January 1960, pp. 42–4.

Holmes, S., *Entertaining Television: The BBC and Popular Television Culture in the 1950s*, Manchester: Manchester University Press, 2008.
Horowitz, D., *Anxieties of Affluence: Critiques of American Consumer Culture, 1939–1979*, Cambridge, MA: University of Massachusetts Press, 2003.
Horowitz, D., *Betty Friedan and the Making of the Feminine Mystique: The American Left, the Cold War and Modern Feminism*, Amherst: University of Massachusetts Press, 1998.
Horowitz, D., *Vance Packard and American Social Criticism*, Chapel Hill, NC: University of North Carolina Press, 1994.
Houlbrook, M., 'A pin to see the peepshow: culture, fiction and self-hood in Edith Thompson's letters 1921–2', *Past and Present*, 207(1), 2010, pp. 215–49.
Howlett, W.P., 'The "Golden Age", 1955–1973', in P. Johnson (ed.), *Twentieth Century British History: Economic, Social and Cultural Change*, London: Longman, 1994, pp. 320–39.
Hughes, G., Lipeitz, A., and Sigh, A., 'The rise and fall of the Golden Age', in S.A. Marglan and J.B. Schor (eds), *The Golden Age of Capitalism: Reinterpreting the Post-war Experience*, Oxford: Clarendon Press, 1990, pp. 39–125.
Hultquist, C.E., 'Americans in Paris: J. Walter Thompson company in France 1927–68', *Enterprise & Society*, 4(3), 2003, pp. 471–99.
Igo, S.E., *The Averaged American: Surveys, Citizens and the Making of a Mass Public*, Cambridge, MA: Harvard University Press, 2007.
IPA, *Agency Employment*, London: IPA, 1966.
IPA, *Agency Employment*, London: IPA, 1967.
IPA, *As Others See Us – a study of attitudes to advertising and to television advertising*, IPA Occasional Paper, 17, London: IPA, 1966.
IPA, *Fifty Years of Growing Responsibility*, London: IPA, 1967.
IPA, *Motivation Research*, London: IPA, 1960.
Jackson, B., *Working Class Community: Some General Notions Raised by a Series of Studies in Northern England*, London: RKP, 1968.
Jarvis, M., *Conservative Governments, Morality and Social Change in Affluent Britain, 1957–64*, Manchester: Manchester University Press, 2005.
Jenkins, C., *Power Behind the Screen*, London: Macgibbon & Kee, 1961.
Johnson, C., and Turnock, R. (eds), *ITV Cultures: Independent Television over Fifty Years*, Maidenhead: Open University Press, 2005.
Jones, G., 'Control, performance and knowledge transfers in large multinationals: Unilever in the United States, 1945–80', *Business History Review*, 76, 2002, pp. 435–78.
Jones, G., and Bostock, F., 'US multinationals in British manufacturing before 1962', *Business History Review*, 70, 1996, pp. 207–56.
J. Walter Thompson, *40 Berkeley Square*, London: JWT, 1967.
J. Walter Thompson, *Shopping in Suburbia*, London: JWT, 1962.
Killick, J., *The United States and European Reconstruction 1945–60*, Edinburgh: Keele University Press, 1997.
Kynaston, D., *Family Britain, 1951–1957*, London: Bloomsbury, 2009.
Langhamer, C., 'The meaning of the home in post-war Britain', *Journal of Contemporary History*, 40(2), 2005, pp. 341–62.
Laski, M., 'Why I hate advertising', *Listener*, 28 October 1965, pp. 653–4.
Lears, J., *Fables of Abundance: A Cultural History of American Advertising*, New York:

Basic Books, 1994.
Leavis, F.R., *Mass Civilization and Minority Culture*, London: Folcroft, 1930.
Le Mahieu, D., *A Culture of Democracy: Mass Communication and the Cultivated Mind in Britain between the Wars*, Oxford: Clarendon Press, 1988.
Light, A., *Forever England: Femininity, Conservatism and Literature between the Wars*, London: Routledge, 1991.
Lockwood, D., 'The new working class', *European Journal of Sociology*, 1, 1960, pp. 248–59.
Mandler, P., 'How modern is it?', *Journal of British Studies*, 42(2), 2003, pp. 271–5.
Marshall, A., *Industry and Trade*, London: Macmillan, 1919.
Mattelart, A., *Advertising International: The Privatisation of Public Space*, London: Routledge, 1991.
Mayhew, C., *Dear Viewer*, n.p., 1953.
McIntyre, I., *The Expense of Glory: A Life of John Reith*, London: Harper Collins, 1994.
McKibbin, R., *Classes and Culture: England 1918–51*, Oxford: Oxford University Press, 1998.
Milland, J., 'Courting Malvolio: the background to the Pilkington committee on broadcasting 1960–2', *Contemporary British History*, 18(2), 2004, pp. 76–102.
Miller, P., and Rose, N., 'Mobilizing the consumer, assembling the subject of consumption', *Theory, Culture & Society*, 14(1), 1997, pp. 1–36.
Mitchell, J., 'Women: the longest revolution', *New Left Review*, November/December 1966, pp. 11–37.
Mort, F., 'The Ben Pimlott Memorial Lecture 2010: the permissive society revisited', *Twentieth Century British History*, 22(2), 2011, pp. 269–98.
Mort, F., *Capital Affairs: The Making of the Permissive Society*, New Haven and London: Yale University Press, 2010.
Mulhern, F., 'A welfare culture?', *Radical Philosophy*, 77, May/June 1996, pp. 29–35.
National Union of Teachers, *The Teacher Looks at Advertising*, London: National Union of Teachers, 1963.
Nevett, T., *Advertising in Britain: A History*, London: Collins, 1982.
Nixon, S., *Hard Looks: Masculinities, Spectatorship and Contemporary Consumption*, London: UCL Press, 1996.
Nixon, S., 'In pursuit of the professional ideal: advertising and the construction of commercial expertise in Britain 1953–64', in P. Jackson, M. Lowe, D. Miller and F. Mort (eds), *Commercial Cultures: Economies, Practices, Spaces*, Oxford: Berg, 2000, pp. 55–74.
Oakley, A., *Housewife*, London: Allen Lane, 1974.
O'Connor, J., 'From minor to major key', in IPA, *Fifty Years of Growing Responsibility*, London: IPA, 1967, pp. 3–15.
Offer, A., *The Challenge of Affluence: Self-Control and Well-being in the United States and Britain since 1950*, Oxford: Oxford University Press, 2006.
Ogilvy, D., *Confessions of an Advertising Man*, London: Mayflower Books, 1966.
Orwell, G., *Keep the Aspidistra Flying*, London: Victor Gollancz, 1936.
O'Sullivan, T., 'Researching the viewing culture: television in the home, 1946–60', in H. Wheatley (ed.), *Re-viewing Television History: Critical Issues in Television Historiography*, London: IB Tauris, 2007, pp. 159–69.
O'Sullivan, T., 'Television memories and cultures of viewing, 1950–65', in J. Corner

(ed.), *Popular Television in Britain*, London: British Film Institute, 1991, pp. 158–81.
Packard, V., *The Hidden Persuaders*, New York: David MacKay, 1957.
Packard, V., *The Status Seekers*, New York: David MacKay, 1959.
Packard, V., *The WasteMakers*, New York: David MacKay, 1960.
Pearson, J., and Turner, G., *The Persuasion Industry*, London: Eyre & Spottiswoode, 1965.
Pells, R., *Not Like Us: How Europeans Have Loved, Hated and Transformed American Culture since World War Two*, New York: Basic Books, 1997.
Piggott, S., *OBM, A Celebration of 125 Years in Advertising*, London: Ogilvy Benson & Mather, 1975.
Pimlott, B., *Harold Wilson*, London: Harper Collins, 1992.
Potter, D., *The Changing Forest*, London: Secker & Warburg, 1962.
Potter, D., *The Glittering Coffin*, London: Victor Gollancz, 1960.
Priestley, J.B., *English Journey*, London: Heinemann, 1935.
Radner, H., 'On the move, fashion photography and the Single Girl in the 1960s', in S. Bruzzi and P. Church Gibson (eds), *Fashion Cultures: Theories, Explorations and Analyses*, London: Routledge, 2000, pp. 128–42.
Rayfield, T., *Fifty in Forty: The Unofficial History of JWT London, 1945–95*, privately published, 1996.
Rogers, D., *Atlantic Crossings: Social Politics in a Progressive Age*, Cambridge. MA: Harvard University Press, 1998.
Roper, L., *Oedipus and the Devil: Witchcraft, Sexuality and Religion in Early Modern Europe*, London: Routledge, 1994.
Roper, M., *Masculinity and the British Organization Man*, Oxford: Oxford University Press, 1994.
Roper, M., 'Slipping out of view: subjectivity and emotion in gender history', *History Workshop Journal*, 59(1), 2005, pp. 57–72.
Rose, J., *The Intellectual Life of the British Working Class*, New Haven and London: Yale University Press, 2002.
Rose, R., *Influencing Voters: A Study of Campaign Rationality*, London: Faber & Faber, 1967.
Ross, K., *Fast Cars, Clean Bodies: Decolonization and the Reordering of French Culture*, Cambridge, MA: MIT Press, 1995.
Rowbotham, S., *The Past is Before Us*, London: Pandora, 1989.
Sampson, A., *Anatomy of Britain Today*, London: Hodder & Stoughton, 1962.
Samuel, L., *Brought To You By: Post-war Television Advertising and the American Dream*, Austin: University of Texas Press, 2002.
Samuel, R., 'Class and classlessness', *New Left Review*, 1959, 6, pp. 44–50.
Samuel, R., 'Dr Abrams and the end of politics', *New Left Review*, 1960, 9, pp. 2–9.
Sandbrook, D., *Never Had It So Good: A History of Britain from Suez to the Beatles*, London: Little, Brown, 2005.
Scannell, P., *Radio, Television and Modern Life*, Oxford: Blackwell, 1996.
Scase, R., and Brown, P., *Higher Education and Corporate Realities*, Milton Keynes: Open University Press, 1994.
Schwarzkopf, S., '"Culture" and the limits of innovations in marketing: Ernest Dichter, motivation studies and psychological consumer research in Great Britain, 1950s–70s', *Management and Organizational History*, 2(3), 2007, pp. 219–36.

Schwarzkopf, S., 'A moment of triumph in the history of the free market', in M. Bailey (ed.), *Narrating Media History*, London: Routledge, 2008, pp. 83–94.

Schwarzkopf, S., 'Respectable persuaders, the advertising industry and British society 1900–39', unpublished PhD thesis, Birkbeck College, Univeristy of London, 2008.

Schwarzkopf, S., 'Transatlantic invasions or common culture? Modes of cultural and economic exchange between the British and American advertising industries 1945–2000', in J.H. Wiener and M. Hampton (eds), *Anglo-American Media Interactions, 1850–2000*, Basingstoke: Palgrave Macmillan, 2007, pp. 254–74.

Sendall, B., *Independent Television in Britain, Volume I: Origin and Foundation 1946–62*, London: Macmillan, 1982.

Shaw, R., 'Sunday persuasion – the adverts', in R. Hoggart (ed.), *Your Sunday Paper*, London: University of London Press, 1967, pp. 95–108.

Shove, E., *Comfort, Cleanliness and Convenience: The Social Organization of Normality*, London: Berg, 2003.

Simons, H., *A Positive Programme for Laissez-faire*, Chicago: University of Chicago Press, 1934.

Smith, A.C.H., *Paper Voices: The Popular Press and Social Change, 1935–65*, London: Chatto & Windus, 1975.

Smith, D., *Aneurin Bevan and the World of South Wales*, Cardiff: University of Wales Press, 1993.

Smith, R.M., 'Elements of demographic change in Britain', in J. Obelkovich and P. Catterall (eds), *Understanding Post-war British Society*, London: Routledge, 1994, pp. 22–38.

Soper, K., 'Rethinking the good life: the citizenship dimension of consumer dissatisfaction with consumerism', *Journal of Consumer Culture*, 7(2), 2007, pp. 205–29.

Soper, K., *Troubled Pleasures: Writings on Politics, Gender and Hedonism*, London: Verso, 1990.

Sparke, P., *Electrical Appliances*, London: Unwin Hyman, 1987.

Sparke, P., *An Introduction to Design and Culture in the Twentieth Century*, London: Allen & Unwin, 1986.

Stavrakakis, Y., *The Lacanian Left: Psychoanalysis, Theory and Politics*, Edinburgh: Edinburgh University Press, 2007.

Strasser, S., *Never Done: A History of American Housework*, New York: Pantheon Books, 1982.

Summerfield, P., 'Women in Britain since 1945, companionate marriage and the double burden', in J. Obelkovich and P. Catterall (eds), *Understanding Post-war British Society*, London: Routledge, 1994, pp. 58–72.

Thompson, D., *Discrimination and Popular Culture*, Harmondsworth: Penguin Books, 1964.

Thompson, E.P., 'Commitment in politics', *New Left Review*, 1959, 6, pp. 50–5.

Thumin, J., *Inventing Television Culture: Men, Women and the Box*, Oxford: Oxford University Press, 2004.

Tiratsoo, N., and Tomlinson, J., 'Exporting the "Gospel of Productivity": United States technical assistance and British industry 1945–60', *Business History Review*, 71, spring 1997, pp. 41–81.

Todd, S., 'Affluence, class and Crown Street: reinvestigating the post-war working class', *Contemporary British History*, 22(4), 2008, pp. 501–18.

Todd, S., *Young Women, Work and Family in England 1918–1950*, Oxford: Oxford University Press, 2005.
Tomlinson, J., 'Inventing decline: the falling behind of the British economy in the post-war years', *Economic History Review*, 49, 1996, pp. 731–57.
Townsend, P., 'The meaning of poverty', *British Journal of Sociology*, 13(3), 1962, pp. 210–27.
Treasure, J., 'American marketing in Britain', *The Grocer*, 8 July 1961, pp. 40–1.
Treasure, J. 'Market research in Britain', *Commentary*, 8(3), 1966.
Trentmann, F., 'Citizenship and consumption', *Journal of Consumer Culture*, 7(2), 2007, pp. 147–58.
Tunstall, J., *The Advertising Man in London Advertising Agencies*, London: Chapman & Hall, 1964.
Turnock, R., *Television and Consumer Culture*, London: IB Tauris, 2007.
Wandor, M. (ed.), *The Body Politic: Writings from the Women's Liberation Movement in Britain, 1969–72*, London: Stage 1, 1972.
West, D., 'From T-square to T-plan: the London office of J. Walter Thompson advertising agency 1919–1970', *Business History*, 29(2), 1987, pp. 199–217.
West, D., 'Multinational competition in the British advertising agency business 1936–87', *Business History Review*, 62(3), 1988, pp. 467–501.
Wheeler, K., *Fairtrade and the Citizen Consumer: Shopping for Justice?*, Basingstoke: Palgrave Macmillan, forthcoming.
Williams, F., *The American Invasion*, London: Anthony Blond, 1962.
Williams, P.M., *Hugh Gaitskell: A Political Biography*, London: Jonathan Cape, 1979.
Williams, R. (ed.), *The May Day Manifesto*, Harmondsworth: Penguin Books, 1968.
Wilson, D.S., 'A new look at the affluent worker: the good working mother in post-war Britain', *Twentieth Century British History*, 17(2), 2006, pp. 206–29.
Wilson, H.H., *Pressure Group: The Campaign for Commercial Television*, New Brunswick: Rutgers University Press, 1961.
Winship, J., 'Culture of restraint: the British chain store 1920–39', in P. Jackson, M. Lowe, D. Miller and F. Mort (eds), *Commercial Cultures: Economies, Practices, Spaces*, Oxford: Berg, 2000, pp. 15–34.
Winship, J., *Inside Women's Magazines*, London: Pandora, 1987.
Worsnick, G.D.N., and Ady, P.H. (eds), *The British Economy in the 1950s*, Oxford: Oxford University Press, 1962.
Wring, D., *The Politics of Marketing the Labour Party*, Oxford: Palgrave, 2005.
Young, M., and Willmott, P., *Family and Class in a London Suburb*, London: RKP, 1960.
Zeitlin, J., and Herrigel, G. (eds), *Americanization and its Limits: Reworking US Technology and Management in Post-war Europe and Japan*, Oxford: Oxford University Press, 2000.
Zweiniger Bargielowska, I., *Austerity in Britain: Rationing Controls and Consumption, 1939–1955*, Oxford: Oxford University Press, 2000.

Index

Abrams, Mark 73, 130, 144, 168–9, 178–9
Adams, Robert 36–7
Advertiser's Weekly 109, 128–31
advertising: central aim of 73; public approval or disapproval of 151
advertising agencies: big players 26, 30; founding partners of 27; graduate staff of 27–8, 39; initial views on commercial television 97, 99; new start-ups 26–7; *see also* American-owned advertising agencies
Advertising Association (AA) 20, 26, 177–81; *see also Journal of the Advertising Association*
advertising expenditure 19–24, 31, 47, 181–2
advertising industry 25–30; criticism of 9–10, 13, 31, 114, 164–74, 178, 181–2, 192–3; defence of 10, 13, 164–6, 173, 175, 181, 192; geographical concentration in London 17–18, 25, 31; internationalization of 18, 28–31
Advertising Inquiry Committee 172
advertising magazines ('ad mags') 110–11
advertising practitioners 16–17, 181, 194–5
Advertising Review 44–5
advertising standards 10, 176–7
Advertising Standards Authority 177, 180

affluence 9–10, 13, 44, 47, 120, 146–7, 164–9, 191–5; dangers of 193
American advertising practice 10, 25–6, 38, 45–7, 96–8, 101–4, 107–13, 188
American commercial culture 7, 120, 123, 136, 189
American economic dominance 18–19, 30, 37, 46
'American invasion' of British advertising 30–1, 44–5
American market research 70, 189
American-owned advertising agencies in Britain 4, 18, 27–31, 44–7, 70, 96
American Tobacco 110
'Americanization' of British commerce and culture 4, 11, 31, 37, 59, 98, 188
animals used in advertising 149–51
animated commercials 109
anti-Americanism 43–9
Antonioni, Michelangelo 57–9
Archibald, James 105
Attwoods (research company) 83

Bailey, David 16, 56, 58
Baron, Barry 103
Barr, Robert 103
Bates, Ted 30, 187
Bauhaus school 122, 188
Baxter, Beverley 98
Beaton, Jane 108–9
Beaverbrook Group 143
Beecham Group 20–3

Bevan, Aneurin 164
Billy Liar (film) 58–9
Bingham, Adrian 148
Birley, Mark 51
Booker, Christopher 16
Bourdieu, Pierre 193–4
Bowden, Peggy 44
Bowden, Sue 122
Bowlby, John 68, 130
Boxer, Mark 16
Bradbury, Malcolm 2, 44
Brillo pads 69, 78–80, 108
British Broadcasting Corporation (BBC) 9, 12, 98–9, 103–4, 113, 144, 146, 165, 171–2; Charter 171
British Institute of Management 23
'British invasion' of the American advertising industry 188
British Market Research Bureau (BMRB) 71–5, 80, 83, 87–8, 151–3, 189
British Overseas Airways Corporation (BOAC) 48–50
Buckingham, A.O. 102
Bullmore, Jeremy 103–4, 107
Burnett, J. 122
Butler, George 104, 106

Cadbury's Group 20, 26, 46
Callon, Michel 8
Campbell's of New Jersey 24, 50
car manufacturers 24, 47
Caron, Denis 45–6
Cawston, Derrick 51
Charles F. Higham (agency) 103, 105
Cheeseborough-Ponds 41, 71
Christie, Julie 58–9
Chrysler 167–8
Clark, Jean 148
class divisions 84–6, 152–4, 158, 194
Coca-Cola 47
Collett Dickenson Pearce (CDP) 25
Collini, Stefan 170
Colman Prentis Varley (CPV) 23, 27–30, 97
commercials 8–9, 31, 89, 95–7, 107, 111–13, 120, 127–9, 134, 137; actresses, models and animals in 148–51; entertainment value of 152–3, 157–8; interruptive nature of 152, 157–8; production companies for 12, 113; reactions to 12–13, 111–13, 141, 149, 151–7, 191; viewers' engagement with 142–3, 159
commission rates on advertising expenditure 101
Conservative Party 149, 191
consumer choice 194–5
Consumer Council 179
consumer culture 3, 191, 194–5
consumer durables 5–6, 122–3
consumer expenditure 6, 19, 146, 173
consumer purchasing panels (CPPs) 66–7, 71–2
consumer research 69, 71, 74; *see also* market research
consumerism 136, 145–6, 165–6, 193–4; American 120
Consumers' Association 165, 170, 180
Cookeen 108
Crawford, Sir William 45
'creative lunches' at JWT 52
Cripps, Stafford 47
Crowther Report (1959) 68
cultural differences between Britain and America 3–4, 38, 74, 113

Daily Express 9, 13, 25, 52, 96, 143–51, 158
Daily Mail 25
Daily Mirror 9, 13, 141–9, 158
Daily Telegraph 96
David, Elizabeth 133–4
David Bailey's Box of Pin-Ups 16–17
de Grazia, Victoria 4, 40–1, 59–60, 120, 136
demonstration-style adverts 108, 153
depth interviews 71–2, 167
Design and Art Directors Association 106
Design magazine 123–4
Dichter, Ernest 72–4, 79, 86–7, 167–8
Dietrich, Marlene 150
Dimmock, Peter 103–4
documentary film making 12, 189

documentary-style adverts 108, 113
Dorland Advertising 102–4
Douglas-Home, Robin 51–2
Duffy, Brian 56
Dunning, Ruth 95, 112

Economics Research Unit (ERU) 23
Egan, Gina 148
Egg Marketing Board 112, 134–5
electrical appliances and electricity prices 5, 122–3
employment in advertising 28
employment trends generally 17, 126
'establishment', cultural 51–2
Ewart, Keith 106
Eyre, Richard 44

Fairtrade organization 195
Fairy Liquid 174
feminism 192
Fenwick's 24
Findus 112, 134
food advertising 19–20
Ford Motors 27, 36–7, 50
Fortune magazine 66
Forty, Adrian 122
Franklin (cartoonist) 149
Fraser, Sir Robert 171–2
Fredericks, Christine 122
Freeman, Alan 108
Friedan, Betty 136, 192

Gaitskell, Hugh 177–8
General Electric 125
General Motors 47
'going native' 4, 11, 38, 60
Granada Television 95, 149–50
Grayton, Larry 103
The Guiding Light 110
Guinness 24, 45

Hailsham, Lord 145
hair care, research on 75–8
Halstead, Sir Ronald 23
Hancock, Tony 112, 135
'hard sell' techniques 3, 9, 46, 113, 193
Hardy, Françoise 58–9

Harrods 2
Havinden, Ashley 44, 106
Havinden, Margaret 45
Heals 123, 133
Hebdige, Dick 43
'hedonic treadmill' 193–5
Heinz 151
Hickey, William 150–1
'hidden persuaders' 167–9
Hilton, Matthew 177
Hinks, Bill 38, 48, 51
Hobson Bates and Partners (HBP) 46
Hoggart, Richard 52, 111, 144–5, 165–75, 179, 182, 191–4
Holland, Mary 131, 149, 157–8
Hoover 135
Hore, L.W. 83
Horowitz, Daniel 73, 168, 181
Hotpoint 122
house building 125
'housewife' role and image 7, 12, 66–9, 72–3, 78, 83–7, 109, 119–21, 127–37, 189–92
'housework enthusiasts' 86
Hull, Henry 103
humour, use of 112, 153
hygiene, domestic 155

Imperial Tobacco 27
Ince, Angela 130
Incorporated Society of British Advisers (ISBA) 99–100
Independent Television (ITV) 19–23, 141–51, 158; initiation of 9, 95–100, 144; hostility towards 96, 143, 146–51, 158, 172; share of television audience 144; support for 147–8
Independent Television Contractors Association (ITCA) 101, 174
Ingman, Dan 173
Institute of Practitioners in Advertising (IPA) 26, 97–100, 111, 151, 173–7, 181
International Refrigerator 122

Jackson, Brian 126–7
Jell-O 110

Jenkins, Clive 96
Jim's Inn 111
jingles, use of 109, 152, 158
Jordon, J. 23
Journal of the Advertising Association 98
J. Walter Thompson (JWT) 1–3, 10–11, 22, 31, 36–60, 66, 69–74, 78–83, 87–8, 95–6, 104–7, 112–13, 119, 127–8, 131, 153, 156, 178–82, 187–9; American-ness of 36–7; high calibre and elite backgrounds of staff 39, 59; management techniques used 41–2; organizational structure 104–7; relations between London office and parent company 39–43, 49–51, 59; reputation 39; use of market research 71–4; *see also* 'Thompson way'

Keith, J.R. 50
kitchens, design and depiction of 12, 120–6, 132–7, 188, 190
Kraft Cheese Whiz 108

Labour Party 145, 165–9, 177–8, 182, 191
Lambe & Robinson (agency) 103
letters from television viewers 142, 154–8, 190
'life cycle' concept 84
'liveness' in television adverts 107–9
Lloyd, Selwyn 98
London Life (magazine) 16–17, 130
London Press Exchange (LPE) 28–30, 37, 97, 105, 109
Lucky Strike Theater 110

MacCabe, Brian 178–9
McCann-Erickson 103, 195
MacDonald, Robert 112
McGowan, Todd 193
Mackay, Josephine 119, 134
MacKenzie, E.C. 45
McMahan, Harry Wayne 103, 108, 111
Macmillan, Harold 147, 171
magazine advertising 24–5
Mandler, Peter 2
manipulation of consumers 168, 174

market research 11, 40, 66–74, 80, 84, 87–8; American 70, 189
Marks & Spencer 6, 23
Marsh, Peter 103
mass consumption 88
Mass Observation 84
Maxted, Stanley 105
Mayhew, Christopher 96
Meek, Sam 39, 48, 50
Milky Bar 153
Miller, Peter 69–70, 89
Mills, C. Wright 168
Mirror Group 143; *see also Daily Mirror*
Mitchell-Innes, Sandy 50
Mitchlemore, S. 175–6
'mobilization' of the consumer 69, 88
Molony, J.T. 167, 175, 178
moralism about advertising 181, 191
mother–child relationships 153
mother–daughter relationships 85–6
motives of consumers and motivational research 69–74, 167–9, 188–9
Moyne, Lord 24
Mulhern, Francis 170
Murray Mints 109
musical extravaganzas 110

nationalism, commercial 43, 48–9
newspapers 9, 143, 145; advertising in 20–2, 25, 47, 101, 114, 130, 145, 150–2, 173, 189; coverage of television advertising 158
Noel-Baker, Francis 172
Norwood Report (1943) 68

Offer, Avner 123, 193–4
Ogilvy, David 29
Ogilvy & Mather (agency) 187
Omo washng powder 108–9
on-screen presenters of advertising 108–9, 152, 158
Orr-Ewing, Charles 100
Osborne & Peacock (agency) 103
Oughton, Hubert 98–9
Oxo 69, 80–3, 120, 130–1, 134, 149, 153, 156–9, 189–90

Packard, Vance 136, 165–9, 182, 192
Pan American Airways (Pan Am) 24, 41, 48, 50
Parker Morris Report (1961) 121–2, 125, 132
Parker Pens 53–6, 59
Patmore, Michael 105
Patterson, Mary 122
Pearson, J. 46
Pells, Richard 2
Pepsodent company 74–7
Perkins, Edward 126
Persil 95–6, 104, 108–9, 112, 119–20, 127–31, 134, 153, 158–9, 174, 189–90
Peusch, Jutta 150
Philip, Norman 73
Pilkington, Sir Harry (and Pilkington Report, 1962) 111, 146–8, 166–7, 171–5, 178, 190–1
Pin-Up home perm 69, 74–8
pin-ups 148, 158
Ponds' cold creams *see* Cheeseborough-Ponds
Pope, George 164
Popular Television Association 99–100
Potter, David 2
Potter, Dennis 165
Procter & Gamble 22–3
psychological approaches to consumer behaviour 70–3, 76, 88, 167, 189
public school education 27–8
public-service obligations 100, 173

Quant, Mary 17, 52

Radner, Hilary 56
Rayfield, Tom 40
recognition agreements 101
Reed, John 103
Reeves, Rosser 46
Reith, Lord (and Reith Commission) 177–80
Resor, Stanley 48
retail audit research 72
Richard Shops 24, 55–9
Riesman, David 136, 168

Robert Sharpe & Partners 27
Robinson, Eric 103–4
Rodgers, John 51
Roper, Mike 27–8
Rose, Jonathan 142
Rose, Nicholas 69–70, 89
Ross, Duncan 102–4
Rowntrees 20–3
Roxena soap 108
Rumble, Crowther & Nicholson 36

Saatchi & Saatchi 187
Sampson, Anthony 44, 51–2
Sanders, Michael 95
Sarrut, André 104
Saunders, Douglas 38, 48
Scannell, Paddy 190
Sedgwick, Ursula 39
segmentation of consumers 72–3
sexuality 76, 132, 148
SH Benson (agency) 29
Shaw, Ken 3, 113
Signal toothpaste 108
sitcom-style adverts 112
'slice of life' dramas 12, 110, 129–31, 135–6, 157, 189–90
Smith, A.C.H. 146
soap operas 156, 190
social change 5, 9, 120–1, 127, 135, 145–6, 166, 169, 189, 194
social consequences of advertising 31, 172, 178, 180, 192
social responsibility of broadcasting 171–2
social role of advertising 165, 173, 181
sociological analysis 87–9, 189
Sorrell, Martin 187
sponsored television 97–9, 110–13, 164
spot adverts 100, 107, 157
Stern, Michael 77
Stobo, Philip 164–5, 173
Stonehewer, J.R. 83
Strouse, Norman 36
subjectivity of consumers 89, 179, 192, 195
Sunday Times magazine 25
Sutherland, Douglas 17

Sutton, Tom 36–7

T-square marketing tool 40
Tarrant, Mollie 84
Tavistock Institute of Human Relations (TIHR) 76–8
Taylor Woodrow 125–6
television: impact on home life 144, 147–8, 157; wider influence of 190
Television Act (1954) 98, 100, 111, 166–7, 171
television advertising 7–9, 12–13, 19–24, 101–14, 120–1, 127, 135–6; belief in power of 31; genres of 107–13; preparations for introduction of 101–7; press coverage of 158; resistance to 23–4; *see also* commercials; sponsored television
testimonial advertising 55, 109–12
'Thompson way' 40–1
Thompson's *see* J Walter Thompson
Til Death Us Do Part 112
Time magazine 111
The Times 8–9, 95–6, 111, 145
Todd, Selina 126
'toddlers' truce' 100
Townsend, Peter 126
Treasure, John 74
Turner, G. 46

Unilever Group 20–3, 26–7, 127
unique selling propositions (USPs) 46
United States *see under* American

Varley, Arthur 27
Vim 108

Vince, Pamela 74
'VIP meetings' at JWT 51–2

Walker, Billy 150
Ward, Peter 51
Warwick, Gina 150
washing up 78–80
Whitehead, Frank 165
Whyte, William 168
Wilding, April 148
Wilkinson, Alan 45
Williams, Raymond 193–4
Willmott, Peter 85, 130
Wilson, Dermot 52
Wilson, Edward 1–3, 40
Wilson, Harold 145, 180
Wilson, H.H. 96–7
Winnicott, D. 68
Wire and Plastic Products (company) 187
Wisdon toothbrushes 104
women practitioners in advertising 28
women's employment generally 126
women's magazines 24–5, 66, 68, 130
women's social role 67–9, 119, 130, 135, 192
Wood, Sinclair 173–4
Woolworth's 60
WS Crawford (agency) 29
Wyndham, Francis 16

Yeo, Peter 187
Young, Michael 85, 130
Young & Rubicam 102, 110
youth markets 72

EU authorised representative for GPSR:
Easy Access System Europe, Mustamäe tee 50,
10621 Tallinn, Estonia
gpsr.requests@easproject.com

www.ingramcontent.com/pod-product-compliance
Ingram Content Group UK Ltd.
Pitfield, Milton Keynes, MK11 3LW, UK
UKHW021848140426
5217IPUK00022B/1658